PRAISE FOR *Cl*

"Roger Noyes has written a compelling and important biography of a nurse, Clara Noyes, who was at the center of all the discipline's early twentieth century achievement. Clara Noyes led nurses to battle during World War I, to scenes of disaster during the flu pandemic and floods, and to the successful recognition of their military authority in the fight to gain officer status. More importantly, Roger Noyes has written a biography of a woman who wielded power and authority at a moment in time when few did. This biography deserves a wide read both by nurses and by those who seek to understand women's leadership in a very public life."

-Patricia D'Antonio, PhD, RN, FAAN,
Director, Barbara Bates Center for
the Study of the History of Nursing

"Roger Noyes writes a compelling biography about one of the leading nurses in the American Red Cross during the early part of the twentieth century. He meticulously researches the work of his great-great aunt, Clara D. Noyes, and her many contributions. Sharing the same surname, the author reflects on Clara D. Noyes' ties to her family, the larger society, and the evolving nursing profession. He contextualizes her life's work within the framework of a world grappling with issues of woman suffrage, class, race, and gender disparities, and a world at war. Roger Noyes weaves a rich historical narrative illuminating Clara D. Noyes' development as a person, a professional, and a global citizen. As he tells her story, he tells the history of the American Red Cross and the vital role nursing leaders like Clara D. Noyes played within this organization. It's not only a must read for those interested in the early twentieth century and nursing, but it is also a great read!"

-Sandra B. Lewenson, RN, EdD, FAAN
Pace University College of Health Professions
Lienhard School of Nursing
Author of *Taking Charge: Nursing, Suffrage,
and Feminism in America, 1873-1920*

Peggy:
trank you for all
you do for
patients.

CLARA D. NOYES, R.N.

LIFE OF A GLOBAL
NURSING LEADER

SHIRES ✺ PRESS

4869 Main Street
P.O. Box 2200
Manchester Center, VT 05255
www.northshire.com

Clara D. Noyes, R.N.
Life of a Global Nursing Leader

ISBN Number: 978-1-60571-350-2
Library of Congress Control Number: 2017936144

Cover photograph Courtesy of the Harris & Ewing
Collection of the Library of Congress, ca. 1922
Cover design by Roger L. Noyes

Printed in the United States of America

CLARA D. NOYES, R.N.

LIFE OF A GLOBAL
NURSING LEADER

-ROGER L. NOYES-

An Iris, for Clara

In Memory of James Brewster Noyes

Roger L. Noyes – who is Clara Noyes's great-great nephew—is Communications Director for the Home Care Association of New York State, an organization that represents visiting nurse associations and other home care providers. His writing has appeared in literary and trade journals and major newspapers. He lives near Albany, New York.

CONTENTS

EPIGRAM

CLARA D. NOYES[1]

Yea – Once in the long history of the race,
There stood "The Lady with a Lamp,"
Strong and Kind of Face.

At that bright lamp eternal-rayed,
Multitudes have lighted
Little candles of skilled aid.

One who but now has laid aside human frame,
So trimmed and fed her bit of flame,
That its blazing rays up-tossed,
Fused into Humanity's beacon;
The American Red Cross.

Hailed amid barren hills
And teeming towns,
Aye, in foreign lands;
Where'er valiant bands,
Seek to bind up wounds of wars,
Or wild nature's aching scars,
Where there's aught that breaks or mars lives
Of puny men, or kills,

The name Clara Noyes
Brought courage, cheer, and poise.

Greeted by courts and kings,
Busied with a great task and all it brings,

From near and far,
Yet ever the warm friend,
Constant as any star.

-Louise P. Yale

ACKNOWLEDGEMENTS

This project was a true labor of love. I came to identify with my subject in a profound way. Reading so many volumes of Clara Noyes's work, I found myself turning to those pages of her writing for inspiration and counsel in my professional life, taking cues from her exceptional organizing ability when it came to my own work in the health care field. Though it might not be reflected in these pages, a thorough read of Clara Noyes's work was instructive for me on so many levels, not the least of which was her approach to organizational leadership.

Writing this book also led to many positive connections with wonderful people who were excited to assist and hear more about Clara Noyes's story.

Candace White, my first reader, gave me so much love and support throughout the entire process. She listened with patience and interest at every moment of sometimes over-eager discovery. These near-daily conversations helped organize my thinking and informed so much of the way this book was written. She was my companion on most of my research trips, and I appreciated her love, support and guidance through it all.

This book was very much a family endeavor. In some cases, those experiences were difficult; but I'd prefer to dwell on those experiences that brought me joy and renewal.

I thank both sides of my family for their support, particularly my mother, Linda Noyes, for inspiring a sense of curiosity throughout my life that rewards this kind of work. I also thank her brother, Terry Powell, my uncle, for repairing Clara Noyes's desk in the first place. Little did he know that restoring a desk would also restore my interest in the very subject of this book? My father, Charles Noyes, a historian, instilled in me an early interest in history which took me many years to appreciate, and for that I am grateful. I also express profound thanks for the Noyes family of Old Lyme, Connecticut, especially my great-uncle James Brewster Noyes for his stories, his loving memory of Clara Noyes, his wealth of knowledge, his source material, and for his blessings and kindness. I am particularly saddened that James passed away before this book came to completion and I dedicate this book, in part, to him and the aunt he was so proud of. I also thank his son Bruce Noyes, Bruce's wife Tammy Noyes, and James's companion Doris Hungerford. They all welcomed me to Old Lyme with warmth as we bonded over stories about a woman, Clara Noyes, whom we all admire so greatly.

This project brought me to several archives where I received excellent assistance combing through primary sources. I specifically thank: Diane Gallagher of the Howard Gotlieb Archival Research Center in Boston; Trudy Hutchinson of the Foundation for New York State Nurses in Albany, New York; Tab Lewis of the National Archives in College Park, Maryland; Andy Harrison of the Alan Mason Chesney Medical Archives at Johns Hopkins University in Baltimore; staff at the New York Public Library's Schomburg Center for Research in Black Culture; and staff at the American Red Cross central headquarters, including independent researcher Jean Schulman who was among the first to take interest in this project and offer guidance. I also want to thank the editor of *Caring Magazine*, Lisa Yarkony, who published my first article on Clara Noyes, which was an impetus for this book-length project.

I also thank Amanda Lanne-Camilli from SUNY Press for her work reviewing the original manuscript and offering vital feedback which added strength to the organization and authority of the writing.

I would also like to thank author Sandra Beth Lewenson who offered additional guidance along the way from her expertise in the area of nursing, feminism and the suffrage movement.

I made one particularly interesting connection through the work of Bulgarian scholar Kristina Popova. In the later stages of my research, I came across one of her papers which cited letters from Clara Noyes in the Bulgaria State Archives, related to Noyes's work helping to develop a nursing school in Sofia, Bulgaria, as Noyes did in scores of European countries. It was fascinating to find that Kristina Popova was also writing about Clara Noyes, for further research in this area (specifically, women's relationships in development and program work), and that we were both mining our own countries' archives for similar source material. This led to an inspiring and helpful series of correspondences and information sharing. I can't help but reflect on the fact that these exchanges are a continuation of the work that Clara Noyes pursued in her exchanges with Bulgarian nurses during the 1920s and 30s, if on a smaller, more focused scale. I'd like to think that this book led to a next phase, and continued discussion, about the history of development work across nations, akin to Clara Noyes's own correspondence with Bulgarian nurse leaders nearly 100 years ago.

W e share a last name and bloodline, but Clara Noyes's story entered my life through a more physical means: her desk.

My uncle, Terry Powell, a craftsman and engineer, restored this desk through months of meticulous work plugging holes, refinishing rich grains, bringing a proud furnishing back to its original splendor.

When it came to me in 2004, I knew little about the desk, other than that it was once owned by my great-great aunt, a famous Red Cross nursing leader whose profile I discovered on the website for the Foundation of New York State Nurses. Intrigued, I printed out Clara Noyes's one-page bio and kept it in the right, top drawer of the desk, bearing "mute testimony that the owner's hands, once proud and eager for Red Cross Service, are now forever quiet," as Clara Noyes herself would remark[1] about the vast catalog of nurses who died in the Red Cross Nursing Service she led. Every now and then, when someone inquired, I would slide open the desk's long drawer to reveal her small biographical sketch; but my knowledge of Clara Noyes remained limited to a few words on a single sheet of paper.

After a stint working as a press officer in the New York State Senate, I took a position, in 2007, as Communications Director for the Home Care Association of New York State, a trade organization representing providers of home and community based services, including many of the state's visiting nurse associations. Immersed in the nuances of home care nursing, I kept returning to that wooden desk in my living room, and the name of its first owner, Clara Noyes, whose status in the nursing field continued to intrigue me – even more so, now that I had entered a similar professional orbit, almost exactly one-hundred years later.

In 2012, Hurricane Sandy hit New York City and Long Island. As I wrote in an article for *Caring Magazine*, a publication of the National Association for Home Care and Hospice (NAHC): "Communities on the coast were decimated; power outages turned high-rise buildings into dark and frigid towers where many people were forced to shelter in place; evacuation orders displaced thousands of others from their homes; flood-waters engulfed and paralyzed New York's transportation networks; bridges were log-jammed by traffic surges; and fuel supplies dwindled."[2] The New York metro region was in crisis, putting home care nurses, aides and therapists into a vital relief role as thousands of chronically ill, disabled or frail-elderly New Yorkers lost power, heat and needed care. Many of the bridges were impassible, streets were flooded, and nurses found their day-to-day duties hobbled by a storm that made their work harder – and the needs of their patients even greater. Diabetes sufferers required insulin injections, as refrigerator outages had spoiled their home supply, and others lacked basic necessities like food, warmth and human contact. I would fire off e-mails to thousands of nurse clinical managers and home care executives about storm preparations, locations for obtaining supplies and other relief needs to help their patients at home. Fielding calls from reporters about the hurricane and its impact on vulnerable populations, I connected NPR health care correspondent Richard Knox with the president of the Visiting Nurse Association of Long Island, Orael Keenan, RN, who explained that "80 percent of the area lost power ... Thirty-two of her 400 clients were evacuated from their homes to a family member or another caregiver's home."[3]

It's unclear what prompted me, two years after the hurricane, to return again to Clara Noyes's desk. But it appears that the memory of Hurricane Sandy, the physical artifact of Clara Noyes's desk, and a shared profession in the nursing world, particularly disaster nursing, would all combine in a flash of inspiration. One of the first news accounts I found was a 1927 Associated Press (AP) feature about the American Red Cross's response to the devastating Mississippi flood of that same year, with the headline: "Woman Heads Red Cross Aid: World-Wide Activities Center at Desk of Miss Clara D. Noyes."[4] The article referred to "The broad desk at which Miss Noyes sits," which was "a keyboard contacting nurses in all corners of this country and nursing organizations in a score of countries abroad."[5]

That "broad desk," featured symbolically in a widely published wire story, some 90 years ago, was now sitting in my own home, not only a physical object, but, as I would soon realize, a powerful symbolic marker of my connection to Clara Noyes, in our bloodline and in our shared professional domain.

I found that she was a prolific writer, reporting, for instance, vividly about the Mississippi Flood – how "Nurses frequently went from house to house in boats, caring for those who were marooned on second and third stories." From her broad desk, Clara Noyes would "press a button," as she told the AP, firing off wire messages to local divisions of nurses, calling nurses into relief action, just as I, nearly 100 years later, would be using the more modern method of e-mail alerts to inform nurses and their home care managers about crisis nursing, during Hurricane Sandy. My connection to Clara Noyes was growing more and more profound, and it inspired me to dig even further into her life, leading me to pen a feature story about her for NAHC's *Caring Magazine*, the same publication that ran my article about the home care response to Hurricane Sandy.

Clara Noyes's story continued to stick with me, and I frequently found myself uncovering strong links between my life and hers. At first, I was particularly drawn to her remarks on "district nursing," or what we call today home care nursing, my area of professional expertise. I later learned that during her time at Bellevue Hospital, Clara Noyes had associated with the likes of Lillian Wald, founder of the famed Progressive-Era Henry Street Settlement. Wald is a household name in the home care nursing field. She helped sow the seeds of what would later become the nation's largest not-for-profit home care agency, the Visiting Nurse Service of New York.

Clara Noyes's most shining and dramatic impact, however, was in wartime nursing, mobilizing more than 20,000 nurses through the Red Cross to help repair the battle wounds of soldiers in World War I. For millennia, wartime officers were exclusively men, but here was a woman operating as a "lieutenant" of sorts to Red Cross Nursing Service Director Jane Delano, and this duo, Clara Noyes and Jane Delano, became the first women to prepare other women for war on a global, systematic scale. They did so within an organizational apparatus that was virtually indistinct from the War Department structure that they worked with to aid, supply, and support the allied cause in war-ravaged Europe.

When I decided to take on a larger book-length project about Clara Noyes's life, I found myself without a lack of primary sources. Clara Noyes was a prolific, often lyrical, writer. She was a frequent presence in the public sphere whose work was recorded in piecemeal events throughout the mainstream press, nursing journals, nurse history scholarship and in the massive 1,500-page tome, the *History of American Red Cross Nursing*, which she co-wrote and edited in 1922.

In 1919, Clara Noyes, as this book will later document, played a pivotal role in securing military rank for Red Cross nurses who had enrolled for duty under the Army Nurse Corps, so that their authority was recognized in the field of duty at base hospitals overseas. Unranked enlisted men, amid the hyper-masculine context of war, served as hospital orderlies, in many cases loath to follow the commands of young women nurses tending to the battle wounded.

One hundred years later, my organization, the Home Care Association of New York State, had learned a similar lesson about the authority of nurses during disaster: when emergency curfews, restricted zones and the traffic chaos of Hurricane Sandy created an obstacle for nurses to travel to patients in need. Like the campaign for nurses' rank 100 years prior, my "broad desk" was communicating to nurses in New York State about the need for legislation granting "essential personnel" status for nurses in disasters, so that these clinicians didn't face the same obstacles in future emergencies as they attempted to fulfill their duties to reach patients in need – a duty and authority that was not recognized in the existing emergency management protocols and planning efforts.[6] As President Taft remarked a hundred years ago, when working with Noyes on the rank issue for nurses, "rank is the remedy and rank they should have"[7]; home care nurses felt a similar remedy was needed, a designated authority, to secure their status and official role when executing duties amid more recent disasters.

Writing this book exactly a hundred years after Clara Noyes's own enrollment of 20,000 nurses for duty during World War I, I found myself feeling like I was reliving her experiences – on a profound, yet far more modest, level. Clara Noyes had collected and reviewed the enrollments of thousands of nurses, whose applications were recorded and filed in "manila jackets" at National Red Cross headquarters in Washington, DC. In similar form, I was building my own personnel file at home, in New York's capital city, organizing my records in manila folders, except that my own growing catalog was focused on just one Red Cross Nurse: Badge No. 6215, Clara Dutton Noyes, RN.

Manifest Destiny is an intoxicating concept in the great American story. As I argue in this book, Clara Noyes was in many ways manifestly destined to assume the "broad desk" of leadership in the American Red Cross's early years. Like the biblical story of Genesis – whose themes run throughout Clara Noyes's life story, the ideologies of her father's service in the Civil War, and back even further through the centuries of our shared heritage – origin stories and a sense of calling all contribute to our understanding of how Clara Noyes ended up at this "broad desk" that she and I share.

My hope is that this book offers readers a glimpse at the way one person, molded by the conditions and causes of global events and contingencies, can add new shades to our understanding of the Great American Story, by examining not just the history of professional nursing but also the psychology of leadership, the women's suffrage movement, the work of women's organizations to achieve equality in Progressive Era America, feminism, political science, the intersection of political currents with race and ethnicity, and, of course the role that war plays in all of these important episodes of American life.

But overall, my main purpose is to shine a light on the story of a woman who experienced fame in her lifetime but is little known to the general public today, other than in very specific circles of nursing scholars. Her story is compelling because it touches so many aspects of American life, ideology and organizational work during the early twentieth century. My intention is not to present a full personal biography, given that so many aspects of Clara Noyes's private life are unknown. Few letters or other personal artifacts survive; yet Clara Noyes's personality nevertheless surfaces in her copious writing for trade journals, American Red Cross archival materials and correspondences, and other primary sources. These all help to convey a picture of Clara Noyes: her zealous protection of nursing's status and its professional standards during the early phases of nursing education; her often-autocratic leadership approach; her pragmatic methods for achieving political aims on behalf of nurses and women broadly; and the life experiences which propelled her up the ladder of leadership positions in nursing and disaster relief.

Rather than establishing a straight chronological narrative, I have taken a somewhat episodic approach with this book, to present Clara Noyes's life thematically using the main sources of information available to me – specifically the vast record of her professional life, as she was very much a private person almost wholly driven by professional interests. These professional interests had the greatest influence on the larger trends in American history, during the early professional development of nursing, the cataclysm of war, and in the movements that drove women to organize professionally for the first time in a substantial way, through the American Nurses Association and other groups that Clara Noyes led.

This book is a legacy to Clara Noyes. At least one other man would memorialize a woman named Clara Noyes: H.P. Sass, the famed horticulturalist, who developed and thoughtfully named several hybrids of irises, including a variety registered in 1930 as the Clara Noyes Iris. It is not known whether the Clara Noyes Iris was named for my great-great aunt or (more likely) an agriculture extension agent in Nebraska who went by the same name, possibly one of Sass's peers in the Omaha region. The Clara Noyes Iris is described as "a medley of peach and apricot tones," in coloring, "suggesting perhaps the rich and brilliant blendings of the rose 'Talisman.'"[8] As one writer remarked, it was "a very brilliant and beautiful iris that everyone wanted at sight."[9]

Regardless of its inspiration, for this author, the Clara Noyes Iris will forever remain connected to a farm girl from Maryland who rose to the top ranks of nursing. And so, this book delivers a flower of my own ... an iris ... of peach and apricot tones ... for Clara.

The author at Clara Noyes's desk. *Photo by Candace White.*

MOUNT ARARAT

"**A**n estimated 55.5 million people around the world die every year," but the *New York Times* obituary pages "acknowledge about 1,000 of them."[1] That's one in 55,000 people of note. Many of these people are celebrities, political figures or cultural icons. Still others led lives operating behind the scenes in the larger backdrop of world events – all of them, no doubt, worthy of fuller examination.

In early twentieth-century America, and throughout the world's nursing profession, Clara Dutton Noyes was known to many as an American Red Cross nursing icon, at a time when nursing was embedded in the very iconography of the American Red Cross. Uniformed nurses were what the public saw in grand parades along major city thoroughfares, and depicted on fundraising posters during World War I. Nursing was what the Red Cross meant for much of the broader public.

Clara Noyes's *New York Times* obituary ran twelve paragraphs. It notes, first, her dramatic death at the wheel of a 1936 Chevy, her preparation of more than 20,000 nurses to serve in World War I, and her work directing the Red Cross nursing response whenever "fire, flood and tornado struck at various parts of the country," during her tenure as American Red Cross Director of Nursing.[2]

It tells of her various service medals; her leadership posts at premier nursing schools (at a time when professional nursing was still new); her pioneering work as president of the American Nurses Association (ANA);

1

and her chairmanship of a "National Committee on Rank for Nurses."

But *The Times* doesn't specify what this committee did. Namely, it succeeded in pressing the case that nurses needed military rank because, as women, their authority was not recognized without it: not by Army officers, nor enlisted men operating in the field of wartime medical relief. In her role as chief of the world's largest body of professional women – the ANA – Clara Noyes mobilized women to push for recognition of their authority, and a bar on their shoulders.

America's newspaper of record also does not mention Clara Noyes's work in post-World War I Europe where she developed schools of nursing in scores of countries that did not have nursing schools, at least not by American standards imported to the U.S. from Florence Nightingale's reforms in London.

The Times does not – nor could it, nor would it, in twelve paragraphs – tell of Clara Noyes's work to battle unfair pay practices for military nurses; nor her efforts to professionalize the practice of midwives (and help open the first school for midwives in the U.S.); nor her rebuke of the medical community's paternalistic tendencies as "hospital men," she called them, were bent on reducing the status of nurses as a means of cheap labor.

Between the compact lines of her obituary, we find a rich story worth knowing and examining further: of a person, a woman, with exceptional organizing ability and vast knowledge of the nursing profession, in its early stages, who mobilized tens of thousands of her sisters to battle the flu epidemic of 1918, aid refugees during the Mississippi Flood of 1927, respond to countless other disasters – and, of course, bring women into their first major experience with war. It is no exaggeration to say that

Clara Noyes's life work touched just about every major question pertaining to nursing in the first quarter of the twentieth century, with lines of influence affecting larger trends and historical currents during wartime America.

This work intertwined with broader themes about the role of women in public life and, more specifically, the cause of women's suffrage, in which nurses played a pivotal advocacy role. Though Clara Noyes was by no means an icon of the suffrage movement, she spoke reflectively of its aims, doing so almost entirely to foster respect for the nursing profession, not necessarily for any social-justice or ardently feminist purpose. This distinction is very important, as the nursing profession grappled extensively with the issue of suffrage, and its early leaders represented a full spectrum of approaches, from principled feminist methods to a more pragmatic and profession-oriented rationale for championing the suffrage cause. This aim for women's professional respect (specifically, white women) also collided with questions about race: the role of African-American women in both the nurse professionalization movement and in the war effort during an era of entrenched segregation and conservatism affecting all areas of public life.

Before rising to the highest levels of nursing at the American Red Cross, Clara Noyes's life began as a farm girl in rural Maryland. But her story was forged much earlier in the crucible of history, with ancestral ties to colonial America and the strong influence of her father's war as a Civil War captain. The war of her father ushered the next generation of women into new relations with the nation-state. Women's burgeoning sense of patriotism during this period helped spawn social reforms in Progressive-Era America and the creation of modern nursing. These movements were influenced by Florence

Nightingale's own wartime experiences during England's Crimean War, and, of course, American Red Cross founder Clara Barton's service to war-wounded in the South during the Civil War. Each of these historical currents aligned very precisely with Clara Noyes's birth in 1869 (a bellwether year in the suffrage movement), her upbringing in a post-Civil War household as professional nursing schools first sprung in the United States (in 1873), and her entrance into the professional sphere as one of the world's most prominent early nurse leaders when a new cataclysm of global war drew a generation of young women into service.

Whether it was the cascade of war wounded during World War I, or submersions of life and property along the Mississippi in the 1920s, Clara Noyes's story is connected to the lore of floods and near-biblical origin stories emanating from a small corner of the world north of Baltimore. There, in the tiny town of Port Deposit, Maryland, Clara Noyes's parents briefly owned a large tract of farmland overlooking a 200-foot-high riverside cliff called Mount Ararat, named after the towering 20,000-foot mountain in Turkey where, says the *Book of Genesis*, Noah's Ark "came to rest."[3] Locals speculate that Mount Ararat provided high ground for citizens of low-lying Port Deposit whenever flood waters rose from the Susquehanna River basin, akin to Noah's biblical landing place.[4] For a culture bred on the idea of manifest destiny, it seems particularly fitting that a line of the Noyes family came to occupy this land at Mount Ararat, even though the Noyes lineage was firmly rooted in Yankeedom – specifically Old Lyme, Connecticut, where Clara Noyes's father and several generations of Noyeses were born and raised. Mount Ararat, as the setting for Clara Noyes's birth and early life, is fertile ground for the imagination. Indeed, the Noyeses were altogether obsessed with a link between their surname and Noah of the Bible, with both the Noyeses and Noah landing atop a fabled Mount Ararat, thousands of miles – and millennia – apart. Fittingly, the English name Noyes roughly translates from its French word origin, "noyer," meaning "to drown" or the "drowned persons,"[5] lending a certain mythology to a family named Noyes farming the land on Maryland's version of Noah's mountain resting place.[6] Early Noyes genealogists cite another theory: "I have heard that the name was originally De la Noye, or from the drowned – saved from drowning; which takes us back to the flood, and the ark, and the name Noe (Noah). It is said that some of the family took the name Delano."[7] This link to the Delanos not only ties the Noyeses to another prominent surname in American history (with bloodlines crossing through the lives of American presidents, like Franklin Delano Roosevelt, and other leaders); but, most importantly (for Clara Noyes's life), we find a possible ancestral connection between Clara Noyes and one other early nursing icon who played a lead role in Noyes's professional development: Jane Arminda Delano, Clara Noyes's mentor at the American Red Cross.

From birth and by ancestry, Clara Dutton Noyes inherited a near biblical sense of duty and mission, steeped in her family's Calvinist roots, extending back to Puritan America. She would refer to this sense of mission repeatedly, later in life, dubbing it her "Macedonian Call," a reference to Acts 16:9, 10, where Paul saw a vision drawing him to preach the gospel in Macedonia. These biblical allegories seemed to follow her from birth and childhood, at Mount Ararat, and throughout her career, with a "Macedonian Call" to serve her country while deploying nursing's response to more contemporary disasters, including America's Great Flood, along the Mississippi in 1927.

War being a central figure of Clara Noyes's story, it is important to consider the impact of nineteenth-century warfare on future generations of twentieth-century leaders, similarly affected by wartime demands. While in name, Clara Noyes seemed biblically destined to race toward the flood of disaster, the war of her father's generation would also have a profound historical impact on Clara Noyes's sense of duty, with distinct parallels between her father's fighting along the ditches of the Mississippi Valley in Louisiana and Europe's trench warfare, which later led Clara Noyes to mobilize tens of thousands of nurses for service. Both her father's battle – at Port Hudson, Louisiana – and the larger campaigns of World War I involved grinding, and, in some cases, futile or reluctantly devised strategic aims, to gain ground against a foe. And these lessons certainly colored Clara Noyes's ideas about war, its contingencies and its consequences.

Before purchasing the land atop Mount Ararat from his older brother Henry in 1864, Clara Noyes's father, Enoch, was drawn from his Old Lyme, Connecticut birthplace to wartime service in the South, serving in the longest siege in United States military history, thirty miles north of Baton Rouge. There, the Union Army sought to choke Confederate access to the Mississippi River between Vicksburg and points southward. The forty-nine day siege ended on July 9, 1863, after the Confederates learned that Union General Ulysses S. Grant's army had taken Vicksburg, plunging Southern hopes of holding on to the mighty Mississippi.[8] Union victory at Port Hudson opened the Mississippi River to northern forces from the source in New Orleans: a strategic event, if anticlimactic in its execution. Confederates, holed up in the fort, may have otherwise been starved into submission had Grant not achieved victory upstream. Of the seemingly futile campaign, Enoch confessed in his diary that the invasion of Port Hudson was a mistake, dispatching several letters back home to his wife in Connecticut, Laura Lay Banning Noyes: "We went right over the top of them ... and peppered away at them for three hours and half but it was no use," he told her. "They swept our lines with canister and we had to fall back ... It fairly rained Iron hail."[9] This sense of duty in the face of futility must have certainly shaded Clara Noyes's view of war as an "abhorrent" enterprise that had to be dutifully answered, regardless of "causes," because "conditions" demanded it, as she would later remark during speeches when recruiting young nurses for Red Cross service in Europe.

Drawn to his brother's property, at Maryland's Mount Ararat, Enoch was determined to resume the quiet farming life he led before the Civil War broke out, trading his blue uniform for the vestments of a gentleman farmer in 1864 when he purchased the land from his brother for $4,000.[10] At Mount Ararat, Enoch and Laura Lay Banning Noyes raised nine children (though a tenth child, Jennie, died at a young age). Few of Clara Noyes's siblings would live to see her rise in the world of global nursing leadership at American Red Cross headquarters. William Curtis and Enoch Noyes, Jr. were the eldest sons. When young Jennie passed at age four, in 1872, Clara Dutton Noyes (born on October 3, 1869) became the eldest daughter, putting her in a key domestic role assisting her mother with child-raising work, caring for six younger siblings: Johnnie, Harry, Martha, Francis, Laura Banning and Charles Reginald Noyes, the youngest, born in 1883, when Clara was seventeen.

The Noyeses at Mount Ararat Farm. *Photo courtesy of the Noyes family.*

It is only in 1894 – three years before his death and about the time Clara Noyes applied to nursing school – that Capt. Enoch Noyes again drew widespread public notice, but for a purely natural occurrence on his property. "What was supposed to be the largest walnut tree in Northern Maryland was felled on the farm of Col. [*sic.*] Enoch Noyes, near Port Deposit," reported the *New York Times*.[11] It's a small detail, a minor footnote in the historical record and seemingly inconsequential. Nevertheless, this curious little news item lends further shades to our imagination in seeing the Noyes family as manifestly destined to settle this particular corner of the world, with biblical storylines running throughout the early years of

Clara Noyes's upbringing and the cultural ideologies that defined her. In addition to "drowned persons," the French word "noyer" also means "walnut." Noyes genealogists point to the name "William de Noyers," in the *Domesday Book* of England in 1086, which, "translated, means, 'William (of the) Walnut trees.'"[12] It is fitting that Enoch Noyes would live and die on this near-mythic parcel of land in northern Maryland, with its Promethean cliffs, rolls of green hillside, proud stone silos, and giant, ageless trees, seemingly as old as origin stories. Like his biblical namesake – Enoch, the son of Jared and the great-grandfather of Noah – Capt. Enoch Noyes "walked with God; and he was not, for God took him."[13]

Laura Lay Banning Noyes remained on the farm for a few more years after Enoch's death. Her son, Harry, inherited a parcel in May of 1898.[14] He, too, died in November of that year.[15] Enoch Noyes, Jr., also lived out his life on the farm, passing in May of 1902.[16] Three years later, Laura Lay Banning Noyes was already back in her hometown, near New London, Connecticut, the large Enoch Noyes family slowly dwindling – and expiring their time at Mount Ararat.[17]

Laura Lay Banning and Enoch Noyes (left and middle; *Photos courtesy of the Noyes family*). Clara Noyes (at right; *Photo courtesy of the Harris and Ewing Collection of the Library of Congress*).

Judged purely on facial likeness, Clara Dutton Noyes strikes a close resemblance to her mother, Laura Lay Banning Noyes. Photographs of the two women in adulthood show the same sparkling, deep-set eyes beneath a curving brow line, a steep nose, and slit mouth. But this mother-daughter resemblance is easily supplanted in one's imagination upon spotting the uniform that Clara and her father, Enoch, would each don in service to their country. His was a uniform of dark blue with golden epaulettes signifying the Union cause, posed in a family photograph clutching his sword from one arm bent on a table. Hers was a dark cloak, buttoned frock, shirt and tie, a brimmed hat crowned with the emblem of the Red Cross, and a gloved hand extending from a similarly bent elbow. Except her glove is clutching not a sword, but a pair of spectacles, pinched between her thumb and forefinger, as if to show us, without obtrusion, the full force of her piercing gaze.

While Clara Noyes may have inherited her mother's facial likeness, one cannot help but see a strong identification with her father, Enoch, in their shared vestments of wartime service and posture. Indeed, a 1924 booklet published by Yale University, showcasing twelve leaders in nursing, makes this paternal connection, as do other records: "Perhaps from her father who had fought in the Civil War, Miss Noyes inherited the love of country which impelled her in 1916 ... to go to National Red Cross headquarters."[18] Susan Zeiger, author of *In Uncle Sam's Service*, explicitly connects Enoch's war with the service of Clara Noyes and others from her generation. In many cases, these young women who grew up in post-Civil War households were bred on stories of American Red Cross founder Clara Barton and wartime patriotic ideologies: "The Union cause specifically was a vital family tradition for many women," writes Zeiger, telling of one Red Cross enrollee whose grandfather was pushed from the fields of battle in a dumpcart handled by Clara Barton. The young woman said it was no small wonder why she "naturally gravitated to the Red Cross service" from hearing her grandfather's stories about Barton. "Indeed, both principal leaders of the American Red Cross Nursing Service in World War I, Clara D. Noyes and Jane Delano, were daughters of Union soldiers," Zeiger adds.[19] The daughters of Civil War veterans would, in essence, be responsible for leading Civil War granddaughters' service in a future war.

The ideology of Civil War-era patriotism clearly influenced women across generations, even from mother to daughter. Union soldiers' wives, like Laura Lay Banning Noyes, found themselves participating in new relations to property and commerce while their husbands were away fighting Confederate forces. Their daughters – perhaps modeling either parent, through identification with the father's wartime service or the mother's enlarged role in both domestic and public spaces – were inspired by a new sense of citizenship. This sense of citizenship helped spark, or further fuel, the many political and social movements of America's Progressive Era, not the least of which was the women's suffrage campaigns.

Clara Noyes's generation was the first cohort of professional nurses; and they guarded the hard-fought practice of nursing zealously, an important professional inroad for women. Through this gateway, fostered by a band of early nursing leaders who mentored them, women of Clara Noyes's generation led nurse education movements and helped consolidate major professional organizations of nursing to form political powerhouses. They would hold executive positions in the American

Red Cross Nursing Service and the Army Nurse Corps; and they would enlist another generation of young women nurses, trained on a now-standard system of nurse practice, who were drawn to service by their identification with Civil War relief icons, like Clara Barton and Dorothea Dix. These post-Civil War ideologies of public spirit prompted measured changes in the domestic role of women, their civic duties, their work life and their experience in the traditional male domain of commercial transactions. During the Civil War, "with so many Northern men making explicit their ranking of country over home, women also had to learn to separate and reexamine their own priorities," writes historian Nina Silber who refers to a new "political mentality" in women who sacrificed their husbands for war service, no doubt leaving this legacy to their daughters. "The evidence is subtle: a mother's growing attentiveness to local politics, a wife's heightened interest in reading war news."[20] Laura Lay Banning Noyes was among those wives receiving first-hand accounts of "war news." This growing sense of duty to the nation-state gave women a determination to seek out new professional and domestic roles, especially the few career opportunities that welcomed them during this period – foremost among them, nursing.

As the oldest daughter in a large household, Clara Noyes would be responsible for many of the domestic duties traditionally reserved for daughters, especially for the second-eldest woman in the family: cooking, cleaning, teaching her young siblings, as well as informal "nursing" and caretaking roles. With her father's death, and as she reached adulthood, Clara Noyes was increasingly compelled to relieve her family from the economic strain of supporting an unmarried, adult daughter. Clara

Noyes's younger sister took over the domestic chores. Her brothers assumed the farming tasks. And young Clara Noyes soon forged a professional path, trading her apron in the wilderness of Mount Ararat farm for the white uniform of a nursing student in the bustling city of Baltimore.

Clara Noyes in her nursing school uniform. *Photo courtesy of the Noyes family.*

CONTAGIOUS WORK: JOHNS HOPKINS

By the time Clara Noyes was a small girl, in 1873, American institutions and pioneer nursing leaders began efforts to professionalize the practice of nursing, which had largely been an informal trade. The first training schools for graduate nurses began in New York City, Boston and New Haven, all based on a system forged by Florence Nightingale in England.[1] That system included a two- or three-year course of practical and theoretical study. To pave a more lasting legacy, "The better graduate nurses were to help establish and run schools in other hospitals," explains historian Susan Reverby, describing a pattern that eventually facilitated Clara Noyes's early rise to top positions at New England and New York nursing schools following her education.[2] While top nursing graduates were tapped to lead the nursing schools (and cultivate the Nightingale model), a larger class of graduates ended up working in the demanding career of private-duty nursing.[3] Only later were hospital reforms initiated, along with technological advances and new theories about business management. This led to better administered hospitals, productivity standards and reforms which made hospitals more appealing places to work – to the diminishment of the private-duty trade. By contrast, the earlier nineteenth-century hospital, especially, was an unsanitary environment. There, patients more often than not got sicker rather than better. As Susan Reverby notes, "dirt, vermin, and rampant cross-infection, known as 'hospitalism,' were common. Benevolence did not necessarily mean comfort or cleanliness."[4]

Clara Noyes entered the profession just as these changes were taking hold. In this new system, a more elite class of nurse graduates found open doors at other nurse training schools, or at their own institutions, where they served as school superintendents. Part headmaster and part dean of students, the nurse training school superintendent prepared the curriculum and generally administered the nurse education programs, readying nurses for careers; in some cases, they even played an active role in hospital governance, as did Clara Noyes, who held Superintendent seats at the New England Hospital for Women and Children, St. Luke's Hospital and the elite Bellevue Hospital nurse training school at the start of her career.

Johns Hopkins School of Nursing, where Clara Noyes applied in 1894, generated (along with the Bellevue Training School in New York City) the true cream of the crop: "Of ninety women identified as the key leaders in nursing between 1873 and 1945, nearly 50 percent ... trained in only six major large nursing schools located in teaching hospitals," explains Susan Reverby. "Nearly one-third had trained at Bellevue or Hopkins."[5] Hopkins was especially fertile ground for cultivating early nurse leaders, in large part due to personalities drawn to the school, most notably three of its early leaders: Isabel Hampton Robb, Lavinia Lloyd Dock and Mary Adelaide Nutting. These three women actively mentored one another, maintained close professional contact and were responsible for the rise of many graduates who completed the Johns Hopkins program, especially those who excelled naturally into seats as superintendents of other nursing training programs budding throughout the nation. As Susan M. Poslusny explains, "Johns Hopkins Hospital Training School of Nurses was the birthplace of a professional relationship among three women that would grow to a personal friendship and would eventually influence the direction that the nursing profession would follow in the twentieth century."[6] By seeking her fortunes at Johns Hopkins, Clara Noyes would enter into a clique of personal and professional contacts that would propel her rise through the early academic ranks of nursing – what Poslusny, and others, have called early nursing's "esprit des corps," which was manifested through "interpersonal support" among the early nursing leaders. These women shared a core set of values about the importance of their profession and a shared aim for women's advancement.[7]

As a young, unmarried white woman from rural America, Clara Noyes also distinctly fit the profile of nursing school applicants in the burgeoning late-nineteenth-century movement for standardized training schools, distinct from the prior period of "untrained" nursing. Historian Susan Reverby explains: "Untrained nursing was an occupation into which older, urban, native- and foreign-born women, often widows, drifted toward the end of their lives. In contrast, trained nurses were younger, native- and rural-born, single women who were 'selected' by the nursing schools."[8] Clara Noyes didn't "drift" into nursing. She actively pursued it; and she was "selected," supporting her application to Johns Hopkins with commendations from local clergy, along with the imprimatur of her family's status as landowners in northern Maryland. The Reverend George Coulson, pastor at Perryville Presbyterian Church, stated in support of her application: "Miss Clara D. Noyes is a young lady of good moral character and in every way worthy of the fullest confidence. The family is one of the best families in Cecil County and one I've known of more than twenty-five years."[9]

Speaking on her own behalf, in her 1894 application letter, Clara Noyes described herself as twenty-seven years old, five-feet-five-inches tall and, "as for strength, I possess more than the average woman and have always lived a very active life. Though slender in appearance, I belong to a loving and long-lived family noted for their endurance."[10]

Her application letter went on to provide a real window into the life of a young woman in a large late nineteenth-century farming family. Just as her pursuit of nursing would fit a profile, Clara Noyes's home life also reveals the domestic role of an eldest daughter in rural America at this time. On the farm, she served as a kind of adjutant to her mother. "I have never held any position outside my own home," Noyes went on in her letter of application. "As the oldest daughter in a family of eight … I have filled every position, from nurse to house keeper, from teacher to cook," she said, chasing her statement, almost parenthetically, with an afterthought: "It is hardly necessary to add that I am single."[11]

Unmarried she would remain. For life. By pursuing a career in nursing – and still single by age 27 – Noyes's lifestyle was akin to many women in her chosen career who were "primarily unmarried … bound to their profession, not unlike nuns in a religious order."[12] But the culture was also slowly changing in regard to occupational roles for older, single women, particularly as the nursing profession drew women away from traditional domestic realms, albeit measuredly. Seventy-one percent of women born 1861 to 1870 had married by ages twenty-five to thirty, according to a statistical analysis on *The Effect of the Civil War on Southern Marriage Patterns*. Though women were marrying later, or not at all, the changing domestic patterns at this time, though small, suggested "the importance of long-run economic factors such as rising farm prices and increasing participation of single women in the paid labor force." In the generation before Clara Noyes, about seven percent of women remained single at older ages. This rose to about 10.7 percent of women born in 1871 to 1880.[13] Clara Noyes, who never married, was on the cusp of these slow-changing shifts in the role of women in the workplace and at home, especially as nursing created a new avenue for professional self-determination.

Noyes's conviction to enter nursing was strong; but household and economic factors were in play. Timing, too. Noyes's younger sister was, by 1894, then old enough to take over the household chores. This presented an opportunity for Noyes to relinquish herself of family duties and any further financial burden for her parents: "My younger sister having reached an age when she can assume responsibilities, and as it is necessary that some of us should leave home, owing to financial distress, it is my desire to learn the profession of nursing, not on the impulses of the moment or from any passing fancy, as I have given it long and serious thought."[14] Nothing in Clara Noyes's life would be decided on the "impulses of the moment," and, even from her application, we see the roots of a cautious, deliberative personality. She carefully reviewed the application requirements. She made painstaking efforts to ensure that she was making the right decision, for herself as well as for her family's domestic integrity. Nursing, it seems, gave her a chance to both strike out on her own *and* relieve her parents of economic burden. These domestic considerations aside, by earning selection to Johns Hopkins School of Nursing – one of the nation's premier schools – Noyes took a first step on a path of leadership in the nursing wards of Baltimore. There she traded her work "cooking and teaching" on the farm for duties in the training school, where hours were grueling and little free time was afforded for social interactions beyond the nurses' quarters.

When Noyes enrolled at Johns Hopkins, in 1894, Mary Adelaide Nutting was superintendent of its nursing program. Nutting would later be Noyes's peer in some of the first major organizations for nursing, including the National League of Nursing Education (NLNE), the Committee on Nursing of the General Medical Board of the Council of National Defense, and in other prominent venues. Nutting, herself a Johns Hopkins graduate from its first class, is credited with expanding the Hopkins curriculum from two years to three,[15] an important aim of the NLNE for nursing schools broadly during the early twentieth century. Nutting sought other reforms, such as shorter workdays for nursing students, who were clocking 60 to 105 hours a week at a time when pupils were exploited to staff the hospitals,[16] oftentimes assigned to servant-like work. These attitudes and views of the nursing trade saturated the culture of Johns Hopkins, influencing the reform-minded ideologies of later generations. Noyes, too, would remark several times about the piteous condition of nursing students exploited by teaching hospitals. Sensitive to this issue, Noyes stated, on a later occasion, how "too often schools have used the training idea for a means of cheap labor."[17] From Nutting, and others, Noyes began to develop ideas about nursing – its role, status, opportunities and possibilities for career advancement – that resonated within the tight-knit community of her peers and mentors.

The Johns Hopkins medical institution was also born with the nurse training concept, and vanguard views about nurse professionalization, even before its hospital broke ground. The hospital's namesake, Johns Hopkins, left specific instructions in his will to finance a university and hospital, with specific mention of a nursing program that would "secure the services of women competent to care for the sick in the hospital wards" and "benefit the whole community by supplying it with a class of trained and experienced nurses."[18] Hopkins left his final requests in 1873, when the first Nightingale model schools were imported to the United States. It took sixteen more years for Johns Hopkins School of Nursing to open, in 1889, following a period of consultation with at least one associate of Nightingale in London.[19] Johns Hopkins School of Nursing was imbued with the Nightingale spirit; and this spirit was apparently much impressed upon its graduates, like Clara Noyes, who summoned Nightingale's name exhaustively in speeches, letters and articles on nursing issues. "Two thousand years ago, a man gave the world a message of mercy, indulgence and love," she said quite poetically in 1922 about the teachings of Jesus Christ, "but it remained for a woman born 102 years ago" – Nightingale – "to give the practical application of those principles to suffering humanity."[20] Noyes later displayed a portrait of "The Lady with a Lamp" prominently in her Red Cross offices.

Much like its peer training schools built on the Nightingale model, especially the revered Bellevue Hospital nursing program in New York City, Johns Hopkins began with a two-year course of study (later extended to three years), enrolling students between twenty-five and thirty-five years of age, with an eye toward the "purely intellectual part of the nurse's training," so that "nursing may be elevated into a profession and raised as far as possible above the standard of a mere practical trade."[21] The school's administrative offices drew top names in nursing. Nutting's predecessor as Johns Hopkins superintendent, Isabel Hampton, and her assistant superintendent Lavinia Dock wrote influential nursing textbooks and served as leaders in the nurse education field.[22] Dock later became a coauthor, with Noyes and others, on the massive 1,500-page *History of American Red Cross Nursing*, a seminal volume for nursing scholarship. The school was very much a center of intellectual growth in the field of nursing, and one reason why so many of its graduates went on to key roles in organizational nursing.

The rigorous three-year course of training at Hopkins, in effect by the time Clara Noyes graduated in 1896 (though it appears her class was still under the two-year schedule, based on her entry and graduation dates), consisted of practical training in medical, surgical and gynecological wards with weekly class work in anatomy, physiology, hygiene and dietetics during year one. Year two would continue the practical training, but added work in the children's ward, the infectious ward and the dispensary, with classes on medical, surgical and gynecological patients as well as care of infectious diseases. The senior year included "practical work in operating room and dispensary; private wards; maternity and children's wards; further training in whatever direction it is evidently more needed." Physicians lectured on topics as wide-ranging as ventilation, anatomy and physiology, elementary principles of medical nursing, diseases of the eye and ear, and care of infants and children in health and disease.[23] This interdisciplinary approach and division of practice in education was important. Clara Noyes would later counsel nursing staff about the importance of this division as she oversaw nursing school development work in foreign countries during the 1920s. With her trademark candor, she advised one of her associates in Czechoslovakia to be sure that the Czech nursing program (under the auspices of the American Red Cross) relied less on physicians for nurse training, given that "highly qualified nurses teach bacteriology, chemistry, anatomy, physiology, and the purely medical subjects only are given to physicians," adding: "Very little of the work in our best schools, at the present time, is being given by medical men."[24] In one early episode at Johns Hopkins, Noyes recalled being thrust, with little preparation, into a clinical leadership position. The challenge proved her mettle and executive capability, one of the first important milestones in her rise through the nursing ranks. Even in her early training, Noyes was bitten by the infectious bug of leadership. The opportunity to prove herself – her clinical competence, her leadership in the wards – presented itself almost accidentally. Writing a decade later, she reflected how "A feeling of anxiety seems to take possession of me as I face once more in retrospection the responsibilities ... laid upon me. After a few weeks in the old operating room, Miss Sharp broke her leg – she was the head nurse – imagine my surprise to be put in charge, where I remained without losing my reason, for three months. From there, or soon after, I was sent to take charge of Ward 1 ... I stayed about three months, perhaps longer, and I look back on it as a most valuable experience, and the knowledge gained there from grappling with contagious work with almost no supervision has stood me in good stead ever since."[25]

Clara Noyes forged lasting friendships with classmates, who later recalled Clara's wry sense of humor as a young nursing student. "Her enjoyment of humorous situations found its climax perhaps in reminiscences of those early days when we were students but served also to ease and brighten the tension of awkward or bizarre situations encountered in her work."[26] A class of 1896 photo shows Noyes in the front row, seated on the lawn alongside classmates, a billowing white skirt stretched across her tented knees, torso erect, staring firmly at the camera with her trademark piercing gaze. Classmate and friend Anna C. Jammé recalled Clara Noyes in like form. Noyes, an upper classmate, Jammé said, was "tall, thin, very erect, doing her work with precision and dispatch."[27] The two worked closely and kept in touch throughout their lives.

Johns Hopkins School of Nursing Class of 1896. Clara Noyes is at front row, seated, third from left. *Photo courtesy of the Alan Mason Chesney Medical Archives of the Johns Hopkins Medical Institutions.*

At one point in their training, Jammé, who was a year behind Noyes, caught typhoid fever, a deadly bacterial infection and public health menace prior to the development of a vaccine in the early twentieth century.[28] As Jammé remembered, "In the lucid period of violent delirium I found that instead of being my fellow worker," Clara Noyes "was my nurse."[29] Jammé's peer had moved from student-colleague to caregiver. "In those days of ice sponges, and tubs with bumping ice around you, starvation and plenty of whiskey, nursing was a difficult art and even a stupefied typhoid could realize the blessing of good care."[30]

The two often spent leisure time around the "chafing dish" on the floor of the nurses' quarters. There, Jammé observed Noyes's humor, impersonating hospital staff during lighter moments. Like her class photo, Noyes "seemed to look beyond the days' work into a future; yet that future was very different from what she even could imagine at the time," Jammé said. "Could she see a Red Cross Nursing Service in the years to come?"[31]

Noyes and Jammé often boarded the trolley at rare leisure periods to talk and catch a welcome breeze during the hot Baltimore summers. On one trip, Noyes mentioned being offered a position at the New England Hospital for Women and Children in Boston, which would become her first big executive post. The nursing programs at institutions like the New England Hospital for Women and Children were floundering, as the Nightingale models of nursing were still just beginning to take hold and had not reached fulfillment of proper nursing standards. These institutions tapped top nursing students from prestigious institutions, like Hopkins, to shore up their nursing curriculum and better prepare the growing cohort of women seeking opportunities in professional nursing. Noyes was one of them. Initially, she appeared reluctant to leave Johns Hopkins, where she was already on the rise as acting head nurse,[32] later assuming the position fully "immediately on receiving her diploma."[33] Her growing management role at Johns Hopkins had been noticed in the tight circle of women working to actively recruit young leaders who were enculturated in the Nightingale model of nursing. Though Noyes was reluctant to move on from Johns Hopkins, Jammé encouraged her friend to pursue new opportunity. The conversation was one of several episodes where Noyes was actively selected for new appointments but expressed initial reservations, given the status she had already gained in climbing her career ladder.[34] She was cautious, deliberative and thoughtful in her approach to virtually all major decisions in her life. She made a move only when the timing was right, when she had built up the expertise, and she shunned any premature overreach that would have doomed her success. In the spirit of her application to Johns Hopkins, Noyes would never be overtaken by "impulses of the moment or from any passing fancy." She always gave her decisions "long and serious thought."

Taking her friend's advice, Noyes arrived in Boston in 1897 where she "found conditions the likes of which had never for one moment entered into my conceptions of training school work."[35] The Massachusetts program was, in Noyes's estimation, a mess. While Johns Hopkins School of Nursing was firmly rooted, Noyes's recollections show the growing pains of other fledgling nurse training schools during this early period. "I found no school, simply a collection of miscellaneous material," she remarked. A labor strike six months prior had resulted in every nurse leaving, and a training program in ruins. One superintendent after another had given up "in despair," she said. Virtually any resident "presenting herself had been taken into the school, from middle aged women to young girls." After developing the program over three years, "I left a school that was well worth being proud of," she said. "I felt that my work there for me was finished and I wanted a broader field."[36] Like her trial-by-fire in the wards of Johns Hopkins, she had again proven herself. Her familiarity with the curriculum standards and Nightingale reform culture at Johns Hopkins yielded an early success in Boston, especially given what were altogether low expectations for the nascent training program.

Three years after arriving in Boston, Noyes returned Jammé's advice – and a favor – to her young friend, recommending Jammé as her replacement at the New England Hospital for Women and Children. Noyes, having turned things around in Boston, was headed 60 miles south to St. Luke's Hospital in New Bedford for her "broader field" of hospital executive work. Noyes mentored Jammé through the transition; but Jammé, a southerner, confronted a new reality of nursing work in Boston. "I remember well the shock I received when Miss Noyes conducted me through the hospital to find a colored head nurse in charge of the surgical pavilion and colored pupil nurses in the wards," Jammé recalled, confessing racial views that were not uncommon among white women trained at segregated institutions, especially in the South. Women of color found the doors shut to them at mainline nursing schools and professional organizations, especially elite institutions like Johns Hopkins and Bellevue. "Coming from Baltimore I was not prepared for the attitude of New England toward the colored race," Jammé said. "I was reassured by Miss Noyes, and through her eyes I soon saw the value of colored nurses in the scheme of nursing."[37]

Boston's school, compared to other institutions, had an unusually progressive view of this "scheme." Mary Mahoney was the first black nurse to graduate from the program, in 1879.[38] Like many American institutions in the late nineteenth and early twentieth centuries, racial discrimination was rampant at nurse training schools. The disparate treatment of aspiring black nurses resulted in movements to develop separate hospitals, education programs and organizational affiliations. Organizations like the National Association of Colored Graduate Nurses (NACGN) sought integration of the schools and an eventual merger with the much larger, mainline organization of nursing, the American Nurses Association (ANA), in 1951. One of the first training schools for black women opened in 1883 and was connected to Spelman Seminary in Atlanta. By the 1890s similar institutions for black nursing students sprouted throughout the United States.[39]

Clearly the New England Hospital for Women and Children was a unique case, though it was not entirely free of racial conflict; and Noyes's seemingly progressive "New England attitude" regarding "colored nurses in the scheme of nursing" is complicated by other events in her life amid the highly segregated environment of late nineteenth-century and early twentieth-century America.

The Noyes Family at Mount Ararat Farm. Clara Noyes is standing at center. Her sister Laura Banning Noyes is seated, far right, with racquet. *Photo courtesy of the Noyes Family.*

A YOUNGER SISTER, BOSTON AND NEW BEDFORD

While Clara Noyes was racking up executive experience at New England schools – well before she'd garner headlines at the American Red Cross – her younger sister, Laura Banning Noyes, was the first sibling to gain public notice as a nurse outside the insular field of early professional nursing. Laura Banning, the second-eldest daughter of Enoch and Laura Lay Banning, had inherited her older sister's household duties in the large Noyes family at Mount Ararat. She had also followed her older sister's path into nursing, but the contrasts in

Clara's and Laura's life pursuits tell a meaningful story about the status of nursing during this period as well as the changes that were taking hold in the profession. In many respects, Clara's sister, Laura, though younger, would ironically assume a more traditional path toward nursing and domestic life that was being summarily changed by professional nurses of Clara's ilk.

In 1905, the *Washington Post* and *New York Times* were following the story of Laura Banning Noyes, a young nurse connected to a big name in Baltimore politics. "Ex-Mayor Davidson Weds: Baltimorean Marries the Nurse with Whom he Eloped in This City," reads a page-one headline in the November 16 edition of the *Times*.[1] The scandal, embroiling Clara's sister, was major news from May to November of that year.

In a divorce saga made public, the wife of former Baltimore mayor Robert C. Davidson was alleging that her husband cashed in $175,000 worth of stocks and bonds[2] and eloped to Europe with Laura Banning Noyes, "a beautiful trained nurse," the *San Francisco Call* reported. "Miss Noyes is a brunette, about six feet tall, and is a friend of Davidson. According to Mrs. Davidson, her husband and Miss Noyes have been seen frequently in public places recently. They have been noticed driving in David Hill Park, she says, and have been seen at luncheon in the fashionable hotels."[3] The betrayed wife even hired a private investigator, having her husband "shadowed by detectives."[4] Despite a brief reconciliation after the ex-mayor returned from Europe, the Davidsons eventually parted ways.

Laura Banning Noyes was Davidson's private nurse at a time when the private-duty trade still dominated nursing occupations. Word-of-mouth referrals and doctor's registries made private-duty work a more amenable option over hospital service, where the hours were grueling, where nursing roles were primarily staffed by students from the training programs, where these students were exploited as cheap labor, and where nurses operated with little autonomy. "Most nurse historians agree that the move of graduate nurses from private-duty home care to hospital care meant a loss of independence, autonomy, and authority," writes historian Susan Malka.[5] "In the hospital, the nurse, within clearer lines of authority, served a patient population of primarily working-class men and women," adds Susan Reverby. "In the home, however, most nurses worked for families whose social position was usually higher than their own."[6] As patient care moved more in the direction of hospitals, private-duty nursing experienced a downward slide, especially with reforms and improved medical and sanitation practices in hospitals.[7]

By the time the Davidson scandal erupted, Laura and Clara's mother, Laura Lay Banning Noyes, had returned to her home state of Connecticut. There she was confronted by a reporter: "Mrs. Enoch Noyes ... when asked today concerning the elopement of her daughter, Laura, expressed great surprise." She said, "I do not believe the report. I am certain there must be some mistake."[8]

There was no mistake.

The Davidsons' divorce was imminent. Robert Davidson transferred all his business interests to New York, leaving his ex-wife with $50,000 alimony.[9] The Noyes-Davidson wedding soon followed at New York's Riverside Baptist Church. Laura Banning's mother and her brother, Charles, were witnesses. "Two sisters and another brother of Miss Noyes were also present."[10]

Laura had only two sisters at this point. One of those sisters must have been the thirty-six-year-old Clara

Noyes. Whether or not Clara was present in the church, witnessing the ceremony, one wonders if she ever considered the different course her life had taken from that of her younger sibling, both in their work as nurses. The episode brings forth a study in contrasts. One sister – a young, decidedly attractive brunette with a taste for society life named Laura Banning – nabbed headlines in a sensational story of elopement, divorce and, ultimately, her marriage. Laura Banning also represented the traditional practice of nursing, working in private-duty where she reportedly crossed the boundary between private and professional. The other, older sister, who would never marry, was already leading the charge of nurse education, forged in grueling hospital-based nursing work. Her career trajectory was beginning to sow changes in the very practice of professional nursing by raising the standards of programs like the New England Hospital for Women and Children and others. These larger movements brought nurses to the hospital for training, to the diminishment of private-duty work.

A family photo of the sisters shows Clara Noyes receiving a pour of tea from her mother on the grounds of Mount Ararat estate. Her younger sister, Laura Banning, is seated off to the right, cross-legged on the ground, with a badminton racquet leaning against her knees, elegantly cradling a teacup. By the time of this photo, it appears that Enoch had already passed, as the family matriarch is surrounded by daughters and sons, all neatly dressed for a summer tea party on the lawn.

By 1905, Clara Noyes was running what is today the oldest still-operating nursing school in the United States. When the St. Luke's Hospital training school in New Bedford opened in 1884, it was the nation's fourth, following the establishment of pioneer institutions at Bellevue, New Haven and Massachusetts General Hospital. Writing at about 1908, Noyes describes how it has been a "joy to develop this place. From 45 beds, we have grown to one hundred and eight."[11]

"It has been interesting work here," she adds. "I formed good material, which had never been developed waiting for me, a training school in which such a thing as a final examination or any was managed along the same course." She described a working school which had become the "apple of my eye," connected to an "ideal laundry, a pathological laboratory, and operating room extension giving us three beautiful operating rooms," a children's ward, and a maternity ward.[12] Like her work at Massachusetts Hospital for Women and Children, Clara Noyes was proving her skill turning around a fledgling nursing school that lacked the exacting standards possessed by Johns Hopkins. Beyond curriculum improvements, she was also overseeing important program capacity growth. St. Luke's was, indeed, a "broader field" for Noyes, as she earlier described it. She not only headed the nursing school but assumed an unusually commanding executive post at the hospital, especially unusual for a young nurse, controlling the internal governance of the institution.[13] From her perch at St. Luke's, Noyes kept in touch with colleagues at Johns Hopkins. She also observed the rise of other nursing schools, including one being built in "Fairhaven, a little town across the river" from New Bedford, endowed by local philanthropist Henry Huttleston Rogers, whom she called "the good fairy" who built St. Luke's "beautiful nurses' home in which we are now ensconced."[14]

Her "broader field" began to include connections with charitable networks and peer nursing leaders, such as former colleagues at Johns Hopkins, while she endeavored to breathe life into nursing programs short on funds, materials and basic facilities to operate effectively. In 1907, Rogers consulted with Noyes, seeking an executive to run the new Fairhaven school. Noyes reached out to her alma mater in search of a candidate, penning a letter to Georgina C. Ross, who was then Acting Superintendent at Johns Hopkins, suggesting the same kind of peer outreach that brought Noyes to her first superintendent role in the closely connected Johns Hopkins professional network. Ross had taken over the Hopkins school after Mary Adelaide Nutting departed to become the world's first professor of nursing, at Columbia University's Teaching School. Noyes's letter to Ross remarked on the bellwether achievement for the "dearly loved Miss Nutting," stating that "We all know what it will mean for the course there."[15] As for the Fairhaven position, Noyes indicated that Rogers is looking for "preferably a widow … I think he would prefer a protestant," adding: "I almost wish I could take the position myself."[16] Her ambition continued to grow, watchful of new opportunities at other nursing programs budding throughout the Northeast, and we see one example of many, noted by other scholars, of the collegial and interpersonal contact maintained by early nursing leaders and their alma maters to pass the torch of the Nightingale model to young graduates, fulfilling their own ambitions in the superintendent seats of early nursing academia.

Noyes would later write Ross again, in 1908, inquiring about the style of portable tubs in use at Johns Hopkins, as St. Luke's was building a "room especially for the treatment of such cases." Those cases – likely for typhoid fever treatment – had previously been put "into the ward bath tubs with canvas slings, which is extremely trying, as you may infer, although ideal as far as running water is concerned," Noyes said.[17] The mechanics of a bathing room may seem mundane by modern medical standards. But these rudimentary facilities were a lifesaver during a time of rampant typhoid fever. The bacterial infection spread among polluted water sources and tenement overcrowding, especially in America's larger cities. Hydrotherapy and chlorinated water were among the chief agents for fighting the infection. Citing an article in the *Medical Examiner and Practitioner*, Tennessee physician Dr. H.P. Coile wrote in 1903 that "there are only two factors that have produced any material effect upon the death rate of typhoid fever during the past half century; the first of these is hydrotherapy ... and the second is the more careful attention to nursing and the regulation of the diet."[18]

Noyes had clearly put both regimens to use in caring for her classmate Anna Jammé – when her friend was in the grip of infection and fever. The practice area of nursing was a primary line of defense and intervention for typhoid, and even a good nursing student was as capable as any medical professional to treat these cases. We are reminded again just how much the simple hygienic and sanitation practices – which we take for granted today – were among the primary methods for disease control and prevention in Progressive Era America, especially before the advent of effective vaccines. The simple matter of bathing facilities, for the care of typhoid and general infection control, put nurses in charge of disease management using methods entirely within their domain of training.

In one of Clara Noyes's earliest published articles for the *American Journal of Nursing*, a new source of media for the nursing masses that was reporting ideas and news updates in the field, she shared a schematic diagram of St. Luke's laundry facility, taking pride in her hospital's neat and orderly approach to the question of hygienic and sanitary practices. The article, entitled "A Modern Laundry," aimed to be "of some assistance to the busy superintendent of the smaller hospital, who is perhaps interested in a new building or the reorganization of an old laundry."[19] In characteristic form, Noyes meticulously described the new sixty-foot by forty-foot room and all of its appurtenances: granolithic floors, copper piping with brass strips, Dover River brick, one-hundred-shirt capacity washers, starching tables, and twelve-horsepower engine "accessible from all sides and sufficiently far from walls to prevent spattering," all at a cost of $15,618.06. Three employees handled 5,000 pieces of laundry weekly,[20] a well-oiled machine assuring proper sanitation and a supply chain for the hospital.

Her impact at St. Luke's was as broad as it was deep, overseeing growth in the number of hospital beds, improving the school's curriculum standards and, even, absorbing the minutia of facility operations. Once again, she had proven herself ready for an even "broader field" of training school management work, and it would take her from the fledgling programs in Massachusetts to one of the nation's more firmly established nursing programs, in New York City, where she became an increasingly prominent voice in organizational nursing education.

BELLEVUE AND THE MIDWIFE SCHOOL

The professional standards, education, role and status of midwives remains hotly debated even today. Its history is tangled in the politics of class, race, gender, religion and the pitting of establishment health care professions against non-establishment healers. Clara Noyes played a public role in this debate during her time as a nurse training school superintendent at Bellevue Hospital's nursing school in New York City. She took over the Bellevue training school for nurses on October 1, 1910 following Annie Goodrich's departure to become State Inspector of Nursing,[1] once again seizing a new career path at the right moment, credited for her work growing the New England programs in Boston and New Bedford and improving their standards. But Bellevue was a different animal. America's first modern nursing school at Bellevue had evolved to become the most revered institution for education in nursing. There, Clara Noyes lived and worked at the nurses' residence on East Twenty-Sixth Street.[2]

Noyes was beginning to gain a public voice on the issue of maternity-newborn nursing care. One of her first major public appearances reported by the national press, in 1912, was capped with the headline "No Conservation of Life of Child: Midwife not recognized." The press was covering a New York City conference of the International Congress of Hygiene and Demography.[3] At this time, the role of midwives was an area of prolonged and targeted debate. 1912 to 1914 were especially prolific years for this debate, as the so-called "midwife problem" cropped up repeatedly in both medical and nursing professional literature. Two years into her tenure at Bellevue, Noyes was instrumental in organizing the nation's first academic, not-for-profit school for midwives at the hospital where she was running the general program of nursing. The outcomes were promising: Bellevue-educated midwives attended births with lower mortality rates than in births generally in New York City.[4] Clearly the city's high infant mortality rate registered prominently in Noyes's concerns. Though she was not herself a mother – and would never marry – public health concerns for child welfare were a major concentration of her life's work. This included not only her nurse education role but also her household reference book *Home Care of the Sick: When Mother Does the Nursing*, published in 1924 as part of Funk and Wagnalls' "National Health Series."[5]

"In America, with characteristic disregard of our natural resources, we have not protected and conserved our child life," Noyes declared at the 1912 conference on hygiene and demography. "We have not recognized the midwife as a necessary part of our social structure. Attempts have been made from time to time to eliminate her, always unsuccessfully, however. We have closed our eyes and let her alone, without means of education and without adequate laws for control and supervision."[6] Here, as elsewhere in her advocacy work, Noyes relied on arguments of national interest, referring, first, to the callous disregard of our nation's "natural resources." These themes cropped up later in her remarks, as she bemoaned of midwifery "that fifty percent of all the births are attended by a class of untaught and untrained women, who, as a rule, are densely ignorant and unspeakably dirty. We are neglecting at the fountain head the health and possible wealth of our nation."[7] At the time, untrained midwives came largely from the immigrant classes, at least in Bellevue's case,[8] and midwives in the South were mostly African-American women. In Mississippi, for instance, about 90 percent of midwives were black, according to a study conducted from 1916 to 1918.[9] Thus, much of the rhetoric dealing with the "midwifery problem" focused on racial and ethnic dynamics. Along these lines, Noyes used a form of nativism in her arguments about the "untaught and untrained women" who were "densely ignorant." She and other trained nurses were largely native-born women of privilege, at least by dint of their race and ethnicity, if not economically. In contrast, healers outside of this group were largely urban-born, non-native women who had "drifted" into their work. However, this rhetoric belied the fact that "those who learned their midwifery in Europe were very well educated compared to U.S. trained physicians attending women in childbirth during the same period," explains scholar Katy Dawley. "Obstetricians seeking to develop the medical specialization of obstetrics and public health nurses aspiring to establish a specialty in midwifery joined in a campaign to eliminate traditional midwives" and their journals "published articles accusing immigrant and African American midwives of being ignorant, dirty and dangerous." Dawley explains that this was "a racist campaign based on the now discredited theory of eugenics," ignoring "data that showed immigrant and African American midwives provided good care."[10]

By 1912, doctors had also begun voicing increasing concerns about midwifery using similar rhetoric. However, those concerns were a bit different from the nursing community's. Many physicians were grappling with fears about the status of their profession in relation to the midwife. Training in obstetrics was poor, and physicians reported, quite frankly, that their work was no better in terms of mortality rates compared to the untrained midwife. Midwifery was a threat to their professional domain. One physician studying the issue recommended the "gradual abolition of midwives in large cities and their replacement by obstetric charities," along with medical-education reforms to make this possible. His findings and recommendations, based on a survey of physicians, were reported in the January 1912 edition of the *Journal of the American Medical Association*. "If midwives are to be educated, it should be done in a broad sense, and not in a makeshift way. Even then disappointment will probably follow."[11] A year later, Dr. Charles Edward Ziegler raised even louder alarms, citing "great danger" in the "possibility of attempting to educate the midwife." Dr. Zeigler went on record to agree with one of his colleagues that midwives were a "menace to the health of the community, an unnecessary evil and a nuisance." If the midwife "becomes a fixed element in our social and economic system," he added, "we may never be able to get rid of her."[12]

The nursing and medical professions were coming at the "problem" from different angles. But Noyes was keenly aware of the fearful threat to physician practice and prestige, as words like "evil" and "menacing" had punctuated the debate, even among those physicians who saw no way around the "midwifery problem" and grudgingly acknowledged that their obstetrics practices were no better at reducing mortality. By highlighting the medical profession's attempts to "eliminate" the midwife – and the feeling, by some, that midwives were an "evil" and a "menace" – Noyes lays bare the ambivalent, at times racist and contradictory views held by establishment authorities during this period. However, one other solution to the "midwife problem" was "not to eliminate midwives but rather to train, license and regulate them," Noyes said, providing a different tack from the other establishment medical views.[13] Just as the nursing school movement was still in its formative phases, the physician field of practice, particularly in obstetrics, similarly lacked formal training institutions to meet the nation's health care needs. But the nursing community more actively welcomed midwives into their practice area. Midwives were, indeed, necessary, even if a "necessary evil." Simply put, there were not enough obstetricians and other trained physicians to attend to all the births.[14] Noyes saw education and regulation as an antidote.

In one of her most influential articles on the subject, Clara Noyes took up the "Midwifery Problem" in the March 1912 edition of the *American Journal of Nursing*. This constant refrain of a "problem" recalls W.E.B Du Bois's famous phrase about the color line in America and his response "To the real question, How does it feel to be a problem? I answer seldom a word."[15] Like white America's attitude towards race, the medical establishment had its own "problem" areas, and it sometimes handled them not only with racist hostility but also a degree of coded ambivalence, especially as race and ethnicity were concerned. In the case of midwifery, race and ethnicity were, indeed, a factor that the medical literature couldn't help but convey in its nativism.

If Noyes's reference to the "unspeakable dirtiness" of midwives seemed disparaging in this racial and ethnic context, she cast a more sympathetic light in her *Journal* article when describing the plight of these women of color and from the immigrant classes.[16] "For years in America the medical profession has fought the midwife, struggled to suppress her, restrict her, eliminate her and what

Bellevue and the Midwife School 41

not, yet the midwife continues to flourish. It seems strange that in America, the so-called 'Home of the brave and land of the free,' she has met this reception." She adds: "There seems little chance of eliminating the midwife except by education of both the midwife and the people."[17] A pervading sense of "fear" and "eradication," at least professional eradication of midwifery, had permeated class-based debates about the status of these women even into the early twentieth century. Clara Noyes, like others, nevertheless opted for a more assimilationist approach, seeking, instead, "education, examination and registration, and supervision and control."[18]

She also raises the concept, though not in name, of a new professional designation, the "nurse-midwife," which did not come into practice until 1925.[19] The idea was revolutionary, in blending nurse training with the traditionally untrained practice of midwifery. It became an emerging concept for professionalizing home childbirths, embraced by Noyes and other nurse leaders like Lillian Wald. A link between midwifery and "district nursing" – what we call home health nursing or visiting nursing today – was first introduced in Noyes's *Journal* article:

> The large number of nurses engaged in district nursing are engaged in instructing the prospective mother and giving nursing care during pregnancy and puerperium. They find themselves seriously handicapped at times, not so much from lack of knowledge, but from lack of legal recognition. If our visiting nurses were also certified midwives, would not the mothers and babies of the less favored classes be infi-

nitely safer in their hands, than in the hands of the majority of midwives?[20]

Reading her *Journal* article, as well as Clara Noyes's full speech to the International Congress of Hygiene and Demography, it appears that many of Noyes's quotes, as they appeared in the mainstream press, may have been cherry-picked, perhaps as an unconscious reflection of contemporary establishment sentiments. The full version of the 1912 speech, along with Noyes's *Journal* article, lean more on the side of championing the midwife. Noyes clearly understood the effectiveness of midwives, in spite of their lack of training, which she appeared to regard as a structural cause rather than as a defect on the part of the midwife: "In justice to the midwife, we find from all reports that midwives are responsible for less injury to mothers and children than that laid to the door of the medical profession," she writes, calling it "criminal negligence" that the medical profession ignores her existence. "If the midwife does better work untrained than the general practitioner, what type of work would she do after six months or one year of careful training?"[21]

Noyes ends her 1912 speech with an exhortation, again drawing on the theme of national interest:

> Our spirit of citizenship is at last stirred, the pitiful cry of the neglected infant has, at last, touched our hearts, and it is for this reason that we urge the education of women, whether as the midwife pure and simple, or as a further development of the nurses' work, in the practice of normal midwifery, not as a means of livelihood … but fundamentally as a protection to the

strength and health and wealth of the nation.[22]

In its nursing school, Bellevue was forged by a curriculum of standardized practical and theoretical training, hallmarks of the Nightingale model. Noyes clearly understood the applicability of this model for midwife training, too, seeing the professional uplift of midwives as akin to the evolution of nurse training schools in the last quarter of the nineteenth century: "Education means elevation and progress. It has not been a very long time since doctors were barbers and the nursing care of the sick was rescued from degradation by Florence Nightingale." Mindful of establishment class fears, she adds: "There seems to be no fundamental reason why the technically educated midwife should be feared any more than the technically educated physician or nurse."[23] Health care scope-of-practice issues have always held a kind of sacred status, and this episode reveals one of many times where a threat to the medical practice area drew protectionism. However, some nurses, unlike many physicians, appeared open to the inclusion of midwives in their professional ranks, though this was by no means a universal view. At a convention on infant mortality, nurses supported a resolution "that the nursing profession be asked to extend its field of usefulness by including training for the practice of midwifery for normal cases. Further that a minimum standard of training be required for all who are permitted to practice midwifery and that all midwives be under state or municipal control."[24] Some voices in the nursing community landed on this regime of "education, examination and registration, and supervision and control," distinct from the protectionism of the physician community.

By 1912, Bellevue's School for Midwives had been operating for little more than a year. The number of beds increased from eight to twenty. The first midwife graduates, in 1911, completed a six-month course where they observed sixty cases and engaged in eight deliveries. A year later, the most recent graduates had observed 104 cases and delivered twelve.[25] Though it was separate from the nursing program, the midwife school was overseen by the General Superintendent of Nursing, in this case, Clara Noyes. The school consisted of a small hospital, "with a house in the rear in which the pupil midwives live," at 223 East 26th Street. The second-floor ward had room for twelve patients. Administrative offices were on the first floor. A graduate nurse directed the nursing and housekeeping instruction, while medical training was directed by the resident physician in a kind of inter-disciplinary approach. "Great attention is paid to teaching the pupil midwives practical housekeeping, simple cooking, cleaning, laundry work, sanitation and hygiene, in addition to the care of mother and babe, preparation for confinement, making dressings, sterilizing, etc.," wrote Noyes about the program in its first year.[26] "Although this is the first School of Midwifery in America, and is in the embryonic stage," Noyes added, "it is, perhaps, too early to prophesy the ultimate results, yet there seems to be no practical reason why it should not succeed."[27]

But these efforts notwithstanding, the movement to professionalize the practice of midwifery succumbed to other evolutions in medical practice, driving down the number of births attended by midwives. Bellevue's school, while successful in its outcomes, ended up shuttering due to a lack of students and other issues in 1936.[28] The closure reflected a larger trend. As health care historian Laura E. Ettinger points out, "The use of midwives rapidly declined in the 1910s and 1920s. In Washington, DC, midwives attended fifty percent of births in 1903 but only fifteen percent in 1912; in New York City, midwives delivered thirty percent of the babies in 1919, but only twelve percent in 1929."[29] In its twenty-five-year history, the Bellevue school graduated 796 students.[30] Midwifery also continued to draw opposition from the medical community, even as physicians noted Bellevue's positive outcomes. Seven years into Bellevue's operation, one physician, J. Clifton Edgar, presented his study of New York City's "midwife problem" at a May 1918 meeting of the American Gynecological Society. He prefaced his remarks with a clear indication of bias: "We are opposed to the midwife; opposed to any plan or system by which she will be permanently retained and perpetuated as practitioner of obstetrics," Dr. Edgar wrote, acknowledging, however, that "She is a necessary evil for traditional, social and economic reasons."[31]

By Dr. Edgar's assessment, it appears that more and more foreign-born women were opting for hospital maternity care than in the pre-war period. The number of New York City births was level between 1914 and 1917, but midwives cared for fewer cases, a reduction from 37.6 percent of births to 32.3 percent attended by midwives, he reported. "There are two main causes for this decline, namely the extension of substitute measures to replace the midwife," Dr. Edgar wrote, "but especially the increasing tendency and willingness of the foreign-born woman to employ a doctor who is a man, and not a midwife because she is cheaper and a woman."[32]

Despite his stated opposition to midwifery, Dr. Edgar pointed to Bellevue's successes. In the seven years since it opened, 235 midwives had graduated by 1918, attending

5,125 births with a maternal mortality rate of 0.7 percent. "The influence of 235 Bellevue alumnae is generally for good among the existing 1,656 midwives" in New York City, he said. "We unhesitatingly affirm that an obstetric patient, normal or otherwise, is safer in the hands of a graduate Bellevue midwife than in those of the casual and indifferent practitioner."[33] Nevertheless, appalled by the high infant mortality rate generally in the city, Dr. Edgar believed that midwives were in no position to determine normal versus complex labors. "For safe obstetrics the obstetrician must ever perform the prenatal examination and care."[34] Period.

Her work at Bellevue gave Noyes a new platform, not just about midwifery, but she began lending her voice more broadly to a host of other issues concerning nurses. Noyes's articles and commentary began appearing with increasing frequency in the *American Journal of Nursing*, and, to a new extent, in mainstream media, where she spoke to nursing issues of the day on the pages of the *New York Tribune* and other dailies in the New York City market. For the nursing public, specifically, the Bellevue post also opened doors for her to lead the early organizations for nursing education, like the American Society of Superintendents of Training Schools and the National League of Nursing Education (NLNE), both of which focused on educational concerns but parlayed into later alignments of organized nursing which fought for fair employment, practice-area legislation and other aims. Beyond the niche area of midwifery, perhaps the more abiding aim of Clara Noyes's work – in these and other venues – was to press for educational standards and measures to combat hospital exploitation of student nurses, which was an ongoing source of angst for nurse education leaders. Her voice was assertive and took seeming delight in the mechanics of argument and advocacy positioning, sprinkled at times with folksy analogies and rhetorical turns of phrase, showing a leadership voice that was becoming increasingly articulate and knowledgeable about the issues of her profession.

In 1912, a committee of the Superintendents' Society was formed to address hospital management issues. The gathering of superintendents from nurse training schools denounced hospital executives for breaking their contracts with student nurses by "putting students into the kitchen" for non-nursing work. "The nurse should be confined to nursing work," Noyes said at a June 4, 1912 conference addressing the issue. "There are no splendid opportunities offered her in answering the telephone and tending the door," she quipped, noting that the hospital executives often assigned nurses to kitchen duty because the nurses "do the work better and with less pay than a regular servant."[35] Noyes was also continuing to fight overtures by hospital executives bent on lowering the bar of nursing education in order to meet nursing shortages – a constant battle throughout her career. "We have to make bricks without straw right along," Noyes said in 1912, conjuring a "Three Little Pigs" folk-tale analogy: A protective structure of nursing standards was needed to guard against dispersive outside forces seeking to diminish the trade. She noted that the nursing schools, if they had the liberty to do so, would actually be inclined to "refuse many of those [nursing students] we do admit," for their lack of solid qualifications. Lowering the bar, as "hospital men" suggested, would just further diminish the quality of candidates. "As for the people who are opposed to the entrance requirements of the Board of Regents," she added of New York's standards, "I do not believe they are really opposed to high standards, but they are hospital men, who must necessarily look at the question from a more or less commercial point of view. They have to consider its economic impact," adding that higher standards actually draw more students into nursing, not less, contrary to conventional wisdom. "By the maintenance of high standards we make our schools more attractive to a high class of women. As a matter of fact, the dearth of pupils appears to be greater in the schools of low standards."[36] Furthermore, weakening of nursing standards would not affect the salary equation for nurses, no more than it would help with shortages, she said. Better standards draw a better class of woman who are less motivated by pecuniary interests. "I have found it is the higher type of woman, the one who can easily meet the present requirements, who takes a scientific and a humane interest in her work and is not so influenced by the money," Noyes remarked.[37] Class-consciousness suffused the question of nursing education at a time when young girls still sought to enter the trade with minimal secondary education, and as hospital executives welcomed lower educational standards in order to staff their hospitals' wards with pliable, cheap labor.

The NLNE aimed to stop this campaign for weaker standards. By 1912, thirty-three states had laws regulating nursing, a byproduct of organized nursing and, specifically, efforts of the NLNE.[38] During this period, the organizations of nursing also strived to promote college affiliation for training schools, shorter workdays for nurses, a standardized curricula and improved graduate-to-student nurse ratios.[39] These efforts culminated in the NLNE's influential 1917 report on the *Standard Curriculum for Schools of Nursing*.[40] Noyes was president of the organization from 1913 to 1916 as these efforts took hold.

Later, the NLNE's grading committees, in the mid-1920s and early 1930s, prompted important improvements in the standards of training schools. This grading process revealed areas of curriculum, staffing and student life where many schools fell short.[41] "Giving impetus to the report was the Great Depression, which brought about many small and large school closings, although many nurse training 'mills' continued to operate,"[42] explains Sarah Slavin in her profile of the NLNE's work during this period. Although the NLNE "was not entirely successful in preventing the exploitation of student nurses for the benefit of hospitals," adds Robert Piemonte in his history of the organization, "it had a very decided effect on limiting the practice."[43]

Noyes would later lock horns with Red Cross officials over the role of charity-minded laywomen in the Red Cross as she tried to maintain the purity of nursing standards.[44] Even though, to her mind, untrained society women had no place in the Red Cross Nursing Service, class-consciousness nevertheless influenced Noyes's view of the ideal nursing school applicant. It appears the nursing profession tried to strike a balance between drawing a "higher" sort of candidate, using Noyes's words, but not the type of "society women" seeking to offer charitable services without requisite training.

By 1915, the NLNE and organized nursing leaders were also stepping into the debates about women's suffrage – a debate that was long simmering. 1869 was not only Clara Noyes's birth year,[45] but it was also a formative year in the suffrage movement. As women generally fought for the ballot, their concerns began to echo in the major nursing organizations throughout the first two decades of the twentieth century.

The suffrage debate, materializing so closely after the Civil War and Reconstruction-era social changes, also unsurprisingly intersected with the issue of race which had a profound impact on the evolution of women's professional aspirations through nursing. The question of suffrage brought to light some of the competing interests between social justice for women and social justice for black Americans. Race, in particular, created a fissure in the suffrage campaigns, as the nation, during the Reconstruction era, was considering ratification of the Fifteenth Amendment, which would grant voting rights to men regardless of color. One side of the suffrage movement, represented by Susan B. Anthony and Elizabeth Cady Stanton, opposed the Fifteenth Amendment's course on the grounds that if white women must wait for the vote, so, too, should black men.[46] Absent from this debate were black women, whose interests didn't even register. A second camp, led by Lucy Stone and others, held a competing pro-Republican/abolitionist view of the role that black-American rights would play in their aim for women's suffrage. This camp saw the Fifteenth Amendment as a necessary step (at least, it seems, in terms of political expediency) to women's suffrage.[47] From these competing schools of thought emerged two suffrage organizations in 1869: the National Woman Suffrage Association and the American Woman Suffrage Association.[48] The internecine conflict – again, with black women on the sidelines – foreshadows later debates about the role of black women in the nursing profession, as the intersection of race, class and white privilege would trickle through virtually every question pertaining to the roles of individuals in public life.

These political divisions also gave rise to a distinct mode of feminist suffragism. This more feminist ideology was distinct from the post-abolitionist-Republican form of suffragism that was driven by a goal of advancing a precedent-setting Fifteenth Amendment, as a glide path for women's ballot rights.[49] Eventually the movements for nurse professionalization and the larger question of women's suffrage came into alignment. But nurses were not uniform in their support of women's suffrage – nor were they uniform in their methods for obtaining it – and the professional institutions of nursing grappled with the matter frequently.[50]

By 1915 Clara Noyes, too, was making an important connection between nurse professionalization and women's suffrage; although, other nurse leaders, like Noyes's colleague Lavinia Dock, made more emphatic appeals – in Dock's case, picketing the White House and getting arrested three times in 1917 and 1918 for her more aggressive tactics.[51] Clara Noyes's early arguments over suffrage, alternatively, reflected a vision for women's advancement revolving almost entirely around the status of her profession: nursing. On two separate occasions, as president of the NLNE, one of the early organizations of nursing advocacy, Clara Noyes made the connection between her profession and suffrage. She was by no means a leading icon of the suffrage movement – or even a major figure in the nursing wing of the suffrage movement – but her remarks nevertheless lay bare some of the different ideological lenses through which nursing leaders viewed the ballot question and its impetus for advancing women's professional and personal interests. Addressing delegates at the NLNE's annual conference in San Francisco in 1915, Noyes devoted part of her speech to the collective movement for standards of nursing education, regulations, licensure and professional recognition, adding: "Nothing ever gains the respect of the world or becomes practicable or reaches beyond the purely practicable until it has been fought for," citing "equal suffrage" among her examples.[52] Noyes takes the connection further in 1916, standing before a similar audience at the NLNE's annual conference in New Orleans: "We have been told that 'when women really want suffrage, they will get it.' The same thing has been said about nursing laws, that 'when nurses really want good nursing laws, they will get them.' But we might as well face the fact that we will never get good nursing laws, proper recognition or good schools of nursing until we stand together, shoulder to shoulder."[53]

The New Orleans speech, using an inclusive "we," conveys a "shoulder-to-shoulder" affinity with the suffrage cause, but, again, it is almost exclusively circumscribed by concerns about Noyes's profession: nursing. This emphasis on promoting public policy (i.e., nursing laws) as a rationale for women's social justice (i.e., suffrage) was a main current of Clara Noyes's advocacy work in later years. She often fought for women's causes using methods that overshadowed social-justice issues by casting light on more professional interests, for the sake of political expediency, necessity, or both, and she often connected women's causes to more amenable public policy issues (e.g., professional standards, patriotism). As historians have observed more globally, especially Sandra Beth Lewenson, one way to convince nurses of the need for suffrage – and to mobilize for it – was to argue that voting rights were necessary for protecting and improving their professional space. By possessing the right to vote, women were strengthened in their advocacy role, as constituents, to help prod nurse registration laws, nurse practice acts, local health board participation, licensure and other regulatory controls.[54] This connection is echoed in Clara Noyes's remarks at New Orleans.

The practice of nursing was fundamentally changing. At the time of her New Orleans speech – in 1916, as the nation was on its reluctant path toward entering a global war – nurses of Clara Noyes's generation expressed caution about the zeal of young women to serve. Many younger women were taken with romantic-patriotic notions and eager for wartime duty without having undergone proper training. Noyes was constantly reminded of the need for a properly trained class of professional nurses, so that soldiers had the most skilled care possible, so that resources were best put to use for civilian populations, and so the practice of nursing wasn't diluted in the mania of war. The enthusiasm of women to enroll in the American Red Cross during the war years even raised an existential concern. "Everyone seems to have gone mad," Noyes wrote her colleague and former mentor, Mary Adelaide Nutting, in 1917. "There are moments when I wonder whether we can stem the tide and control the hysterical desire on the part of thousands, literally thousands, to get into nursing … The most vital thing in the life of our profession is the protection of the use of the word nurse."[55] This concern appears to have preoccupied Noyes well before she came to the Red Cross, and especially as America's participation in the war was drawing closer. Noyes and others took heed of British practices as nurses were already pressed into duty. They observed in England "the unskilled and untrained lay worker from all grades of society quite generally made responsible for the nursing of the sick soldier in the present conflict."[56] In the British example, Noyes found herself astonished that Florence Nightingale's home nation had resorted to untrained nurses caring for its battle-wounded. The lesson certainly stuck with her as she prepared U.S. nurses for war two years later; but it was one that concerned her very early in her career. As she told delegates quite colorfully during the 1915 NLNE convention, almost in Rip Van Winkle fashion: "We, who have viewed this extraordinary situation from afar, have rubbed our eyes and wondered if we have been sleeping and had dreamed that a Florence Nightingale some fifty years ago had risen to the rescue of the English soldier ... Through the protection of our schools, our professional rights and duties, we protect the community, both in peace and war, from charlatanism and quackery."[57]

Superintendent Clara Noyes (center) with students at Bellevue Hospital Training School for Nurses. *Photo courtesy of the Noyes Family.*

BELLEVUE AND THE COLOR LINE

Regardless of the somewhat inclusionary race practices that Noyes experienced at her first job in Boston, the color line was a factor in Noyes's decisions at other points in the first half of her career, due in large to existing institutional practices and cultural attitudes at more established, mainline institutions like Bellevue Hospital. One case was even referred for investigation by the National Association for the Advancement of Colored People (NAACP). Senetta Anderson, a black high school graduate,[1] sought entrance to the Bellevue Hospital school in 1914. Noyes reportedly discouraged Anderson from applying. The case even brought forth a vigorous defense from Lillian Wald, famous in the nursing world as founder of New York City's Henry Street Settlement (a precursor to the Visiting Nurse Service of New York,

56 Clara D. Noyes

which, today, is the nation's largest not-for-profit home nursing agency). The somewhat cliquey and guarded network of early nursing leaders, so vital to the uplift of one another in the ranks of nursing academia, had also conspired to protect the profession from what they deemed "outside" threats, with racial consequences that limited the advancement of black women seeking the same uplift and career opportunity.

The arguments of both women in the Anderson case, Noyes and Wald, each products of Progressive Era yet segregated America, tiptoe around the social-justice issue for black nurses. Leaning on practical considerations, it's as if they felt separate from the culture of racial bigotry and merely confronted a delicate custom of American life, and, thus, did not want to upend the established social order in any way disruptive of their own aspirations to raise the status and education of nurses broadly. In August 1914, Noyes wrote to Wald, defending her call in the Anderson case, having sidelined Anderson's application. Noyes's letter begins with a mixed expression of racial sympathy and ambivalence: "Ever since I have been in New York ... I have feared that such a request as made by this young colored woman might come – not that I have anything but the greatest sympathy for them as a race – but because of the complications that might arise, should such a demand be made."[2] Noyes added: "Legally, I presume [Anderson] could force the issue, and although I did not refuse to consider her, I told her that colored students had never been admitted [to Bellevue] in the past. She seemed intelligent; consequently, I discussed the matter with her, and gave her a list of schools offering good training,"[3] ostensibly a list of segregated nursing schools.

The matter was brought to NAACP Counsel Chapin Brinsmead, where it was reported Senetta Anderson "had been refused." In her technical arguments, Noyes contended that Anderson was merely dissuaded, not outright rejected, given that no formal application was received.[4] And as evidence of her racial goodwill, Noyes cited her time at the New England Hospital for Women and Children, proving that she had "grappled" with the color line before and did not arrive at the Anderson decision lightly. "There in Boston, sympathy ran high for the negro. A southern woman was rarely admitted to the school, yet I lost many good students, because they were forced into such intimate relations when off duty." And on duty, she said, "military discipline prevails and the colored student sooner or later rose to the rank of 'senior,'" making it "almost impossible to preserve the discipline; and open insurrection, despite my most earnest efforts, occurred again and again, and if I did my duty, it meant sacrificing the white pupil for the colored."[5]

There's a lot to unpack in Noyes's statement of defense. But it appears that a primary concern was ensuring stability and maintaining Bellevue's roster of students: by not "sacrificing" qualified white students for the sake of equally qualified black students. As with the suffrage debates of the 1860s, we see here a striking interference of America's color line within women's causes – in this case, Noyes's work to advance (white) women professionally as nurses at Bellevue.

Noyes's letter goes on to reference other concerns, such as endangerment to patient care and the potential suffering for Anderson who might be the target of racist insults. She repeatedly emphasized concerns about the status and stability of her institution, "which, after a brief period of re-adjustment, is only beginning to stand upon a firm basis." She concluded: "I believe in fair play and giving the negro every chance in the world, and I have lived up to this wherever I could, but I think that they have not yet reached the place where they should try to force the issue, particularly where so much that is vital is concerned. There are good schools provided for them; their doors are open; thus every colored woman who desires studying nursing can do so, if she qualifies"[6] – except, of course, not at Bellevue, nor at many other premier nursing institutions divided by color.

Wald, though a board member of the NAACP and a proponent of the National Association of Colored Graduate Nurses (NACGN),[7] nevertheless agrees. She prepared a letter to the NAACP's counsel, first sharing her arguments with Noyes that "there are good training schools for colored women, and their graduates rank well," while also emphasizing fear that southern students would leave if the doors were open to applicants of all races. Also, "many patients would object to colored nurses."[8]

In an August 13, 1914 letter, Wald concluded: "I believe in giving colored people every chance," adding that "we have consistently lived up to our belief whenever possible, but I would deplore any entanglement that would bring the matter to an issue in the training schools, particularly those training schools where the superintendents are friendly and broad minded, and themselves have no prejudice."[9]

Wald offered to bring the issue to the NAACP's executive committee. In a letter to Brinsmead, on August 18, 1914, Wald said she had "not changed" her opinion. "However, the young woman has the right to make her application formally, and if she feels strongly that she wants to go to Bellevue, I presume that there is nothing more to be said."[10]

The letter appears to have been a last word on the matter.

In justice to Senetta B. Anderson, this chapter warrants some truly final word on her life and family. She lived in Washington, DC, where the 1930 census recorded her occupation: "trained nurse," though it is not clear through which avenue.[11] She married Emanuel E. Nelom, a citizen of British Guiana[12] who was a member of Marcus Garvey's renowned Universal Negro Improvement Association (UNIA) and signer on its *Declaration of Rights of the Negro Peoples of the World*.[13] Their daughter, Gloria, pursued a teaching career.[14] Gloria also enlisted for war service: in the Women's Army Corps (WAC), as an "aviation cadet" during World War II.[15] While stationed at Fort Des Moines, Iowa, Gloria joined a WAC band. She was its drummer.[16]

The 404th Army Service Forces Band performed throughout the United States to raise money for war-bond drives. After a sold-out show at the University of Chicago, connected to an NAACP conference, the unit was told to pack up their instruments, at a time then it was outshining the other (all-white) WAC group at Fort Des Moines, the 400th band.[17] An outcry from black newspapers got the band reinstated.[18]

Like her mother, Gloria Nelom encountered an iteration of the color line, extending from early twentieth-century nursing education, and, even, to a group of young women at a segregated WAC camp during the Second World War. There, despite opposition, they sought to "bend that military instrument into a beam of lyrical sound,"[19] as Ralph Ellison would later describe the symbolic importance of Louis Armstrong's horn and his music's cultural contributions, with their patriotism blaring in a chorus of trumpets, piccolos, trombones, clarinets, tubas, and, perhaps the ultimate military instrument, the marching of a drum.

Senetta B. Anderson indeed became a "trained nurse." Her life was connected to the pan-Africanist movement of Marcus Garvey, an early incarnation of "black pride." And her daughter would proudly offer service to the U.S. cause in the Second World War, pushing back against the color line in patriotic duty during her generation's moment of wartime sacrifice.

'CONDITIONS, NOT CAUSES': A PATH TO WAR AND RED CROSS SERVICE

I n 1913, Columbia-University-trained psychologist Cora Sutton Castle wrote the first *Statistical Study of Eminent Women*. Castle analyzed and indexed the records of women who were cataloged in several reference books, from the *Encyclopedia Britannica* to biographical dictionaries. She found that this existing record of so-called eminent women – those "high in rank, office, worth or public estimation" – included a mere 868 entries. "It is a sad commentary on the sex that from the dawn of history to the present day less than one thousand women have accomplished anything that history has recorded as worthwhile," Castle wrote. "One cannot evade the question – is woman innately so inferior to man or has the attitude of civilization been to close the avenues of eminence against her?"[1] It's an earnest question, but the answer today is quite obvious. Structural, social, professional and domestic reforms were slow moving in establishing a pathway for women's advancement. While the Progressive Era birthed women's organizations and a new level of women's participation in the public sphere, only in extremely rare cases were educated women leaders welcomed as actors within mainstream institutions, such as government bureaus, non-government organizations, the business world or legislative bodies.

But the tide was slowly changing.

In 1916, Montana elected the first woman ever to Congress, Jeannette Rankin. Four days after taking her historic seat in Congress, Rankin cast one of her most defining votes amid her overall defining moment in the history of women's aims for high office. It was a 'no' vote: on the congressional resolution to enter World War I.[2]

The response to Rankin's pacifism revealed deep fissures within the women's suffrage movement when it came to the issue of war. Suffrage arguments, both pro and con, were laden with the notion that war and voting-rights were bound together, rightly or wrongly so: The "bullet" was somehow linked to the "ballot." Many women who were regarded as "militaristic" believed that an enlarged role in so-called "home defense" would naturally offer a link to full citizenship, providing yet another shade to the link between bullet and ballot, observes historian Kimberly Jensen.[3] Asserting a strong connection to the nation-state through militant preparedness and patriotism, some women thought, would logically extend to broader recognition and support of their right to vote. But many pacifist-suffragists disagreed that martial participation was a necessary criterion for the right to vote.[4]

In the early twentieth century, women were increasingly present at shooting clubs and ranges, rifles in hand, seeking to train for the eventuality of home-defense. Despite the fervor of some to bear arms, women nevertheless found themselves in a complicated relationship to war. Yes, they were drawn by a sense of patriotic duty; but their role remained largely separated from the fields of violence. Nursing was one of the few areas where women were being inserted into a more proximal relationship to the fields of battle. These first expeditions included the early American Red Cross mobilization of nurses as part of the Spanish-American War and on a special mission, known as the "Mercy Ship," to provide aid to combatant nations in Europe, already in the throes of World War I by 1914.[5] The United States wouldn't formally enter the war for another three years. But in 1914 the *SS Red Cross* (as the "Mercy Ship" was more formally known) sailed for Europe with 170 nurses and surgeons aboard to provide relief for all sides in the conflict, under the aegis of the Geneva Conventions, long before a U.S. soldier set foot on the European continent in service to the Allies.[6]

Once Rankin cast her pacifist vote, some women's groups even shunned her or kept her at arm's length, including Carrie Chapman Catt, the suffragist leader, who, ironically, was among the more prominent opponents of the "bullet and ballot" argument. She and others saw Rankin's decision as politically damaging because it stood at odds with prevailing views of the (male) voting public, including Rankin's 373 House colleagues who had approved the war resolution and whose support was needed to carry a suffrage bill.[7] Though Catt argued forcefully against the idea that war service was a criterion for suffrage, she nevertheless worried about the political impact of Rankin's vote in an environment of patriotism.

Indeed, some suffragists theorized that war provided an avenue for advancement. Proof of this advancement would later be shown in the far larger-scale mobilization of nurses and other women Red Cross auxiliary volunteers for war after the Mercy Ship. This broader recognition of women's work – their professional contributions, as well as some of the advocacy efforts that nurse leaders staked out on behalf of women amid wartime – would help propel the women's suffrage movement forward. While Rankin's vote complicated the syllogism between the "bullet and the ballot," her relationship to the suffrage movement was later repaired when, by 1918, she reopened congressional debate on a Nineteenth Amendment for women's right to vote.[8]

As the United States was readying for battle, Clara Noyes expressed views of her own on the moral dimensions of war. Those views were vital as she and her mentor, Jane Delano, would soon became perhaps the most prominent two officials involved in the enlistment of fellow women for war. "I personally abhor war and all its paraphernalia," Clara Noyes told nursing school graduates in one speech. "I deplore the waste, the destruction of life and property and the shattering of our ideas of peace and love," Noyes said.[9] "Yet we are now engaged in war," she added, highlighting the struggle to reconcile private views with the public need to act. "We are dealing with conditions, not causes, and much as we dislike it, we must as individuals and as a nation meet these conditions and deal with them efficiently."[10] Put another way, now wasn't the time to debate the cause of war. Others had made this decision for reasons outside nurses' control. Nurses could control, however, their responsiveness. And so, just as her father's Battle of Port Hudson had been a mistake – storming the Confederate bastion unnecessarily, costing lives in the process as "iron hail" pounded the foggy trenches along the Mississippi – Clara Noyes's generation would understand that a duty to act, serving troops in the trenches of Europe, would trump any debate about causes. For Clara Noyes, war was a contingency that had to be answered. Without a response, far greater suffering, loss of life, and prolonged damage were inevitable. Perhaps her expression of hatred for war was an important way of persuading American Red Cross enrollment from young women who felt unprepared or disinclined for war service. For many young women, the pursuit of a nursing profession was surely driven by economic considerations and healing the nation's sick, not ministering to the army or navy wounded. Noyes's rhetoric of "conditions, not causes" would reinforce a sense of unavoidability – the urgency of conditions that needed to be addressed, following causes long since decided.

Regardless of "conditions or causes," a line of division was emerging among suffragists and other women's rights advocates over the war. These divisions were aired on several specific occasions. One, in particular, surfaced during a February 1917 meeting of the Brooklyn Woman Suffrage Association. Mrs. Henry Clarke Coe, President of the National Society of New England Women, rose to speak, extending an invitation for her fellow suffragists to arm themselves with rifles as part of a preparedness effort in wartime. "It is our duty to get ready for what may come and if you are a suffragist you must be as good shots as the men," she told attendees, speaking on behalf of the American Rifle Defense Club.[11] Her remarks underscore the very heart of the "bullet-for-ballot" syllogism and all of its variations: i.e., if you are a suffragist, then you must be willing to take up arms.

Coe's invitation must have certainly raised eyebrows. Others at the suffrage meeting clearly took umbrage with her appeal to militancy. Mrs. Emily Brewster was among those who responded to Coe from the standpoint of a "peace-at-any-price pacifist," stating: "Why can't we women stand shoulder to shoulder and urge peace? Peace with honor. I love my son, and I am disappointed in women who are so militaristic and so ready to give up their sons."[12] As Kimberly Jensen notes, "anti-imperialist suffragists defined citizenship as democratic, not militaristic, and used their critique of American empire to call for democratic and inclusive U.S. citizenship."[13] Some, like Emily Brewster, appear to have represented the views of this camp.

Coe and others, on the other hand, saw an arms-bearing role for women in time of war; but it is uncertain whether this more militant appeal was made strictly in terms of home defense or whether Coe, like others, envisioned the prospect of actual overseas combat. Her mention of getting "ready for what may come" is cryptic. Nevertheless, at no point during the war was a combat role for women seriously considered. When the Navy Nurse Corps began imposing strict eyesight requirements for nurses enrolling, Clara Noyes quipped to its nurse leader, "Does the Navy contemplate making sharpshooters out of your nurses?"[14] Such a notion was restricted to a mere punchline.

A 1918 postcard showing composite images of Clara Noyes, Florence Nightingale and Jane Delano.

A 'MACEDONIAN CALL'

A postcard from 1918 shows three proud women in staggered formation against a background of rising steps. At the top is Florence Nightingale; on the next rise down is Jane A. Delano; and on the ground floor, by Delano's side, is her protégé, Clara Dutton Noyes.[1] By 1918, this trinity of nurse leaders loomed large in the public imagination, enough to give them featured placement on a postcard. But why these three? Only two – Delano and Noyes – were directly affiliated with the American Red Cross. If the image was intended to enshrine women leaders at the American Red Cross, where is its founder, Clara Barton? Nightingale, probably the most household name in nursing history, did not have an official role in the American Red Cross, though she is credited as a fountainhead of nursing education, a field of practice she honed from her own experiences in battlefield nursing.[2] Clara Noyes and Jane Delano were direct beneficiaries of Nightingale's model of nurse training – unlike Barton, who was branded by some Red Cross leaders and historians as an "amateur nurse," even after she ministered courageously to the sick and wounded during the Civil War and Spanish-American War. Criticism over Barton's lack of professional standards would later lead to her ouster from the organization she founded in a well-documented feud with ascendant leaders at the American Red Cross during the pre-World War I years.

Both Delano and Noyes attended and subsequently led nursing schools firmly rooted in Nightingale's formulation of practical and theoretical training, Noyes as a graduate of Johns Hopkins and later as superintendent of

69

Nightingale-based programs at Bellevue Hospital and elsewhere; and Delano, a few years older than Noyes, who graduated from Bellevue and also led its elite program. If Nightingale was the founder of modern nursing education, Noyes and Delano were two of its most famous beneficiaries from this period. They chased similar paths of advancement, from their training on the Nightingale system, to their executive positions at Bellevue, and, ultimately, their close collaboration at the American Red Cross. These parallels are among the reasons why Noyes was an obvious choice to arrive in Washington for Red Cross duty – ultimately joining the Nightingale-Delano-Noyes trinity of leaders. It was Jane Delano who recruited Noyes to Washington. Overworked and anxious about the demands on nursing in the lead-up to America's foreseeable engagement in war, Delano needed a lieutenant serving with her who was well-connected to the nursing establishment (as Noyes was, especially through her rise in the NLNE and the networks she forged in the New York City nursing world with Lillian Wald and others). Delano also wanted an executive with experience in the superintendent seat of a prestigious nursing program, and no program was more lauded than the Bellevue training school, where Noyes was already familiar with the nurse enrollment work happening in New York to begin getting nurses ready for battle. Delano also needed a staunch protector of nursing and professional standards, so that the best nurses were recruited from graduate programs and hospitals to serve the war effort, and Noyes's Bellevue post put her in connection with the leaders of foremost nurse-training programs who could martial the forces needed from their graduate rosters and other regional connections to supply war-ready units for duty.

At Bellevue, Noyes had already begun answering the Red Cross's call for wartime preparedness and she had gained notice for speaking eloquently about its aims and strategic needs during her NLNE convention speeches. In its strategy to organize units for overseas operations, the Delano-led Red Cross Nursing Service (which started in 1909 under Delano's leadership in partnership with a forerunner organization of the ANA) worked with military officers and their nurse service corps to engage the heads of hospitals on assembling home-based personnel for enlistment. The idea was to form war-ready hospital nursing units at the local level, much as Clara Noyes's own father, Enoch, did in organizing a company of Connecticut troops during the Civil War. This strategy transplanted a tight-knit community of health professionals from their home hospitals in a similarly unified "company" of recruits for service at the Army base hospitals, known as "cantonments," which were being hurriedly assembled throughout the United States. This strategy created an "esprit des corps," so that personnel from the same hospital formed a working core together in the army and navy operation. As Red Cross historians explained: "The underlying principle of organizing such units was a recognition of the clan instinct. War seemed less formidable when a nurse could go out with a former room-mate or a friend who had been trained in the same wards."[3]

In mid 1916, a call came in from U.S. Army Col. Jefferson Kean for a medical unit comprised of Bellevue's hospital staff. The unit organized at Bellevue was the nation's first to officially form under the aegis of the army and its Red Cross auxiliary. It would be called "Base Hospital No. 1" when commended for overseas duty. Bellevue's Dr. George D. Stewart had begun selecting medical staff for the unit while Clara Noyes was charged with enrolling her nurses.[4] This role would have made her chief nurse of Bellevue's unit had she joined Base Hospital No. 1 when it was assigned travel orders for France, and if Noyes hadn't already exceeded the Red Cross age threshold for service overseas. Rather elliptically, the book *Bellevue in France, an Anecdotal History of Base Hospital No. 1* notes that Noyes, soon after recruiting nurses for Base Hospital No. 1, was "called away for other duties," the enrollment task falling to her successor at Bellevue, Carrie J. Brink.[5] This history does not mention those "other duties," which would ultimately entail work with hospitals, nursing school superintendents and organizations of nursing to recruit more than 20,000 nurses on a national level at Delano's newly formed Red Cross Nursing Service in Washington, DC.

Meanwhile, Bellevue's unit, though the first to organize, did not arrive to France until March 1918.[6]

Noyes had already enrolled in the Red Cross Nursing Service as a volunteer at the local level. Her enrollment slip, tendered by the New York City branch of the American Red Cross in March 1916, assigned her with badge number 6215. On the back of the slip is a running tally of Noyes's changing home address over the next ten years, listing her movements from New York City to new locations in Washington: first residing at 1726 M Street NW, and, in March of 1929, her more permanent home at 1411 Twenty-Ninth Street NW.[7] To enroll in the Red Cross, nurses needed references. Mary Adelaide Nutting, Noyes's superintendent at Johns Hopkins, signed her credentialing form. She attested to Noyes's executive experience as "substitute head nurse" at the 300-bed Baltimore hospital. In the blank left for remarks, Nutting simply wrote: "I know of no one more capable."[8]

Delano shared Nutting's assessment, setting her sights on Noyes for a broader field of Red Cross work, but her appeal took some persistence. In an exchange of letters with Noyes, Delano worked vigorously to convince the 46-year-old Bellevue leader to leave her influential post in New York. "I do wish that you could come over to Washington to talk the matter over and see something of the work," Delano wrote to Noyes on June 7, 1916. To coax the Bellevue superintendent, Delano suggested that the job may last for as little as one year, allowing Noyes to return to Manhattan; U.S. war involvement was imminent, but the magnitude and length of that involvement was not entirely foreseeable.[9] Delano trusted Noyes with the daunting task of overseeing the war preparations by her side: "The work has grown to such proportions during the past two years that it seems to me most unsafe to have only one person with a knowledge of its various ramifications."[10]

It appears that Noyes herself had underestimated the magnitude of this demand, prompting Delano and Mabel Boardman (the Red Cross's general administrator at the time) to "laugh" at Noyes's "fear that there might not be enough to occupy one if the preparedness wave should subside."[11] A driven individual like Noyes did not anticipate being pulled into an all-consuming war-response effort and, ultimately, an extended career at the American Red Cross – a career that lasted the remainder of her life – no more than the American public could foresee the extent of its wartime sacrifice.

The work at American Red Cross Headquarters, wrote Delano, "needs an organizer such as I know you to be and someone with strong convictions and courage."[12] It would entail preparing nurses for enrollment, reviewing their qualifications and enrollment forms from local committees, keeping meticulous records of nurse enrollees, standardizing surgical methods of nursing, and firing up local Red Cross units to recruit more nurses for service from local institutions. Aware of Noyes's zealous regard for the professional status of nursing, Delano used it to advantage in persuading Noyes to join her at Red Cross headquarters: "I believe there is a distinct menace to our nursing standards in the development of this lay personnel unless it is carefully directed and supervised and that at this time no work in the country compares with it in far reaching results or importance."[13]

This wasn't Delano's first time approaching Noyes about joining the Red Cross effort. On June 1, 1916, Delano had already written to Noyes with a strong appeal: "We must have a strong woman in Washington! There is too much at stake now to take any chances and I feel in my very soul that you are the person for the place."[14] As the *History of American Red Cross Nursing* made clear, "Miss Noyes, however, was not at first disposed to give up the work at Bellevue, with its large branch hospitals at Harlem, Fordham and Governeur, and its specialized schools of midwifery and of male attendants."[15] Like that long ago conversation with Anna Jammé on a Baltimore trolley, Noyes proved yet again a hesitant bargainer. But after initial reluctance, she eventually traveled to Washington in mid-June 1916 for interviews. Noyes then received a follow-up missive, again from Delano. This time Delano pleaded in bold patriotic appeals punctured with exclamation points: "There is a tremendous piece of work to be done and your country certainly needs you!"[16]

By 1916, Noyes had already been outspoken in her own appeals to nurses for war preparedness. Her address to colleagues of the NLNE in New Orleans was especially focused on the "vital question" of preparedness. She told attendees: "Profiting by lessons learned from the great war, which is still wasting the strength and sapping the forces of all Europe, the American Red Cross has assumed the responsibility of organizing base hospitals, medical and nursing units ... In case of great medical necessity, which, let us hope will never arise, the numerical strength of our organized Army and Red Cross Nursing Service would probably be insufficient to assume all nursing responsibilities."[17] Noyes was also aware of the balance between the huge enlistment demands and the threat of diluting hard-fought training standards for nurses. Properly trained nurses needed to enroll; otherwise, "lay workers" may take their place. Noyes was already attuned to the major questions that would occupy her attention as the nation got pulled reluctantly into war, and this certainly caught Delano's notice.

Aside from professional qualifications, there were other factors – on a more personal level – that surely must have sparked Delano's interest in Noyes as her hand-picked assistant. Noyes "came of Connecticut parentage," the *History of American Red Cross Nursing* notes. "Her father served, as had Miss Delano's, in the Civil War."[18] Both women were raised in similar households, likely reared on a common narrative of service and patriotism. But the connections go further. Well before the era of Jane Delano – or her more famous cousin, President Franklin Delano Roosevelt – Noyes genealogists speculated a bloodline link between the Noyeses and the Delanos, a heritage that extends throughout the dynasties of American history, the Delanos being descended from Philippe de la Noye (of the "drowned persons"). Philippe de la Noye was an early American settler, akin – and possibly kin – to Clara Noyes's ancestors seven generations prior. Daniel Delano, in his 1946 book *Franklin*

Delano and the Delano Influence, also makes the Noyes/Delano connection. He notes how the ancient town of Alnetum in France later "became Lannoy, the de la Noyes became Delanos ... Some branches adopted certain of these forms and use them to this day. One line dropped the first syllable of the name and retained Noye, adding an 's' and coining the name Noyes."[19]

Indeed, as former President William Howard Taft noted in a statement announcing Noyes's appointment to the Red Cross: "Although born in Maryland, Miss Noyes comes of New England ancestors who have been prominent in the history of this country for several generations."[20] Clara Noyes's *New York Times* obituary remarks that she was "a descendant of William Brewster, who came to America on the Mayflower,"[21] as did Philippe de la Noye's uncle, through marriage, Francis Cooke.[22] All of these genealogical strands are culled from multiple sources across the centuries; and it is a dizzying enterprise connecting two people on the basis of a common surname, especially when dealing with far-back family histories. Whether or not Clara Noyes and Jane Delano had a common ancestry is immaterial. What we can say for certain is that the top two positions at the Red Cross Nursing Service were occupied by predominately white, Anglo-Saxon, northern, protestant women, trained on the Nightingale system, with executive experiences leading elite nurse training schools, and roots extending back to the early American colonies. In fact, this demographic makeup of nurse leadership appears to have been a point of focus for nurses. The *History of American Red Cross Nursing,* written by women of Noyes's generation and completed in 1922, frequently emphasized heritage in identifying nurses among its ranks: "Miss Goodrich came from pure New England stock"[23]; "A New Englander by birth and ancestry, Mrs. Harris was graduated from the New York Infirmary for Women and Children."[24] Similar words are used to describe other Red Cross functionaries, like Ida F. Butler, and even Jane Delano herself. These connections may simply reflect what has otherwise been observed in the early professional nursing movement: that educated nurses were white, native-born and recruited.

Nevertheless, the imagination leads one to consider whether Clara Noyes and Jane Delano ever once exchanged a moment of light conversation in the marble hallways at the Red Cross headquarters on Seventeenth Street in Washington, possibly during a brief exchange of candor, to make mention of their common heritages and place in the great American story, both descendants of the "drowned persons," and both figuratively engulfed by the momentous work before them.

There's also a certain poetry in the fact that Clara Noyes shared a first name with American Red Cross founder Clara Barton, as well as a linguistic, if not genealogical, connection to the woman who brought her to the American Red Cross, Jane Delano. For anyone with a providential mind, destiny seemed very much at work in bringing Noyes to the Red Cross's "marble palace," as the Red Cross headquarters was called.

Genealogical considerations aside, historians later noted that the two Red Cross nursing leaders worked hand-in-glove, exhibiting complementary personality traits. While Delano in many ways provided the vision, it was Noyes who shined at executing: "A woman of clear judgment, of excellent organizing ability and jealously ambitious of her chosen profession, she was wholly relied on by Miss Delano, with whose more intense and dramatic nature the exceeding reserve of Miss Noyes was in striking contrast." Like Delano, Noyes "was tall and of commanding presence. Like her, too, her gray hair became snowy white during her Red Cross labors."[25]

Delano clearly saw the work at Red Cross headquarters as an extension of the superintendent's role at nurse-training programs – and no other leader would fit the bill better than Noyes, who was, by then, well past the age limit for overseas duty but unequaled in her experience improving the standards at New England training schools and, now, leading the foremost Nightingale-based school of nursing at Bellevue. "This branch of the work has become so large and important and the burden of it so great that Miss Delano felt it advisable to secure a Superintendent for the Nursing Bureau, to be, if possible one of the ablest Training School Superintendents," former President Taft remarked in a press announcement picked up by the *New York Times*. "We are fortunate to secure for this office Miss Clara D. Noyes."[26] Having firmed up her commitment for duty, Taft authorized Clara Noyes's appointment at $4,000 a year salary.[27] Noyes accepted the position in July 1916 and arrived in Washington in October. Her title: Director of the Bureau of Field Nursing.

During his presidency, Taft served as the Red Cross's honorary chairman, starting a tradition for future presidents. He was Woodrow Wilson's rival, and lost resoundingly in the 1912 presidential election, stepping down from his honorary post on inauguration day in 1913. But his experience working with the relief agency proved needed at a time when the country was entering a major new war and as the newly elected President Wilson was consumed with military preparedness. Taft found himself ushered back into the Red Cross hierarchy, at Wilson's request.[28] Later, Taft and Clara Noyes would serve as chair and vice-chair, respectively, of a committee to pursue military rank for enlisted nurses in the war effort, a watershed moment in the history of military nursing.

As the drumbeat for war was growing louder, the American Red Cross found itself continually reshaping its mission, role, and administration. Since its Congressional charter in 1905, the Red Cross served as a private organization but with close ties to the government. Its treasury was filled not from government sources, but from donations solicited during annual "roll calls" and fundraising appeals delivered through popular magazines, presidential addresses to the public, newspaper articles and other organs of publicity, including the popular *Red Cross Magazine*. These efforts hit their stride in mid-1917 with the help of fundraising expert Charles Sumner Ward who brought energy to the first major development work.[29] But its status as a private organization, birthed by the Geneva Conventions of neutrality, was complicated by non-neutral demands of the nation-state, particularly for a country at war. The demands of war brought the American Red Cross into closer alignment with the U.S. Army and Navy Nurse Corps. Out of patriotic need, the American Red Cross War Council, appointed in May of 1917, officially suspended the Red Cross's neutrality clause for the duration of the war.[30]

The Red Cross is not – and has not been – a government bureau. But its wartime status as the sole auxiliary for army nursing was enshrined in government statute, further blurring the lines of division between it and the nation-state. As author Portia Kernodle vividly explains in her mid-century history of the American Red Cross, "a discerning eye might see that army nursing, Red Cross nursing, and professional nursing could be like Chinese boxes, each inclosed by a larger. Although the boxes did not fit perfectly and there were surplus pieces, the possibility of the neat arrangement existed."[31] This imperfect fit often resulted in conflicts over turf and administrative confusion from multiple bureaucracies operating worlds apart, both literally and figuratively. In one instance, officials simultaneously recruited two different women to head Red Cross nursing operations at the Paris office. Amid the confusion, and crossed communications, Martha Russell eventually set sail for France, on Jane Delano's recommendation. She found herself hamstrung by a lack of authority, and eventually tendered her resignation, essentially forced out by Red Cross brass over conflicts involving the use of nurses' aides. During a period of manpower shortages, the Commission for France was calling for more and more partially trained aides whose orders for service in Europe were "requested through various sources," and Noyes drafted a letter stressing that it is "highly important that these [requests] should be secured through Red Cross Nursing Service at Washington or their representative in Paris."[32] The Red Cross Nursing Bureau in France was being divided to include a sub-bureau for nurses' aides, led by "an untrained woman as director." This prompted Noyes to reiterate that: "Bureau Nursing feels strong inadvisability separating hospital auxiliary workers from Nursing Service. Establishes precedent contrary to Red Cross regulations and policy of Surgeon Generals."[33] Russell's office in Paris soon "became the subject of a cross-fire of cables and letters." It appears that Delano and Noyes had close contacts with members of the War Council and others, assuming their representative in France brought the same level of authority to her efforts, but evidently didn't.[34] This break-down in the chain of authority resulted in

Russell's resignation. The episode drew a frank response from Julia Stimson, chief nurse at Base Hospital No. 21, who was consulted in the matter. Officials "grasped and said they saw I was right," said Stimson, who asserted a new organizational plan and soon took over the Red Cross's nursing operations in France. Stimson would later become the first woman to achieve the rank of major in the U.S. Army.[35] Much like Kernodle's "Chinese Box" analogy, Red Cross historians referred to this episode as "an imperfect tool." Russell "tried to reshape the tool to the pattern upon which she knew Miss Delano and Miss Noyes were insistent ... Miss Stimson took up the tool and worked with it as it was as well as she could and with her nurses accomplished a brilliant piece of work."[36] The "controversy" was at least one instance where parties in the American Red Cross or military organization sought to employ non-nurses for executive work in the nursing realm, thus overstepping a key tenet of the professional nursing model – that trained, graduate nurses are responsible for managing their own profession, including the work of nurses' aides.

Clara Noyes with Red Cross Nurse in regulation uniform. *Photo courtesy of the Library of Congress.*

Even before America's war declaration, plans for 25 base hospitals were well underway in the winter of 1917, with nursing units overseen by Red Cross-enrolled nurses.[37] But the demand was growing, especially for domestic duty at army training camps. A few months after the war declaration, Noyes embarked on an extensive public speaking tour, addressing women's groups, nurse graduating classes and community organizations to drum up enrollment through local Red Cross committees and chapters. Thousands of local American Red Cross chapters were operating by war's end in all forty-eight states. Each functioned in wartime medical and relief service much like the localized organization of military companies during the Civil War, conscripting nurse enrollments for approval and travel orders by the Delano/Noyes-led

American Red Cross Nursing Service at national headquarters. The difference between these local organizational units often created confusion. As Noyes explained, nurses did not enroll through chapters but through local committees on Red Cross Nursing Service. These committees were entirely made of graduate nurses, while chapters predominately included "lay people interested in the development of nursing in their Chapter" which was in charge of local Red Cross operations in its territory. The Local Committee on Red Cross Nursing Service was primarily designed to "interest nurses in enrollment," she said, but "it has other important duties such as helping to supply the chapter with nurses in time of disaster." The chapters covered smaller territory, but they were more numerous. As of May 1925, Noyes reported, there were 220 Local Committees on Red Cross Nursing Service, with over 3,000 chapters all following orders and guidance from Washington.[38]

As Noyes told one group on her first speaking tour, "women will play a prominent part in the whole question of preparedness."[39] In this early phase, Noyes began serving as one of the nursing world's most public embodiments of a war-relief effort that hinged on the vigorous involvement of women. Her 1917 to 1918 tour, starting in mid-December, sent her on at least 30 stops, according to a printed itinerary in her personnel file. She travelled from Washington to Boston, throughout New England and New York, to Chicago, Milwaukee, Camp Grant (Rockford, Illinois), a return trip through Western New York, back through New York City and Camp Merritt (Englewood, New Jersey), eventually returning to Washington around February.[40]

Noyes made one important stop that was a homeward journey of sorts: back to the Noyes family seat at

Old Lyme, Connecticut, where she spoke to the local American Red Cross chapter in September of 1917. *The Day*, a local newspaper, took note of her homecoming, reporting in its September 5 edition: "Miss Noyes is herself related to so many of the townspeople that she said in her opening remarks it was very hard to speak before an audience of friends and relatives."[41] While Noyes was born and raised in Maryland, her parents hailed from Old Lyme, and her ancestry traces back to one of the town's first settlers, the Reverend Moses Noyes, who was pastor at its Congregational Church, which he founded in 1665.

Perhaps recognizing the town's local connection to a famed daughter – her mother was then a local resident, and her father and many ancestors lay buried in Old Lyme's Duck River Cemetery – *The Day* gave ample column space to Clara Noyes's remarks, as the American Red Cross was by then being drawn up into sixteen divisions nationwide, each with a nursing director to communicate with local Red Cross committees. President Woodrow Wilson had already organized the American Red Cross War Council. Headed by H.P. Davidson, the council oversaw a $100 million war-readiness campaign to pay for administrative salaries, equipment and infrastructure related to the mobilization of the entire relief campaign. To her Old Lyme audience, Noyes described the enrollment requirements as follows: Nurses had to be twenty-five to forty years of age and registered through a state association; "only Red Cross nurses are allowed in France and none of German descent allowed abroad," *The Day* reported.[42]

While the speaking tour brought her across much of the United States, Noyes apparently didn't leave her desk much in the first weeks of her Red Cross work, where she occupied a "large and airy" office on the southwest corner of the first floor at headquarters.[43] As explained to the Connecticut audience, she "would dictate letters and telegrams while standing and eating a sandwich. She also said she felt she could now eat before anyone, for she had been seen eating from the president of the United States down to the little office boy." By September, sixteen base hospitals were equipped in France "and ten more were asked for and supplied at a two weeks' notice."[44]

Noyes's duties were growing at a breakneck pace, and she desperately needed help. As she once remarked humorously to a friend, "I will never get to the bottom of these letter baskets, so I just turn the bottom up every morning and answer as many as I can."[45]

To assist in the Red Cross Nursing Division's administrative functions, Noyes enlisted a Johns Hopkins colleague, Vashti Bartlett, to come to National Headquarters in March 1917. Their correspondence offers a lighthearted moment in the Red Cross nursing division's otherwise grueling war-readiness work.

"Miss Noyes's request that [Bartlett] come to Washington brought a smile to the lips of the overworked Director of Nursing," recall Red Cross historians. Noyes had wired a playful message to Bartlett; but it was misunderstood by her Johns Hopkins colleague and taken all too literally. "Will you answer a Macedonian call?" Noyes asked. Bartlett replied: "I will have to consult my family … before undertaking further Foreign Service, especially in Greece."[46] Noyes was citing a biblical metaphor, showing how she regarded the Red Cross work with a missionary's zeal. "Macedonian Call" is a reference to Acts 16:9, 10: "And a vision appeared to Paul in the night: a man of Macedonia was standing beseeching him and saying, 'Come over to Macedonia and help us.'

And when he had seen the vision, immediately we sought to go on into Macedonia, concluding that God had called us to preach the gospel to them."[47]

Noyes was clearly fluent with scripture, reared on the strong Puritan and Calvinist roots of her ancestors. For her, and others, the American Red Cross enlistment demands amounted to pleas of biblical proportions,[48] bringing nurses to new lands and fields of service. Noyes would repeatedly issue her "Macedonian Call" for as many audiences as she could. Thousands of volunteer nurses ended up truly answering this call, by signing up for war nursing with the American Expeditionary Forces. It wasn't until after the war that Noyes would herself function as an overseas missionary, during her first travels to Europe in the early 1920s as she endeavored to repair or build from scratch the undeveloped nurse training infrastructure in several countries and regions.

Perhaps one of Noyes's most rousing stump speeches occurred soon after America declared war on April 6, 1917. On April 30, the ANA held the main event at its biennial conference in Philadelphia, a captive audience of 3,000 nurses at the Academy of Music hall. "On that night, the very air seemed charged with patriotic ardor," states the *History of American Red Cross Nursing*.[49] Following Jane Delano's opening remarks, Clara Noyes took the stage in one of her first major addresses as a Red Cross leader: "As I stand facing you tonight, sister nurses, under the shadow of war, we know not what we as nurses shall be called upon to give. We know, however, that our Red Cross Nursing Service exists for but one purpose – the reserve of the Army and Navy Nurse Corps in time of war."[50]

"We shall be called upon to give fully, to make personal sacrifices," she intoned. "It must be written upon the pages of history for all time that Red Cross nurses were prepared, that in this war our soldiers were not neglected and that they were properly nursed."[51]

The American Red Cross was making full use of its growing numbers in publicity work. Parades have long been features of wartime pageantry, and the American Red Cross knew the value of these columned marches as it sought public sacrifices through volunteerism and donations. Delano and Noyes marched at the head of at least one big parade, in New York City, leading the pack of more than 1,500 Red Cross nurses given travel orders or awaiting mobilization.[52] Of these displays, writes Kernodle: "Although the entire Red Cross organization was represented, the nurses appeared in almost every headline and were more commented upon than any other group."[53] While the Red Cross was communicating to nursing audiences during these parades, it was also showing the might of its broader public appeal for private donations and volunteerism. But no matter what the broader appeal, these parades nevertheless firmly embedded in the American imagination a connection between the American Red Cross and nursing.

By mid-1917, Noyes was travelling to New York as often as three times a week to see off ships loaded with nurses en route to overseas service. "It is an inspiring picture to see the nursing personnel of a base hospital ready to embark," she said. "The dignified uniform of dark blue cloth, the scarlet lining of the cape ... Complete understanding of the nature of the mission is expressed in the face."[54] But sailing orders were delayed in many instances; and the young women found themselves idle at Ellis Island for long periods waiting to embark for Europe. Even though the nurses and other medical staff were desperately needed overseas, military supplies and soldiers sailed first. Battle-ready men took precedence in the trans-Atlantic movement of manpower, leaving many nurses in the lurch during the early fits-and-starts of wartime mobilization.

Surveying the enormous ocean liners and transport ships, women awaiting travel overseas referred to the great "dazzle painting" of seaward vessels,[55] a poignant indication that this was, for many nurses, a novel encounter with the machinery of war.

Arriving in New York, the nurses first reported to the Bureau of Nurses' Equipment at 222 Fourth Avenue. There they received supplies, stocked through an appropriation of $766,000, and later enlarged to meet estimates that $2 million would be needed overall for nurses' equipment, especially during the heavy call for deployments in the summer of 1918.[56] As with the delayed mobilization, American Red Cross nurses had to overcome the secondary consideration given by war officials for basic clothing and supplies. The army uniforms for "outdoor service" were woefully inadequate, and the Red Cross Nursing Service quickly assembled a committee of nurse leaders to adopt regulation attire. This consisted of a blue serge dress, a heavy blue ulster and a blue velour service hat for the first round of attachments, later changed to a dark blue Norfolk suit and gray uniform.[57] These uniforms and supplies were later supplemented with a sleeping-bag, a blanket-roll, a sweater, a raincoat, rain hat, rubber boots and woolen garments, due to the severity of the climate in parts of Europe. Although nurses were enrolled and vetted by the Red Cross, they were employed, upon commission, by the Army and Navy Nurse Corps, which paid $50 per month for domestic duty and $60 for overseas duty, but with no allowance for clothing. This omission compelled the Red Cross War Council to appropriate $200 for equipping each nurse.[58]

In one dramatic episode, nurses escaped the accidental sinking of the ship *Saratoga* at port. While no lives were lost, the nurses' supplies went down with the ship. "Within two hours Miss Noyes had appeared before the War Council, secured a special appropriation and wired orders" to the New York executive to keep the supply going.[59] Many of these first nursing units set sail for England to staff military and evacuation hospitals far from the theaters of war. Carrie May Hall was appointed as chief nurse for the American Expeditionary Forces in England where wounded soldiers were evacuated from France for further treatment or recovery. The German submarine blockade in April 1917 soon prevented transfer of wounded soldiers to the base hospitals in Britain. As a result, the medical relief mission had to move closer to the main fields of battle, in France, where new hospital units raised their stakes, staffed by Red Cross-enrolled nurses.[60]

One other stop on her 1917 speaking circuit brought Noyes back to her alma mater, Johns Hopkins School of Nursing, where she gave a stirring speech about the patriotic duty of nurses to enroll in the Red Cross. On the subject of service, she told graduates, "may I state in anticipation that if I appear to over-emphasize the military aspect of this form of service I trust you will bear with me, as I am living and working very close to the center of things and may I state that I, personally, abhor war and all its paraphernalia. I deplore the waste, the destruction of life and property and the shattering of all our ideas of peace and love."[61] In reaching the crux of her message, Noyes takes inspiration from President Wilson who spoke at a dedication ceremony for the new Red Cross

National Headquarters at Seventeenth Street NW in Washington. Wilson's presence at the ground-breaking occasion, two years prior, served as a bellwether moment in the leadership direction of the American Red Cross, as the Commander in Chief laid the cornerstone for the new edifice, cementing his support and connection to America's largest relief agency. Wilson also used the occasion to share the stage with his former adversary, Taft. Capitalizing on his predecessor's success, Wilson handed over to Taft a dominant role in the leadership structure of the American Red Cross that Wilson, as the current president, would have otherwise assumed. "Whatever their political and personal differences," historian Julia Irwin writes of this symbolically important occasion, "the two presidents wholly concurred on the centrality of [American Red Cross] civilian aid to U.S. foreign affairs."[62]

At the May 1917 dedication ceremony for the completed building, just days prior to Noyes's Johns Hopkins speech, President Wilson offered a strong message of faith in the American Red Cross; and this message clearly resonated with Noyes's own imperative for delivering a professional nursing relief response to the war effort as she listened to Wilson's remarks at the event. For the class of 1917 at Johns Hopkins School of Nursing, her message, like Wilson's, was a special call to duty aimed at a new generation of professionals, in her case nurses. Quoting Wilson, himself a Johns Hopkins alumnus, Noyes repeated a message "so wonderfully expressed by President Wilson." He said, and she reiterated, "This is no war for amateurs; this is no war for spontaneous impulse."[63] Wilson's rhetoric stressing professionalism trickled throughout the entire ethos of wartime preparedness, distinguishing the Red Cross work in a Post-Nightingale system of nursing from the less formalized system of relief in the Civil War and Spanish-American War. Noyes clearly took this message to heart. Just as the Red Cross was raising new structures at the "marble palace" headquarters, it was retreating away from what many deemed an "amateur" past. The Red Cross's chief administrator, Mabel Boardman, was the architect behind this view. Her efforts to professionalize the financial and governing structure of the American Red Cross led to the ouster of Clara Barton, an untrained nurse who founded the very organization. When the new Red Cross headquarters officially opened, Boardman "adamantly refused to include even a plaque commemorating the organization's founder," calling Barton "a skeleton in the closet upon which the doors have been closed."[64] Boardman's views may explain the absence of Barton's name in much of the rhetoric during this period, including the Red Cross's emphasis, in Noyes's words, on a highly trained nursing response to war which offered no space for "amateurs," most especially amateur medical relief personnel.

Personal traits of exactness and efficiency clearly suited the work that Clara Noyes was called to do. Early on, this included not only the management of nurse enrollment activities but also the likely tedious work of standardizing and approving surgical dressings for nurse instructors as they oversaw a major supply and manufacturing operation at local districts for shipment overseas. As chronicled in the *History of American Red Cross Nursing*:

> Before a woman was certified as an instructor, she was required to submit a sample box of the various types of surgical dressings. No sooner had Miss Noyes ex-

amined and cleared her desk of these samples than the Mail Division would send up a hundred more. The top floor of the 'Marble Palace' billowed with cotton and gauze ... To zealous women waiting impatiently in Red Cross Chapter and Branch headquarters for their certificates, the Nursing Service may have seemed over-exacting in their insistence upon perfect dressings.[65]

This standardization process was crucial at a time of resource scarcity, which demanded efficient mass production of wound-care supplies. Nurses near the front lines did not have the time or luxury to repackage unraveled surgical dressings, whose frayed "edges might result in discomfort and danger to their patients."[66] The exactness, regimentation and standardization of procedure, it seems, raised the hackles of surgeons accustomed to asserting their own individualized methods in the field of practice. On the issue of surgical gauze, we see one of several instances where Noyes went toe-to-toe with the physician community: "As this standard had been reached after conference with leading authorities of the Army, the Navy and civilian institutions, Miss Noyes turned a polite but deaf ear to protesting physicians who came to interview her" about the dressings.[67]

On June 23, 1917, Noyes wrote Col. Jefferson Kean, who was responsible for the Army's war-relief preparedness activities, offering further updates about the supply efforts being successfully managed at local districts with orders coming from Washington:

We have divided the country into eight

districts – Boston, New York City, Philadelphia, Baltimore, Cleveland, Chicago, Colorado Springs and San Francisco, for distribution of sample boxes of dressings, patterns, emblems and information ... It would be safe to say that workrooms have not only been established in all of our cities, but towns and country districts have developed in the same direction.[68]

Her work did not go unnoticed, even in the public realm. An editorial memorializing Noyes in the June 9, 1936 edition of the *Wilkes-Barre Record* ends by noting: "Not the least of her services to humanity was the part she played in bringing modern surgical methods into war work,"[69] a point remarked in many biographical summations of her American Red Cross career.

By October 1917, Noyes was making strong appeals to local committees for enrollment of nurses in the domestic cantonments, but it was proving to be a struggle; nurses were more disposed to romantic-heroic notions of overseas service, not duty at home bases where they were most needed for care of soldiers. "We have just received a definite call from the War Department for nearly 700 nurses for immediate cantonment service," Noyes wrote to local committees, bemoaning the anemic response from nurses for domestic duty. She chided: "It is far from patriotic, far from the purpose of the Red Cross to have nurses continue to refuse home service where the need is urgent, in favor of foreign assignment, where the demand is not so great."[70] Many of the soldiers were desperately ill in several domestic base hospitals, most suffering from flu, typhoid fever and other non-combat sicknesses. Caring for them was an average of ten nurses on duty per hospital, Noyes said.

Nurses' reluctance to serve in cantonments continued to beleaguer the Red Cross nursing brass; and Noyes would, at later periods, take to the pages of the influential *American Journal of Nursing* to further press her appeal to "care for the sick or wounded soldiers or sailors wherever they may be." In the *Journal's* January 1918 edition, she told nurses: "The sick soldier in the cantonment is now calling ... more loudly than is his brother in France. It may be your brother or cousin or father. What are the readers of this magazine doing about it? Have you enrolled in the Red Cross Nursing Service? If not, why not?"[71]

But the Red Cross plea bypassed an important group ready to assist. Though eager to serve their country – and despite their services being desperately needed – black women were afforded a limited, sidelined role in the Red Cross Nursing Service. They were later assigned to Red Cross duty at only a few military hospital units, during the Spanish Flu crisis. Only in December of 1918 were eighteen black nurses enrolled for duty. None served overseas.[72]

As one black nurse, Aileen Cole Stewart, remarked of this period: The "story of the Negro nurse in World War I is not spectacular. We arrived after the armistice was signed, which alone was anticlimactic."[73] According to scholar Andrea Patterson, "Black nurses had to fight a twin battle, for they had to win acceptance into both the female-dominated American Red Cross and the male-dominated military – institutions that repeatedly blamed each other for denying black nurses the right to treat soldiers."[74] The record supports Patterson's assertion that the proverbial "buck was passed" between both institutions (the War Department and its medical auxiliary, the

Red Cross) for the blame. Nevertheless, the effect boiled down to one stark and unremitting fact: The grip of American prejudice was too powerful for wartime institutions to permit women with a meaningful avenue of service regardless of race.

Patterson further cites press accounts from black nurses who blamed the supremacist views of the American Red Cross for this omission. One nurse, whose remarks were published anonymously, called American Red Cross Director of Nursing Jane Delano "the dictator of Red Cross destinies [who] refused to consider poor me and my friends," adding that black nurses were "ready and willing to enter the government service without compensation other than our own satisfied consciences, but absolutely not through the condescension of Miss Delano."[75]

In 1922, Lavinia Dock, Sarah Elizabeth Pickett and Clara Noyes, in the History of American Red Cross Nursing, called the deployment of black nurses an "interesting experiment" at Camp Sherman, Ohio, during the influenza epidemic, one of the few instances where black nurses were allowed to serve. "The question of utilization of colored nurses had been the cause of prolonged discussion between the Surgeon General's office and the American Red Cross,"[76] they explained. The National Committee of the Red Cross had earlier contemplated the deployment of black nurses "in connection with base hospitals, if such were organized for colored troops alone," but later modified this position in a resolution which seemed to offer flexibility.[77]

The country's race and gender politics throughout the antebellum and postbellum periods had long involved black women serving in care-giving roles for white men. Yet, this ideology was nullified when it came to military service, as the services of black nurses were conceived at first only for duty in segregated units of black men. Clearly, this age-old domestic ideology of caregiving was seen differently when it came to service in an officially sanctioned capacity under the aegis of the War Department and American Red Cross Nursing Service, with its focus on professional caregivers, even though there existed a growing number of licensed black nurses who were ready, willing, prepared and able to serve. When it came to wartime service roles, racial and gender politics had yet again laid bare many of America's complicated and paranoid ideological inconsistencies.

The *History of American Red Cross Nursing* does go on to extol the work of black nurses who the Red Cross belatedly enrolled for wartime service. "I do not mind saying that I was quite sure, when orders came for the colored group, that I was about to meet my Waterloo," described Mary Roberts, Chief Nurse at Camp Sherman. "My feeling now is that it was a valuable experience for them and for me ... they did valuable service for our patients and it was a service that the patients appreciated. I now find myself deeply interested in the problems of all colored nurses and believe in giving them such opportunities as they can grasp for advancement."[78] Just as women's volunteerism for war was viewed as a lever for gaining career advancement, and eventually a right to vote, black women likewise saw war work as a pathway for eventual cooperation with their white colleagues and wider recognition in American culture.

This, after all, was Woodrow Wilson's America, a few decades after the Civil War, in the throes of the Jim Crow era. Wilson is ignominiously remembered for re-segregating U.S. government bureaus[79]; and this period of American history is generally rampant with examples of the color line interfering at all levels of public life, including in the nursing field. Hand-written conference minutes from the National Association of Colored Graduate Nurses (NACGN) in its early years showed just how prominent the issue of wartime service was for black nurses. At the NACGN's August 1918 executive committee meeting in St. Louis, the group's president, Adah Thoms, "spoke of the attitude of the Red Cross toward colored nurses," adding that "the colored nurse is no slacker and will not be satisfied until she reaches devastated Europe."[80]

By that time, a landmark moment had been reached: Francis Elliot, a graduate of the Freedman's Hospital Training School for Nurses and nursing supervisor at the Provident Hospital in Baltimore, had enrolled in the Red Cross. Though Elliot "wears the first Red Cross emblem of the colored nurses," the NACGN remained uncertain about the role of black nurses generally in wartime nursing even as deployments were escalating. "There will be 1,000 nurses to be sent to Europe weekly for two months. Whether colored nurses will be in that number is not known."[81] During this same meeting, the group recorded "greetings" from Jane Delano, noting that "the Red Cross is blameless for the colored nurses not having been utilized," yet it is not clear whether this summation is a paraphrase of Delano's "greetings" to the group or whether this was the NACGN's own assessment of the situation. Nevertheless, NACGN President Adah Thoms urged "all nurses to enroll for Red Cross work and the applicants to be ready for Red Cross duty."[82]

Expressing strong patriotism, the organization considered several points of leverage for gaining official recognition and inclusion in the Red Cross and Army Nurse Corps. Some members of the NACGN recommended a survey of black nurses who had contributed money for Liberty Bonds, a financial indicator of black nurses' sacrifice. Even after the war, in December 1918, one member of the group noted that though "the Armistice was signed ... we are reasonably sure [there] is no reason why we should discontinue our efforts for wartime nursing. To stop now will mean to lose some of our prestige we gained by our past efforts. One of the best things to do in my opinion is to make a survey of accounts subscribed to Liberty Loans by nurses." Another NACGN member added: "I am somewhat discouraged about the Red Cross appointing colored nurses ... We should let the public see what we have done" in contributing financially and, yet, "ignored professionally."[83]

The eighteen black nurses who ultimately served in 1918 were stationed mainly at Fort Sherman in Ohio and Fort Grant in Illinois, where they nursed soldiers of all races, despite the initial policy of limiting black nurses to duty only in segregated units. The group offered a positive message that transcended whatever hostilities they may have endured: "We hope as encouragement, we as professional women in our walk of life, have nothing to fear, but all things to hope for," they told colleagues at the NACGN. "We were morally efficient, as well as professional ... Our work stood the test, we had obstacles to confront us ... we left the army with commendation."[84]

"As colored women and nurses, we must be firm, tactful, earnest, cheerful and observant in our work," they added, "and if we pray to God for our success, we will succeed."[85]

Other controversies plagued the war enrollment work. Early on, the American Red Cross caught wind of several rumors about sabotage tactics within the nursing corps. They also heard a whisper campaign about nurses coming back from the war zone pregnant, mutilated, or subjected to "white slavery" by the enemy, as one Division Director put it in remarks to the press that raised eyebrows at Washington headquarters.[86]

Several files in the national archives contain letters to and from Red Cross officials who sought to track down the sources of these rumors. Many of the wilder claims were voiced at YWCA meetings, from church pulpits, and other public forums. Some were overheard in private and then repeated. In every case, the Red Cross sought to identify the sources of the rumors, locate the nurses allegedly harmed, and deploy public-relations efforts combatting the more specious accounts.[87] Red Cross officials – lacking evidence recorded in any of their own files or reports – mostly attributed these rumors to pro-German or pacifist propaganda. One file even focuses specifically on German-leaning sabotage tactics occurring within the Red Cross nursing apparatus. Among the reports is a Justice Department communiqué informing the Red Cross that a nurse of Austrian descent allegedly intended to enroll for purposes of poisoning American troops.[88] Another Justice Department report concerned allegations that a woman from Kansas City stated her desire for "transportation to Mexico in order to secure employment in the hospitals there so that she might kill off all American soldiers entering those hospitals."[89] These latter statements prompted an agent from the Kansas City office of the Justice Department to interview the former Mexican consul, Jack Dansiger, who had met the nurse and was "of the opinion that she would do anything that she could to injure this country," wrote Special Agent Arthur T. Bagley. "The matter will receive further attention."[90] Another report told of a dinner in Baltimore where a Mr. Bryant of Durham, North Carolina, "said that his brother, who is an undertaker at Greenville, S.C., had taken care of the body of a nurse who had been executed by a firing squad at Camp Sevier for having poisoned soldiers."[91]

Some of the more gruesome allegations described American nurses who had returned home from the war with their hands dismembered and their tongues cut out, allegedly at the hands of German combatants. Yet the Red Cross was unable to find any physical evidence of the rumor, at least according to internal records. Clara Noyes overheard one of these rumors first-hand while standing on a railway station platform in 1918. After a bit of eavesdropping, she tracked the rumor's source to a resident of Saybrook, Connecticut, not far from Old Lyme where Noyes owned a summer home. As Noyes overheard it, members of Frederick Dorr's family mentioned him witnessing two "Red Cross nurses who had lost their hands and tongues, I believe, on a trolley car," Noyes wrote to Dorr on July 12, 1918. "We have heard this story many times, but have never been able to find anyone who actually saw the nurses. I understand that you were told by a man who was with the nurses that this circumstance was correct," Noyes added, asking for a description of the man who gave the account, the number of the trolley car where this encounter occurred, and any other identifying information. "We feel sure that this is a definite attempt on the part of the enemy to discourage nurses from going into service. So far as we know … no nurses have ever returned from Europe in the condition specified above."[92] A choppy, possibly translated reply from Dorr (penned by his wife), arrived at Noyes's desk on July 15 stating of his remarks that he did "not even know it built upon facts, and stated nothing definite when repeated at my own home. No other place did I mention it. Mean to be careful of stating anything definite."[93]

In the hyper-politicized environment of a nation at war – when government censorship reached new levels and as organizations with tacit government support were sniffing out pro-German (and potentially disloyal) views – a few stray words, even in one's own home, could have dangerous consequences. At least one case of rumor-spreading about Red Cross nurses resulted in a man facing criminal charges of one year in prison and a $1,000 fine. Another individual was questioned before a grand jury. "A few cases of this kind ought to convince the public that there is no basis for rumors," wrote Jane Delano to one correspondent.[94]

Well after the war, populist elected officials like Georgia Senator Thomas E. Watson continued to make disparaging remarks about nurses coming home pregnant, compelling the Red Cross to combat the charges. "I deem it a duty to deny with all vehemence I can summon up, the outrageous lie that special maternity hospitals are apportioned in this country for unfortunate women who have been among our nurses in France," said one chief surgeon, repeating Watson's allegations. "There are just twelve such cases to be found ... among 11,000 women, living under conditions during nearly two years of detachment from their ordinary environment."[95] Noyes even received a letter from Bellevue nurses calling for Senator Watson's expulsion from office.

On one highly publicized occasion, a clergyman based in Los Angeles, Dr. William Evans, claimed from his pulpit that half of all nurses returning from France were pregnant,[96] a figure directly refuted by Red Cross data. After the Red Cross launched an investigation, Dr. Evans clarified that he had stated not "half" of all nurses, but 500, as his figure. A series of correspondences ensued. The pastor's claim turns out to have originated with Doctor Wayland Morrison, a captain in the Medical reserve of the Army. The rumor's source (whether Morrison or another person, it is unclear) told Red Cross officials that he "had heard the report from his wife, who had learned it from another woman, and so on back."[97]

While war preparedness weighed heavily on the American Red Cross Nursing Service in 1917, its two leaders, Jane Delano and Clara Noyes, engaged with peer nurses in other vital organizational efforts. In papers filed on April 28, 1917, Delano, Noyes and three others – Annie Goodrich, Georgia M. Nevins and Sarah Sly – signed the certificate of incorporation for the ANA in Washington, DC, at about same time that the ANA was gathered for its twentieth convention. Goodrich, Noyes's immediate predecessor as superintendent at Bellevue, was by this time also Noyes's immediate predecessor as ANA president, serving from 1915 to 1918. Noyes took charge of the ANA from 1918 until 1922. Once again we see how a tight cluster of nursing leaders circulated in and out of key leadership positions. From her time at Johns Hopkins to her rise through the training schools, Noyes was one of these names in continual running, as "interpersonal relationships" among a core group of women gave rise to a distinct cohort of leaders in nursing, mentoring one another and recruiting each other up the ladder. As Susan Poslusny described the early leaders at Johns Hopkins: "Each shared a sense of history, a common frustration with the exploitation of nurses, a mutual concern for the rights of women, a common goal of unity for the profession. Each worked to develop the major professional nursing institutions; each also maintained a unique professional focus." Poslusny finds evidence that this tight-knit group actively supported one another's advancement,[98] and they certainly chased many of the same career pathways in a kind of revolving door of nursing leadership, akin to an "old boys club," but gender-swapped within the clique of nursing.

The ANA's development is not only important in the history of American nursing but also in terms of the political impact it gave to women within the clique and beyond. During this period, the ANA became the largest organized body of professional women in the world. Its organization roots effectively formed the same year that Noyes graduated from nursing school, in 1896, but under a different name. That year, delegates from ten nurse training school alumnae associations met in New York City to form what was known as the Nurses' Associated Alumnae of the United States and Canada.[99] The growth of nurse alumnae associations was not simply a means for connecting graduates with peers and their alma maters; these organizations, within the discrete professional domain of nursing, evolved into a political powerhouse throughout the early twentieth century, especially as questions of women's suffrage commanded attention, not to mention professional interests at the heart of nursing.

By 1901, state-level nurses associations were organized for purposes of advancing progressive nursing laws in New York, Virginia, Illinois and New Jersey. These were the first states to become constituent associations of the Nurses' Associated Alumnae. That same year, the national organization of Associated Alumnae secured passage of a bill creating an Army Nurse Corps, a statutory basis for the participation of women in wartime nursing. Throughout the first five years of its existence, other states joined the Associated Alumnae's ranks, and nurse registration laws were soon enacted.[100] Jane

Delano became president of the Associated Alumnae in 1909, working with the nascent organization to develop the Red Cross Nursing Service that same year while she also served as chief nurse for the U.S. Army Nurse Corps.

The Associated Alumnae changed its name to the American Nurses Association (ANA) in 1911. A year later, the ANA purchased all of the stock of the *American Journal of Nursing*, making it a fully nurses-owned publication and major organ of communication to nurses countrywide.[101] Before its first edition went to press in 1900, the *Journal* had 550 cash subscriptions. Its circulation grew to over 106,000 by 1950, making it, at that time, "the largest voluntary paid circulation of any professional magazine in the world."[102] Noyes served as editor of the *Journal* for a period. She also published a regular feature column on Red Cross nursing activities to inform the nursing community's growing readership.

By 1917, the ANA had evolved quickly through its humble beginnings in the alumnae associations as it connected with the growth of state-level nurses associations. When Delano, Noyes, Goodrich, Nevins and Sly signed the ANA's articles of incorporation in Washington, the organization had already incorporated in New York State under its current name; though, as ANA historians note, by then it was "readily apparent that a number of problems could not be resolved as long as ANA remained incorporated under the New York laws," which prohibited certain unique structural aspects of the ANA's membership organization. ANA legal counsel recommended a national charter, which failed to pass both houses of Congress (in part because Congress was consumed by concerns over the war), leading Noyes, Delano and colleagues to secure the certificate of incorporation in Washington, DC.[103]

Those articles of incorporation state the following purposes of the growing organization:

> To promote the professional and educational advancement of nurses in every proper way; to elevate the standard of nursing education; to establish and maintain a code of ethics among nurses; to distribute relief among such nurses as may become ill, disabled, or destitute; to disseminate information on the subject of nursing by publications in official periodicals or otherwise; to bring into communication with each other various nurses and associations and federations of nurses throughout the United States of America.[104]

One year later, in 1918, during the height of her war work, Noyes would assume the presidency of the ANA, at a time when there were 83,775 graduate nurses in the United States, some 66,000 of whom were registered nurses.[105] Her dual role as a nursing leader at the Red Cross and at the ANA allowed her to navigate thorny political issues in a flexible, multi-tiered fashion, perhaps one reason why she was selected from within nursing's rarefied clique to assume the highest post in the ANA. She obtained extensive intelligence from her position in the American Red Cross, about such issues as U.S. Army policies unfairly affecting nurses pay and benefits, or the plight of nurses operating with little official power in the chain of command overseas. This she coupled with the political pulpit of the ANA, which gave her a vast reserve of nurses who could mobilize politically through its official organ of publicity, the *American Journal of Nursing,* and other communications channels. While an influential insider at the Red Cross, Noyes found herself seemingly restricted by the Red Cross's allegiance to the preparedness efforts of the Army Nurse Corps and, generally, to the commands of the military apparatus. The ANA, in several instances, gave Noyes an outlet to push political causes for nurses in ways that would have been undutiful from her war-time capacity within the American Red Cross superstructure.

Noyes's presidency also saw increasing interactions between the ANA and the NACGN about organizational alignment and political unification, though it appears these overtures were initiated by black nurses seeking integration in the ANA, and not a gesture of pure beneficence from the ranks of the mainline ANA. The communication between the groups was cordial, though ambivalent, as many prior episodes reveal, especially when it came to the collision between black nurses' aspirations and those of the white nursing community (i.e., Noyes' and Lillian Wald's treatment of the Senetta Anderson case at Bellevue and questions about the role of black nurses in the Red Cross). In meeting minutes from 1920, Adah Thoms, the NACGN president, "suggests that colored nurses attend white nurse's meetings and especially the American Nurses Association to keep in touch with what is going on, as colored nurses are discussed in all these white meetings."[106] Clearly the impetus for integration came from within the ranks of the black nursing community. But by 1921, the NACGN had received a letter from Clara Noyes about the subject of a more formal affiliation. In an executive committee meeting that year, the NACGN discussed the matter and Noyes's letter, recommending that a committee "be appointed from all sections of this country to meet and confer on this subject and advise the national [association] concerning the same and make a report."[107]

A full partnership and inclusion of black nurses within the ANA wouldn't occur until the late 1940s and early 50s when the NACGN disbanded and officially accepted the ANA's proposition that it take over the duties and functions of the NACGN. "Cooperation between Negro and white nurses was, in a large measure, responsible for keeping the membership channels in the ANA open,"[108] wrote Mabel Staupers, a former executive secretary and president of the NACGN. "It would be difficult to say whether the founding of the National Association of Colored Graduate Nurses in 1908 or its dissolution in 1951 gave greater satisfaction to its members."[109] Black nurses sought integration into the mainstream ANA. Even if the NACGN's sole purpose of inclusion would result in the NACGN's elimination, so be it. By the 1950s and 60s, black nurses saw increasing opportunities for participation and membership in the ANA, eventual integration into the U.S. armed forces, and better employment opportunities. As Staupers reflected in 1961, ten years after the NACGN ceased to exist, "negro nurses are no longer generally denied opportunity because of their race. By no means do these progressive steps mean that all the problems have been solved; they do mean that within the profession there is deeper concern for all qualified nurses to share in meeting the health and nursing needs of the American people."[110]

'BAPTISM OF HORROR': REPORTS FROM FRANCE

Clara Noyes was a main point of contact with nurses in military service, receiving countless gripping and dramatic accounts of the war. Using language that put nurses in league with any wartime correspondent, women overseas reported back to the Red Cross with descriptions of war wounds, fear of bombing raids, complications with travel orders, unfair treatment in the military chain of command, and the condition of base hospitals. These issues, especially technical or logistical ones, had to be addressed by the Red Cross Nursing Services' newly opened Paris office, national headquarters, or, at times, through the political channels of the ANA.

From the time of mobilization to the armistice in November 1918, Clara Noyes was a main line of correspondence, and a far-afield witness observing wartime nursing, and these accounts certainly informed her understanding of nurses' enormous sacrifices, further inspiring many of her later advocacy positions on nurses' behalf.

Stretcher cases at No. 9 General Hospital were particularly gruesome, as three nurses helped administer 300 surgical dressings per day. Some patients at the hospital "who had lain in shell holes without medical attention, came with wounds infected with maggots," wrote one of its nurses, Grace Allison. "Others were admitted who had lost both legs, while still others were found with great pieces of muscle and flesh torn away by shell and shrapnel." The hospital was particularly susceptible to night raids. "Every afternoon rough coffins were carried there upon the shoulders of eight British or American soldiers and lowered into a deep trench, three coffins, one upon another."[1]

In 1917, Margaret A. Dunlop, at No. 16 General Hospital, referred to mustard gas cases as a "baptism of horror," describing "horrible pictures of misery." Medical and surgical cases "poured upon us in great numbers, six hundred in less than forty-eight hours." German use of chemical warfare would later escalate during the summer of 1918. Lily B. Crighton, at Red Cross Military Hospital No. 6, told of men streaming in "with hideous blisters extending from their shoulders down. The nurses would clip away all this blistered skin, clean the-then raw surface with antiseptic solution, dry it with the electric blower and spray on the 'amberine.'"[2]

A nurse's proximity to the war depended on which type of hospital she was assigned to: field hospitals, evacuation hospitals, mobile units or the base hospital. Mary T. Sarnecky, a retired colonel in the U.S. Army Nurse Corps, offers a cogent summary of the various units. As Sarnecky explains, field hospitals were close to the action. "Located ideally three to four miles behind the dressing stations of the front lines," Sarnecky writes, "the 216-bed field hospitals used tentage or suitable local buildings for shelter" and were intended to "receive and stabilize casualties from the battlefield."[3] Evacuation hospitals, located in the rear, would replace the field hospitals as they "advanced with their divisions."[4] Mobile units treated the "seriously wounded as close as possible to the front lines. Those with head, chest, and abdominal wounds were potential patients."[5] The largest facilities were base hospitals, at 500 beds, where patients landed for recovery after treatment in the field and evacuation units.[6] When Clara Noyes's alma mater, Johns Hopkins, reached France, it morphed into several different unit types, serving as a base hospital and later as mobile attachments close to the fighting at the height of American bloodshed, during the Meuse-Argonne offensives. Johns Hopkins nurses arrived at Bazoilles-sur-Meuse in June 1917. There, six additional base hospitals were also erected – capable of caring for 20,000 soldiers. "Nearly every member of our staff has served in the front line hospitals just back of the battle line," wrote nurses in the May 1919 edition of the *Johns Hopkins Nurses Alumnae Magazine*, recounting their wartime experiences.[7] As Chief Nurse Bessie Baker noted, their base hospital was supposed to support 500 beds but eventually became a 1,000-bed hospital. It also changed "during the drives" – presumably the nearby Meuse-Argonne offensives – when the base hospital was "used as an evacuation hospital," tending to more serious cases.[8]

At a field hospital's shock unit near the Chateau Thiérry front, Johns Hopkins nurses like Gertrude Bowling cared for gassed patients and men hemorrhaging blood. "To us fell the care of those patients too ill and too seriously wounded to survive transportation farther back, or too badly shocked either from exposure, loss of blood, or wounds."[9] The severity of wounds showed just how close Bowling and her field unit were to the fighting. "Through our paneless windows and the ragged shell holes in our wall, the flare from the big guns and their boom, too novel and resoundingly near, kept us from more than naps the first night."[10] She described a young soldier whose "back bore huge shrapnel wounds alive with maggots," adding: "Words cannot do justice to the gruesomeness of those crawling things in human flesh."[11] Pauline Stock, another shock team nurse, describes receiving patients whose muddy, blood-soaked clothes needed to be cut off, as she wrapped patients in blankets surrounded by hot bags, fed them a quarter grain of morphine, if needed, and atropin for hydration. Blood transfusions often served dual purposes, reviving the donor and resupplying the recipient. "The blood was usually taken from the gassed patients who were really better for it," Stock said. "The boys were very good about offering themselves as donors when the situation was explained to them, and they were always greatly interested in the recipient and whether the blood had helped him." She added: "It was remarkable how quickly as a rule the patient would pick up after a transfusion of blood."[12]

Approximately ten thousand nurses served with the military overseas. Only three were injured in the fighting. The first was Eva Jean Parmelee, of Base Hospital No. 5, wounded by shrapnel. Beatrice Mary MacDonald, while serving in Belgium, lost sight in one eye during a bombing raid. Isabelle Stambaugh of Base Hospital No. 11 was the final combat-related injury, during an attack in March 1918.[13] MacDonald, the most seriously injured, later received the Distinguished Service Cross, the first official recognition by the U.S. government of the bravery of nurses. Noyes wrote about the February 27, 1919 medal ceremony, recounting how MacDonald sustained injury from three bombs that "fell within a few seconds of each other" at Evacuation Hospital No. 2 on the night of August 17, 1917. Two English nurses were also hurt in the bombings. Several orderlies and an English officer were killed. Many others were gravely injured.[14] Noyes later expressed hope that official citations for MacDonald would be the "first of many." She also hoped that the army's recognition of wounded nurses, especially in MacDonald's case, would temper its opposition to providing official military rank for nurses, an important advocacy goal during the latter half of the war. She called MacDonald's medal "perhaps the most convincing argument for the award of military rank."[15]

At a quieter time, two years after the armistice, Noyes wrote perhaps her most tender remembrance to fallen nurses, in the February 1920 edition of the *American Journal of Nursing*. Most nurses' deaths were caused by illness, like Spanish Flu and typhoid. Somewhat out of character for her writing style, Noyes uses a narrative device to take the reader on a virtual tour of the Red Cross headquarters, directing the reader to pause before the service flag of the Department of Nursing hanging above the grand marble steps, where the offices are "as busy as when sixteen months ago it was sending to the Surgeon General's office the papers of 100 nurses a day."[16] She then guides readers to a "white-ceilinged, oak-furnished office space" in the Fourth Annex, where the papers of 36,000 Red Cross nurses are kept. "Were you to open one of the manila jackets, you would probably find eager letters of application" and "accounts full of the humor, the thrill and the pathos of war."[17] To the left is a "cubby-hole of an office" where 530 special records are kept: a catalog of nurses who had died since the Red Cross Nursing Service began in 1909. "An appointment-card, perhaps a little bent and soiled now will bear mute testimony that the owner's hands, once proud and eager for Red Cross Service, are now forever quiet," she wrote.[18] It's an incredibly stirring description, and a touching, evocative reflection, revealing a deep connection to the thousands of nurses she enrolled for service, both living and dead, Noyes's own hands having personally reviewed many of these thousands of records.

Under Noyes's telling, even the stray sounds of office activity near this hallowed room seemed muted, slightly hushed, as if in solemn deference to the dead: "Though for a moment in the chatter of typewriters, the hum of voices, and the creak of a swivel chair quickly pushed back, you may seem worlds away from a hospital, or even a dispensary in Omsk, here you will find the nucleus of the far-flung army of mercy, of which Florence Nightingale," she said, "dreamed as she walked through the wards of Scutari."[19]

Throughout Clara Noyes's career, she wrote voluminously and spoke in vivid, impassioned tones, during stump speeches marked by patriotic flourishes; but perhaps no words are more powerful than this contemplative reflection on the fallen "army of mercy."

By March 1918, fourteen base hospitals were serving in France. There was only one nurse for every 110 soldiers, and the shortage was growing. The need for more personnel led U.S. Army Surgeon General William C. Gorgas, in August 1918, to order 1,000 nurses sent overseas per week for a period of eight weeks. But, as with initial deployments, the nursing shortage was exacerbated by war officials continuing to give right of way to combat troops and supplies before sending medical personnel,[20] one of many instances where the rush of war and the troop supply prerogative had hampered the nursing relief effort. With the medical shortage came exhaustion as "surgeons and nurses literally dropped at the operating-tables from fatigue," states the *History of American Red Cross Nursing*. "War no longer appeared to be a fine, a brave, an heroic thing."[21]

Red Cross officials had already brought the dire situation to the attention of the press, as the *Chicago Daily Tribune* reported, on January 26, 1918, with the headline "Only Third of Nurses Ready Used In Camps." According to the news report, only 5,500 of the 17,000 enrolled nurses had been mustered by the War Department for "actual work" at a time when fatigue was setting in among the active duty ranks. The *Tribune* paraphrases Noyes's assurance that an "unlimited" number of trained nurses are ready for their travel calls, but the apparent "lack of quarters has forced the bureau practically to mark time since war was declared."[22] In a direct quote, Noyes remarked: "I can say truthfully that the Red Cross can supply all of the trained women that are called for and they are the type of competent experts who have completed the rigid requirements of the service," cautioning that "the service we offer is expert service and not the misdirected force of amateur enthusiasm."[23] Once again she was giving breath to President Wilson's dictum, as she did during her 1917 speech to Johns Hopkins nursing graduates: this was "no war for amateurs."

To Clara Noyes and others at the Red Cross, the supply bottleneck and corresponding shortage were in large part the War Department's own doing: its hasty preparation for war and its secondary regard for the transfer and quartering of medical personnel. These decisions were, indeed, threatening Wilson's lofty credo that the war had no place for amateurs, by forcing professionals to bide their time awaiting orders overseas and grounding the urgent need for professional backup to resupply Europe. Noyes made sure to clear the air that, despite shortages, "none of the society women heralded as members of units sent to France to do Red Cross work are with the American Red Cross unless they are trained nurses of proved ability," adding that those nurses, if they are untrained, otherwise may be "identified with the French organization," not the venerable American Red Cross.[24]

Agnes Von Kurowsky and Ernest Hemingway. *Photo courtesy of the John F. Kennedy Presidential Library.*

CATHERINE BARKLEY IN THE MAKING

One poignant set of American Red Cross files concerns the enrollment of Agnes Von Kurowsky. The young nurse's first message in handsome cursive reached Noyes's desk in January 1918.

Von Kurowsky described being "anxious" to enroll for duty. But aside from her eagerness to enroll, one other factor caused anxiety: Her father, though dead for eight years, was German. "I have heard that nurses of German parentage have been refused, and I am very anxious to volunteer for active service in this country."[1] Von Kurowsky was sensitive to the jingoistic sentiments that gripped the United States. Former President Theodore Roosevelt was on record questioning the loyalties of "hyphenated Americanism." American vernacular was being scrubbed of any distinctively German allusions. On a more diabolical level, the federal government was expanding its investigations of German citizens for charges of espionage,[2] and the Red Cross was wary of reports, early on in the enrollment process, suggesting an infiltration of German-supporting nurses who aimed to do harm to American troops. The litmus test of ethnic-national background, as a determinant for patriotic wartime duty, nevertheless remained murky.

"You may remember me as a Bellevue graduate of the 1917 class," Von Kurowsky added. Given the Bellevue connection, this wasn't the first time that Noyes crossed paths with Von Kurowsky, or made decisions about her professional aspirations. Noyes must have seen something in Von Kurowsky's application that made it worthy of approval, despite any complications that might arise in the government's background check on a woman of second-generation German heritage. Encouraging Von Kurowsky to pursue Red Cross service, Noyes said, in a measured tone, "We have always considered applications from American citizens regardless of parent's nationality, but there has been some delay in assigning nurses whose parents were foreign born ... until proof was given which would satisfy the Government." Noyes counseled Von Kurowsky to approach the local Red Cross committee in Brooklyn for an enrollment form.[3]

On this point of nationality, the Surgeon General's policy established that native or naturalized citizens alike are "liable to service" without discrimination "as far as the manner in which the citizenship was acquired," so long as "the loyalty and fidelity of the individual is unquestioned." The policy further stated: "Care should be taken" not to assign "persons who are naturalized citizens of alien enemy origin."[4] The policy did not explicitly prohibit naturalized citizens from foreign service (contrary to press and other reports suggesting otherwise), and it said nothing of second-generation Americans; but the question of Von Kurowsky's German background ultimately did hit a bureaucratic snag – "the German 'Von' threw the Italian consulate into a dither," writes historian Bernice Kert – despite Clara Noyes's instructions for the young nurse to join Catherine DeLong's Bellevue Hospital deployment in Italy.[5]

The bureaucratic snag eventually got freed. Having finally arrived as a bona fide American Red Cross nurse, it was at a Red Cross hospital in Milan that Von Kurowsky would encounter another young Red Cross volunteer, an ambulance driver by the name of Ernest Hemingway, who was convalescing from shrapnel injuries. Letters and diary entries offered conflicting accounts of the relationship between Hemingway, the future author, and Von Kurowsky, the future muse. She is believed to be the inspiration for Hemingway's love interest, Catherine Barkley, in *A Farewell to Arms*. "Miss Barkley was quite tall," says Hemingway's first-person protagonist, Frederic Henry, a lieutenant in the ambulance corps of the Italian Army. "She wore what seemed to be a nurse's uniform, was blonde and had tawny skin and gray eyes. I thought she was very beautiful."[6]

While personal chemistry and the larger backdrop of war had a substantially more direct role in the romance, Clara Noyes, in the very least, held a facilitator's role, albeit of a distant order in a chance encounter that changed literary, and American Red Cross, history. But the Von Kurowsky-Hemingway relationship has long been colored by the mythology of war, the power of fictional representation, and Hemingway's own fabled braggadocio. Red Cross officials were certainly aware of the relationship, as reflected in letters following the publication of Hemingway's book and described by Red Cross historian Jean Shulman. Charlotte M. Heilman, a Johns Hopkins nurse who served in the Milan unit, later wrote that she talked about the book with Agnes, and both nurses recognized in the book "incidents and most of the personnel." Heilman said she and Agnes were "quite sure that [the character of] Miss Gage was none other than myself as we recalled the thermometer incident ... Miss Barkley seems to be fictitious." Heilman added that "Agnes had outings with Hemingway but Miss Delong insisted upon a chaperone because of Italian customs. Agnes had correspondence with him for a while after she returned to the U.S. but destroyed his letters before he published his first book," remembering Hemingway as "impulsive, rude and uncooperative."[7] Writes Kert: "No one has suggested that it was a fully realized love affair. Even as Agnes was drawn to him, she continued to put limits on their physical closeness." According to Kert, a fellow ambulance driver and Hemingway friend, Henry Villard, "recognized the setting and most of the characters" in *A Farewell to Arms*, "but was sure that Ernest dreamed a good part of the story. The part he dreamed, of course, was the fantasy of Agnes sleeping with him, becoming pregnant by him, and fleeing with him to Switzerland."[8]

Von Kurowsky's case is important for many other reasons than her connection to Hemingway, not the least of which is its revelation of ethnicity questions at play in the American Red Cross deployment effort, as with the country at large. But in the context of American Red Cross nursing, matters of ethnicity also intersected with questions of propriety and the role of women in public service roles, as the intimate lives of nurses were subject to enormous scrutiny. (Red Cross nurse enrollees had to submit signatures "vouching for their moral character.") Hemingway's fictional representation of army nursing certainly subverted these ideologies. But Von Kurowsky's private life became a factor in other decisions after the war as well. Echoing previous worry about her father's German heritage, Agnes later revealed to Clara Noyes her anxiety about whether or not marriage would disqualify her for service. During World War I, married women were shepherded into domestic duty as "Home Defense" nurses, deemed unsuitable for overseas assignment in the conservative cultural environment of early twentieth-century America. Ten years after the war, in 1928, Von Kurowsky tied the knot, for the first time, to Howard Preston Garner, while serving under the Red Cross in Haiti. On the matter of marriage, Von Kurowsky's future with the American Red Cross was again dropped on Noyes's desk. Noyes received a letter from Commander K.C. Melhourn, Director General of the National Public Health Service in Haiti, on November 28, 1928. "As this is the first time in the history of our Training School that one of the Red Cross Nurses was married," he wrote, "there is no precedent to guide us. Will you therefore please advise me as to your decision in the matter."[9] Noyes replied to Melhourn that she had already received a letter from Agnes Garner (née Von Kurowsky) telling Noyes: "that she had been married, that you [Melhourn] had been good enough to give her away, and that she was very happy, etc. She seemed very concerned as to my attitude toward the matter, but I immediately replied sending her my blessings."[10]

Noyes wrote personally to Agnes, offering words of encouragement. "Once it was regarded as not quite proper for a nurse to marry while she was working," she said. "Times have changed and our attitude toward such matters have [sic.] undergone a complete adjustment." She closed: "I do hope, my dear, that you are going to be happy, and that ultimately you will have your own home and settle down into a homemaker. Please offer my congratulations to Mr. Garner."[11]

Here we see a second case where Noyes takes special – and, indeed, unusually warm – consideration for Von Kurowsky. Their letters throughout this period reveal a blend of professional matters as well as personal pleasantries, slightly uncommon in Noyes's otherwise very cool, direct manner. Agnes Garner later visited with Noyes and others for a luncheon during a stateside reprieve from her work in Haiti to visit family. Following the visit, she thanked Noyes and Red Cross nurse colleague Ida F. Butler "for your faith in me, and for renewing my inspiration once more," as she planned to return to the Caribbean: "The change has already done me a lot of good, and I feel quite ready for another battle with Haiti."[12] These exchanges reveal an evolution in how the profession regarded the private lives of nurses – in this case, a nurse whose private life not only drew Red Cross scrutiny but an intimate examination, fictionalized and writ large, on the pages of Hemingway's acclaimed wartime novel. Clara Noyes, in her decision-making capacity at Red Cross headquarters, helped establish new precedents for women in service roles, reflecting changes in thinking that took hold in the nursing profession and in the lives of women broadly.

y 1918, a new, silent killer was invading U.S. military camps. It infected young, healthy men who were otherwise resilient to sickness and disease. It came at a time when much of the nation's health profession was occupied by the priority of war. Spanish Flu was the killer; and it didn't merely augment the dangers of war. Its epidemic proportions were made possible strictly because of war. Medical resources were stretched thin, and the confinement of human life in close quarters provided little open space for germ resistance. Public health leaders and military officials had hastily established military training camps throughout the country with little regard for proper health and hygiene measures, paving the way for a more virulent strain of influenza to take hold in young men and civilian communities.

Despite its Iberian name, "Spanish Flu" is an historical misnomer. The disease is actually believed to have first spawned in the heart of America. Its name caught on only after the epidemic hit Spain, the first country that gave widespread press attention to the illness. Censorship by the United States government and other nations at war suppressed publicity about influenza for fear it would project a nation in a weakened state. The moniker "American Flu" would have been fatal to the war cause.[1] The epidemic first surfaced at a military camp near Haskell County, Kansas, early in 1918, where illness began striking troops at Camp Funston.[2] Red Cross reports showed 7,000 cases at this one camp alone throughout the epidemic.[3] A more virulent second wave struck at Camp Devens near Boston, where it took off amid the immense congregation of 45,000 soldiers. According to science scholar Sandra Opdycke: "By September 30 – just three weeks after the first soldier got sick – Devens had had 10,000 cases of flu, 2,000 cases of pneumonia, and 500 deaths."[4] Eight of the twelve nurses attached to flu service at Camp Devens came down with the illness and two died, the Red Cross reported in its internal files. "Those remaining at their post worked 18 hours caring for the sick and relatives of the sick."[5]

In the United States alone, the flu epidemic of 1918 was responsible for 675,000 deaths, far surpassing the 50,000 U.S. citizens killed in World War I combat.[6] Its dizzying path of suffering and death was made possible by certain characteristics of disease that are known to us today when we think of recent Ebola and swine flu scares. Those who caught it showed few signs or symptoms at the onset, often becoming sick only after a few days. Soldiers underwent medical checkups prior to obtaining travel orders overseas or transfer to different training camps, but many did not realize they were ill until they were already en route or had reported to duty at new locations. The soldier would exhibit the typical signs of flu: high fever, aches and chills, coughing and sneezing. But in many cases the illness progressed to a secondary case of pneumonia. Arlene Keeling, a scholar who has written extensively about nursing and the Spanish Flu response, vividly describes the violent course of this so-called "purple death," as "victims often succumbed within 24 hours to a fulminating acute respiratory distress syndrome, their faces purple, blood pouring from their noses and mouths."[7] The disease's virulence within tightly packed military barracks gave rise to the virus's epidemic status: "Literally millions of American soldiers were crowded together in training camps, on troopships, and in overseas bases, ideally situated to catch the disease from each other and pass it on,"[8] says Opdycke.

A second wave of influenza was circulating through the military camps in the early fall of 1918, and it leaped to the civilian population at a dizzying rate. Noyes and Delano understood that wartime demands had to be balanced by a parallel effort of civilian public health planning. Both women served on the Committee on Nursing of the Council of National Defense, which endorsed a plan for domestic nurse recruitment efforts and the establishment of a special domestic relief designation known as the "Home Defense" nurse. These graduate nurses had the same level of training as those serving on the war front, except they didn't meet the military's requirements when it came to their own domestic lives: "Home Defense" nurses were either married, which made them ineligible for overseas duty, retired, physically unqualified, or had exceeded the age threshold,[9] which was forty years of age. For domestic defense, the American Red Cross ensured that 6,000[10] of these public health nurses remained on call in mobile units for natural disasters or incidents like the flu outbreak, which arose at the worst possible time, as so much of the country's medical personnel were engaged overseas. When the flu reached epidemic levels in late 1918, a plan was ready for "Home Defense" mobilization.

Beyond the camps, Spanish Flu was affecting the war operation in other ways. On September 14, 1918, the first major call came in for nurse deployments to fight the flu after an outbreak was reported in Boston Harbor. Illness was "seriously interfering with the work of the men in the ship yards, with which the government is concerned,"[11] wrote the Red Cross Vice Chairman to the Secretary of the Navy. A meeting was quickly called to ad-

Purple Death, Spanish Flu 123

dress the crisis, attended by Clara Noyes, still serving under Jane Delano as the Director of the Field Nursing Bureau. The Vice Chairman of the Central Red Cross Committee, the Assistant Chairman of the Red Cross War Council, and representatives of the Surgeon General and U.S. Public Health Service assembled all relevant staff to determine a plan of action. The Nursing Division was clearly concerned about pulling nurses away from travel orders, needed to serve the war effort. They sought a tight grip on the redistribution of nurse resources from different regions of the country where the need for domestic personnel may be more acute, and as they were balancing the war-enrollment work. Initial calls from U.S. Surgeon General Rupert Blue of the U.S. Public Health Service asked specifically for 600 nurses at an initially estimated appropriation of $500,000.[12]

On September 24, Noyes wired local Red Cross divisions with a brief message: "Suggest you organize Home Defense nurses and those available for Nitro and Marine Hospitals to meet present epidemic," referring to the base hospital in Nitro, West Virginia. "Do not go outside Division without notifying us. Provide nurses with masks. Avoid using nurses who have given date of availability for Army … May use, under direction of Red Cross nurses, those [nurses] not enrolled … wire possible number available."[13] Noyes sent a follow-up cable to regional division directors with further instructions: "We should like you to organize in your Division one or more mobile units of ten to fifteen nursing personnel to be sent to other localities if necessary. Place competent Home Defense nurse in charge and authorize her to secure assistants, undergraduates, attendants, or nurses aids and prepare them for instant service."[14]

As Noyes would later quip to an Associated Press reporter about her work, "All I do is press a button and things happen."[15] Indeed, with a ready, highly skilled force prepared for domestic response, the push of a "button" from American Red Cross headquarters brought the Home Defense nurses into local communities, the cantonments and zones outside the domestic bases.

Well before the flu outbreak, Home Defense and other public health nurses had already been working locally to teach families the principles of hygiene and basic nursing principles through courses using Jane Delano's widely circulated textbook *Home Hygiene and Care of the Sick*. Trained nurses were especially valued in this call to service. This work significantly elevated their status in meeting the nation's domestic health needs, and further enlarging the American Red Cross mission in its by-then already enlarged function beyond the roots of the International Red Cross movement for wartime aid.[16]

By early October 1918, the military camps were reporting 144,095 total cases of flu, with 12,570 escalating to pneumonia and 3,552 deaths from all causes since September 13.[17] At Camp Pike in Arkansas, 64 nurses were called for help. "The situation was complicated by the fact that the entire Red Cross personnel, with the sole exception of the Field Director, was stricken with the disease," explained one report.[18] At Camp Sherman in Ohio, 1,100 soldiers died in less than three months. Forty-five emergency hospitals were organized in that state where 15,993 deaths occurred during October and November 1918. "In Cincinnati 300 mothers were widowed; 1,000 children left fatherless," Red Cross reports add.[19] At Camp Beauregard in Louisiana, 2,000 cases erupted in a mere 24 hours on September 25.[20] One novel technique was used in Arcadia, California where medical personnel attached an automobile compressor to 16 rubber tubes and atomizers from which "6,000 men were sprayed with anti-pneumonia solution several times daily."[21]

While surgeons were needed to repair torn flesh, extract shrapnel, and administer amputations for the battle-scarred at hospitals overseas, medical science had done little by this time to train physicians in combating influenza. Immunizations existed for bacterial infections, but no effective treatment plan existed for viruses. The main treatment theories for flu consisted simply of "social distancing" and "public sanitation."[22] Public health campaigns sought to minimize large gatherings of people, by closing community pools and other places in an effort to keep space between people. Domestic military cantonments included "sanitation zones" to block illnesses from jumping past the packed aggregation of men in the camps to the host communities just outside the bases. As soldiers and civilians alike suffered from high fevers, aches, violent coughing, splitting headaches, and sometimes choking on bloody fluid, physicians could do little else but employ minimal tools then at their disposal: basically, keep people separated, keep spaces clean, monitor the disease progress and apply basic medical practices. With so much resource scarcity, for physicians and nurses alike, the "Home Defense" nurse could do as much to help her patients as anyone else in the medical community could: providing comfort to the suffering, ensuring proper nutrition and hydration, and acting on simple principles of social containment, distancing, ventilation and cleanliness.

An appendix at the back of the *History of American Red Cross Nursing* lists seventeen nurses who died in war-related service. "In almost every case the nurse died of influenza, or pneumonia following influenza, during the

1918 epidemic, just after travel orders for military service had been issued to her, but before she had opportunity to execute the oath." Most had been working to assist influenza cases "while waiting for their travel orders for military service." Noyes authorized posthumous service medals and citations for these women.[23] Like many of their allied soldiers, and the public toll of wartime deaths at large, most of the approximately 260 nurses (total) who died in service during the war (though other sources cite 296) would not succumb to battle wounds but the far deadlier scourge of Spanish Flu.

Throughout her career, Clara Noyes recognized the courageous sacrifices of women in disaster and war relief. And she firmly believed that the nation needed to give back to these women, or their families, for these sacrifices. In the aftermath of the flu epidemic, Noyes appealed for Red Cross funding to cover funeral expenses of nurses who died from flu service, but other officials declined. "Miss Noyes estimates that there are probably 250 nurses who have died from this cause ... It would involve a very large expenditure and I think it would be a dangerous precedent for us to establish," explained one internal memo between Red Cross War Council Member George B. Case and Charles Scott, Jr., Vice Chairman of the American Red Cross in Charge of Finance,[24] as the death toll was still being enumerated. "We all agree that it is a financial obligation which the Red Cross ought not to assume," stated another internal memo, in which Red Cross leaders instead recommended procuring donations from friends of the affected families.[25]

Ninety years later, scientists gained a fuller understanding of the virus that killed anywhere from twenty million to 100 million of the world's population, infecting twenty-five percent of American citizens, many of whom were otherwise young and healthy. Fittingly, modern science was able to reconstruct the genetic structure of the virus from the autopsy tissues of two U.S. Army soldiers who died in the second wave of Spanish Flu. These cases occurred during September 1918, in New York's Camp Upton and South Carolina's Fort Jackson.[26] The military cause of epidemic flu would inevitably hold a key to sequencing the genome. A third tissue sample, providing the final piece of the puzzle, was found in the remains of an Inuit woman interred in the permafrost of Alaska.[27]

These cases all had ties to the Red Cross nursing response. Not only did nurses render service to soldiers in the training camps but their civilian relief role battling influenza included services provided by the Seattle-based Northwest Red Cross division, which mobilized a unit of ten nurses and ten physicians for commission in the hinterlands of Alaska throughout December 1918 and January 1919. There, the suffering of native populations was especially acute, including forty-seven deaths in the remote Kodiak region.[28] Following the December and January campaign, a second expedition to Alaska was called in the summer of 1919. "Permit nurses to proceed from San Francisco to join ship Marble Head at Seattle for work in Alaska with influenza," Noyes wrote in a June 3, 1919 telegram to Lillian White, Nursing Director for the northwest division. "Not to exceed twelve nurses. Salary seventy dollars per month maintenance probably provided by Navy or U.S. Public Health Service."[29]

The expedition was not without administrative headaches for the Nursing Division. At the port, two nurses underwent disciplinary review for deserting their post on the mainland to attend a dance, only to find the next day that their duties were refused by the physician in charge who is described as a "reformed alcoholist," perhaps in explanation for his moral objections.[30] "It is a most unfortunate occurrence and I agree with you 'The less said the sooner mended,'" Noyes wrote White.[31]

The group divided up into units. One arrived at a pretty grisly scene when it reached Alaska: "Numerous villages were found but no sign of life about except for packs of half-starved, semi-wild dogs," stated one report.[32]

At one location, the party "found heaps of dead bodies on the shelves and floors, men, women and children and the majority of cases too far decomposed to be handled," the report went on. "It was quite impossible to estimate the number of dead as the starving dogs had dug their way into many huts and devoured the dead, a few bones and clothing left to tell the story."[33]

Back in Washington, the hard months of the flu epidemic took a toll on Clara Noyes and Jane Delano, tugged as they were between the two poles of home defense and the loud drumbeat from military brass calling for more nurses. August and September 1918 were "oppressively hot" months in Washington, and "the contrast in temperament between Miss Delano and Miss Noyes had grown daily more apparent." Jane Delano was showing the signs of age, and "dark circles deepened" under her eyes, sometimes losing her "usual kindliness of manner." In contrast, "Miss Noyes grew more silent, more poised, in appearance more cool. Her unshakeable control, the result of temperament and circumstance, seemed to render her impervious to vexatious detail."[34] As colleague Alice Fitzgerald would later remark, Noyes, even in the more pressing moments, "never raised her voice or talked sharply but her few carefully selected words conveyed all that was needed and her hearers could not possibly mistake her meaning."[35] She kept her cool, even if, at times, remote or aloof.

Pressure mounted during the long, hot days of early fall 1918, with a second wave of influenza battering civilians and military personnel alike at home and on the European fronts, amid the unrelenting military call for deployments. Neither Noyes nor Delano would have foreseen that peace was imminent. In the climax of war, the Red Cross Nursing Service was handling multiple crises at once and, by that fall, the Chief Surgeon of the American Expeditionary Forces, Merritte Ireland, was yet again calling for 1,500 nurses' aides – what historians at the Red Cross called a "last straw."[36]

The Germans were also mounting some of their biggest offenses in an attempt to unlock the stalemate of grinding trench warfare. Wounded men were streaming into field and evacuation hospitals from some of the bloodiest fighting yet, including the Meuse-Argonne offensives – one of the largest campaigns in U.S. military history, costing 26,277 American lives and 95,786 American wounded.[37] This "last straw" was a final, bloody dénouement, culminating with a sudden end to fighting as the German forces surrendered, themselves dwindling in numbers, piled high with casualties and facing similar odds against Spanish Flu. Indeed, approximately 187,000 Germans are believed to have died from the epidemic.[38]

Noyes's contribution to the American Red Cross Annual Report that year shows the magnitude of enrollments up to this period before and after the armistice: 4,363 nurses staffed forty-eight army base hospitals; 399 were assigned to nineteen hospital units; 4,681 in 130 emergency detachments; thirty in one mobile unit; and a smattering of other attachments, for a total of 9,860 U.S.

Army Nurse Corps nurses who served overseas. A smaller group of 669 nurses was attached to the U.S. Navy, with 263 in five navy base hospital units; 115 in nine naval station units; and 291 in forty-two navy detachments. Nearly 300 nurses were also pressed into foreign-service work in France, Palestine, Italy, Greece, England and Romania. The grand total of overseas attachments, whether in the army, navy or foreign-service work, was 10,974,[39] approximately half of the total who had enrolled for service abroad and at home.

Rumors of peace first arrived at Red Cross headquarters on November 10, 1918. As the nursing staff were conferencing in Jane Delano's office that day or the next (the accounts are unclear, though the armistice was formally signed on November 11), a messenger girl stormed into the room shouting "Peace has been signed!" The nurses and office force "rushed out to confirm the report, for newspaper boys were shouting the extras." The day, long hoped for, is summed up in an almost poetic couplet from the *History of American Red Cross Nursing*: Upon confirming the news, "Miss Delano and Miss Noyes stood looking at each other in the deserted, sunshine-flooded room."[40]

But soon that "sunshine-flooded room" became a den of mourning, as the hopefulness of peace gave way to tragedy and a major transition period for Red Cross nursing.

Clara Noyes (far right) joins colleagues as Dame Emma Maud McCarthy, the British Army Matron-in-Chief (far left), delivers flowers to the grave of Jane Delano at Arlington National Cemetery. *Photo courtesy of the Harris and Ewing Collection of the Library of Congress.*

A PINE-BOARDED ROOM, A LEAD-LINED COFFIN

On January 2, 1919 Jane Delano embarked on her first visit to Europe in the post-war period. She aimed to survey the nursing operations in France, Italy and the Balkans as the military and its American Red Cross auxiliary entered the demobilization period. At the armistice, there were 400 Red Cross nurses still stationed in Europe.[1]

Delano wasn't long in France, when the news arrived by wire that she was ill. Noyes first got word on January 21 in a letter from Carrie May Hall, by then chief nurse of the American Red Cross in France. "In case you hear of it from some outside source," she told Noyes, "I am writing to you that Miss Delano is at the moment sick in hospital," suffering from a severe sore throat and ruptured ear drum.[2]

Delano found herself in the hands of nurses she had organized for war. She soon recovered enough to continue her inspection tour with a stop to review the Red Cross work at Base Hospital No. 27 in Angers. But her condition again worsened. She was transferred to Base Hospital No. 69 in Savenay. There, she was admitted to a pine-boarded room in the nurses' barracks[3] as she recovered from a mastoid operation in February. A steady stream of cables from Savenay offered terse progress notes throughout the first week of March: "Miss Delano's condition slightly improved, temperature normal but night uncomfortable" ... "Condition about the same. Temperature fluctuating. Restless night" ... "Miss Delano's condition unimproved. State of mind sane. Temperature and pulse normal for last eight hours. Contemplating operating if no improvement in next twelve hours."[4]

She was in critical condition for three weeks. Then, on April 17, came the final notice from the medical department certifying her death, caused by a brain abscess. Her last words, on April 15, were: "My work, my work – I must go to my work."[5]

Depending on the source, approximately 260 to 296 nurses – both figures are cited in the literature – would perish in the line of duty, none from combat fatalities, though a few were injured from stray shelling or bombing raids near hospitals. Most died from non-combat illness.[6] Among their number was Jane A. Delano, who, like hundreds of nurses, had fallen while in service to her country.

A Pine-Boarded Room 133

The news was a stunning blow to colleagues. Delano's protégé, Noyes, seven years younger and at her side throughout the toughest early period of Red Cross nursing, became interim director of the Red Cross Nursing Service. In this new capacity, Clara Noyes was among the first to break the devastating news to colleagues nationally. "The death of Miss Jane A. Delano ... comes as an irreparable loss to the nursing profession," Noyes wrote to National Red Cross officials. "She, like Florence Nightingale, combined the highest idealism with the most practical form of every day service. That she should have died in line of active duty at Savenay, France, marks the final sacrifice of a life devoted entirely to service."[7]

Word of Delano's death reached all corners of the nursing world. Letters and cables of condolence began flooding Noyes's office, from nursing organizations throughout the country and abroad, including one of a more personal nature from a former classmate and friend during the Johns Hopkins years. "I was very much shocked yesterday when your telegram came telling me of the death of Miss Delano," wrote Anna Jammé, who was by then working at the California State Board of Health. "I fully realize what this will mean to you and the tremendous burden that falls on your shoulders."[8]

As Clara Noyes was preparing for this "tremendous burden," the body of Jane Delano was temporarily interred in a lead-lined casket in France.[9] Red Cross and army officials later prepared for the safe return of her remains back home on the *U.S. Army Transport Sherman*. The casket arrived in Washington on September 15, 1920. A military commitment ceremony was held at Arlington National Cemetery, where Delano was laid to rest among so many heroes of wartime duty and national service.

She was posthumously awarded the Distinguished Service Cross from the War Department.[10]

Well before Delano's body returned to the United States, American Red Cross nursing faced a leadership question. As Red Cross historians remarked: "To the student of history, no phase of study is more engaging or more productive of speculation than the rise of leaders to fit the changing needs of the changing times." Once again, the differing personalities and aptitudes of Delano and Noyes would suit the purpose of the day:

> War is a spectacular cataclysm, incredibly dramatic, and Miss Delano, in her life and death and personality, had matched it. Demobilization with its unrest and reconstruction, with its uncertainty and indecision, called for sanity and an unerring sense of proportion, by means of which the displaced social order might be neatly arranged again into the normal conditions of peace. In temperament and methods of work, Miss Noyes matched the newer need.[11]

However, it is worth noting, here, somewhat of an inconsistency regarding this stated contrast in aptitudes. In previous episodes, the *History* notes how Noyes helpfully kept her cool among the growing and urgent war-time mobilization demands; and in other instances we see that Noyes's leadership style was more autocratic and less communal than Delano's – these autocratic tendencies being helpful during emergencies, as opposed to post-war relief work which required consensus-building, as was the character of Delano's oftentimes more tactful

A Pine-Boarded Room 135

leadership style. Nevertheless, Noyes's assumption of Delano's post became a virtual inevitability. She had been at Delano's side before war was declared and throughout the intense period of mobilization and the beginning of demobilization. Fresh after the Armistice, with nurses still operating overseas, and with the Red Cross looking to further engage in post-war relief work, the organization needed stability, and there was no greater stabilizing force than Noyes. At its December 9, 1919 meeting, the National Committee on Red Cross Nursing Service unanimously selected Noyes as its chairman. By then, and even before Delano's death, Noyes had already made important structural decisions in the post-war period. From January to April 1919, the first units of the original base hospitals had sailed back to the Port of New York.[12] To prepare nurses for reentry, Noyes helped establish a Bureau of Information, funded by the Red Cross but staffed by representatives of the three national nursing organizations (the ANA, the NLNE and the National Organization of Public Health Nursing). This bureau assumed some of the work handled by the Committee of Nursing of the Council of National Defense, which was being phased out. Impetus for the bureau began a full year before Noyes became nursing chairman. In December 1918, Noyes wrote to Susan C. Francis, Director of the Red Cross's Pennsylvania-Delaware Division, recommending her appointment as an adviser for the new bureau "to which nurses released from war service, as well as institutions and organizations may direct their inquiries."[13] Francis responded eagerly, noting how the war had gutted the nursing units of civilian hospitals. She expressed hope that some organized conduit for reentry into civilian nursing would help replenish the country's institutional nursing needs:

"I have responses from fifty hospitals, and I am appalled at the number of vacancies which exist in the nursing staffs of many of these institutions," she told Noyes. "The Superintendents must have done some heroic work, particularly during the recent epidemic, and I wonder just how much our training schools have suffered as a result of it all."[14]

The bureau opened in February 1919 and its interviews with homeward women provided a window into the psychological toll of wartime nursing, the culture shock of reentry into civilian life, and a feeling that "the present somehow does not fit with the past."[15] By October 1919, Noyes had begun working to transfer this bureau's auspices from the Red Cross to the three organizations of nursing. The change in management was a pivotal moment in the history of organized nursing, as it brought these three groups together at a single location of coordinated activity. As ANA historians note, "with the operation of the Bureau of Information, the American Nurses' Association established physical roots for the first time."[16] According to the ANA, 1,357 nurses applied and 1,275 were placed in positions through the bureau and over 1,544 hospital and other vacancies were made possible directly or indirectly through its auspices.[17] As the *Pacific Coast Journal of Nursing* explained: "That the three national nursing organizations are now housed in a joint headquarters in New York City is ... largely due to Miss Noyes' zeal in that behalf."[18]

Re-entry into civilian life also meant ensuring that nurses availed themselves of important benefits for their wartime service. While nurses were not fully commissioned officers entitled to pensions – at least not for their World War I service, though benefits would change during World War II – disabled nurses were entitled to assistance through the Bureau of War Risk Insurance, as were men. Clara Noyes worked to ensure that nurses took advantage of these entitlements, much as she had sought financial help for families of nurses after the flu crisis. The government asked the Red Cross to canvas the country to locate "every disabled man in order that he may learn of his rights and privileges and be put in the way of receiving them," but Noyes emphasized the importance of identifying women for the same purpose. As she wrote in the *American Journal of Nursing*:

> It cannot be too emphatically or too frequently stated that this same plan of assistance is open to every ex-service woman as well as to every ex-service man. The disabled nurse, quite as sacredly as the disabled soldier, is the obligation of the nation. Every disabled nurse who served with the Army or Navy is entitled to this type of service and it is hoped that all nurses who have been physically disqualified since the war will not fail to bring forward their claims.[19]

The Bureau of Information was a critical clearinghouse to help. Nurses reported to the bureau sick, traumatized, or requiring follow-up care. Some also needed accommodations as they awaited compensation from the Veterans' Bureau, prompting local Red Cross divisions to assist with hotel costs in New York City during their convalescence. Eventually, the Red Cross secured a more permanent location for convalescent nurses on Bay Shore, Long Island. By June 1921, "294 nurses have sojourned there and have derived great benefit from the opportunities for relaxation and convalescent care," Noyes wrote.[20] Nurses were returning home, the Red Cross was downsizing its war-time divisions, and a period of post-war transition, demobilization and advocacy work took hold. As Noyes told delegates at the ANA's twenty-second convention, "While the pressure of actual war conditions has been lifted, the period of reconstruction brings pressure of quite a different type."[21] Approximately 100,000 nurses were by then registered through nurse practice acts in forty-six states. From the 3,000 schools of nursing, 13,000 nurses were graduating each year, she said. Yet, even with these sizeable numbers, Noyes voiced concerns about scarcity, as reentry into domestic life seemed to offer new callings. "We should have at least 28,000 more nurses available for service than we had a year ago," Noyes said of the shortage. "What has become of them?" She added: "Many seem to be leaving the profession entirely, many enter the business field which at present is offering lucrative positions and alluring possibilities ... as secretaries they seem to excel, while matrimony and tea-rooms beguile many from the ranks of active workers."[22] Nursing was again changing, as new opportunities greeted nurses in peacetime America. So, too, were traditional domestic enticements, much to the chagrin of Noyes whose service to nursing was never shaken off course from the "beguiling" draw of matrimony.

But post-war military obligations still commanded nurses' attention. At peacetime, 39,000 graduate nurses remained enrolled in the Red Cross Nursing Service for domestic duties to care for disabled ex-servicemen and those who did not meet the draft requirements because of disability, Noyes said.[23] Approximately 30,000 ex-servicemen remained in hospitals, and Noyes took to the

American Journal of Nursing, appealing for nurses to fill hospital vacancies to serve this ongoing obligation. "It would be a serious commentary upon the patriotism of nurses of this country if they failed to meet this demand," she said. "It is easy to be patriotic during active hostilities, but the aftermath of the war is sometimes more tragic than war itself."[24]

Throughout war, the Red Cross and military apparatus had been helped in its communication efforts by modern technologies. Wire telegram services allowed Clara Noyes's words, orders and counsel to reach Europe and other corners of the globe as she oversaw the work of nurses during the conflict and demobilization period from her broad desk. For the war operation specifically, one thrilling new advancement was radiotelephony, "by which constant communication could be maintained between ground stations and flying airplanes," a new wireless tool for modern wartime communication.[25]

This tool was used to great effect immediately after the war as well.

While Red Cross parades may have been a grand human display in the pageantry of wartime sacrifice, new technologies were also being pressed into service as a vocal means of drumming up post-war monetary sacrifice, in the form of liberty bond contributions from the public. Those bonds were used to pay off war debts.

"During the three weeks covering the recent Victory Liberty Loan drive," reported the May 31, 1919 edition of *Electrical Review,* "the crowds that daily thronged 'Liberty Way' in New York City were accorded the unusual sensation of having spoken messages come to them out of the air."[26] Crowds had gathered in a long stretch outside of Madison Square Park where an arched column was erected in 1918, modeled after the Arch of Constantine in Rome, to honor the city's war dead. From this arch, a grand concourse was extended.

In late April 1919, a set of antennas was stretched over the concourse, along with 112 loud-speaking telephone receivers and a "maze of wires and switches forming the wireless sending and receiving apparatus" in the nearby YMCA building, adjacent to a podium for announcements. At the YMCA building, messages received from Washington "passed over the wires to the control room" at the podium along Liberty Way, "and were there amplified many million times so that they might be heard by the crowds on the concourse through the medium of the loud-speaking receivers."[27]

Using this marvel of wireless technology, several leading officials "talked direct from Washington to the great audiences" outside Madison Square Park, as "a return circuit made it possible for the speakers at Washington to hear other speeches, music and applause from the audience in New York," all routed across the great expanse of the Middle Atlantic States.[28]

Among the voices from Washington were: President Wilson's daughter; Franklin D. Roosevelt, then Assistant Secretary of the U.S. Navy; an official from the French Embassy in Washington; the wife of the Secretary of War; and Clara Dutton Noyes, chairman of the Bureau of Nursing Service of the Red Cross, whose "every word was clearly heard by a crowd of 10,000 people" in New York.[29]

Clara Noyes spoke from her office, describing the work of the Red Cross nurse. "She, too, like the soldier, has made a supreme sacrifice," Noyes said over long-distance telephone, switched to a wireless transmitter and a set of loudspeakers along New York's Liberty Way.

A Pine-Boarded Room 141

"Over 200 American Red Cross nurses have died during the war. Some sleep quietly among the American dead in France, others in England, many here in the United States. Now the most tragic loss comes in the death of ... Miss Jane A. Delano, at Savenay, France, in line of duty. That these nurses may not have served and died in vain, and that the work begun by America may be completed now, buy Victory Liberty Loan notes!"[30]

The leadership of Jane Delano – "once proud and eager for Red Cross Service" and "now forever quiet" – was taken up in the capable frame of her successor, Clara Noyes, in words of triumph, spiked with loss, cascading across cheering throngs of Americans now experiencing a new phase of sacrifice and involvement in world affairs.

And so, a new day was dawning. A nation would gather to remember its war dead, continue making monetary sacrifices for a national cause, celebrate peace, and marvel as voices from America's two great centers of power – New York and Washington, miles apart – mingled in mid-air, amid cheers, music, and a sense of triumph.

Clara Noyes. *Photo courtesy of the Harris and Ewing Collection of the Library of Congress.*

'RANK IS THE REMEDY AND RANK THEY SHOULD HAVE'

W as Clara Noyes a feminist? A proto-feminist – meaning that she embodied feminist ideals before such a label was used? Certainly she expected others to value her authority, and she spoke authoritatively. She cared deeply for the professional standards of nursing, a vocation dominated by women. She fought to secure this professional space, often against onslaughts from male establishment figures, whether it was her feud with Dr. Charles H. Mayo about nursing standards,[1] volleyed on the pages of a popular woman's magazine, or when she voiced insistence to doctors about the best method of surgical dressings.

Clara Noyes saw herself in league with the women's suffrage movement – or, in the very least, echoed its goals in the context of nursing advocacy – and she was an official representative of Red Cross nurses at the National Convention of the Woman's Party in 1921 where delegates laid wreaths at statues commemorating America's pioneer suffragists.[2] Later, she was elected chairman of the Women's Joint Congressional Committee, which, at the time of her incumbency, included nineteen organizations, among them the ANA. They advocated for bills on food and drug safety, education initiatives and other measures. The committee was at one time considered the "most powerful lobby in Washington,"[3] serving as an information clearinghouse for coordinated women's groups to monitor legislation.

Well before Clara Noyes took a leading role in the committee, though, the press accused it of communist leanings, a damaging propaganda campaign that prompted Carrie Chapman Catt to pen a response in the May 31, 1924 edition of *The Woman Citizen*. Catt and others pegged the rumor's origin to a "subordinate in a bureau of the War Department" who had branded the committee as part of "The Socialist Pacifist Movement in America."

To inoculate criticism, Catt published the committee's plainly stated mission statement as:

> A clearing house for seventeen national women's organizations which have representatives in Washington ... the Committee, as such, initiates no policy and supports no legislation and no organization joining it is committed to any policy except that of cooperation, whenever possible ... After a measure has been endorsed by five or more organizations of the committee, a sub-committee of representatives of endorsing organizations is organized ... and carries out a campaign of action.[4]

The explanation is slightly contradictory, as it says, on the one hand, that the organization "supports no legislation" but, on the other hand, describes a process of endorsement. Regardless of the committee's own level of activism, clearly its constituent organizations got on record in support of or against discrete legislation.

The War Department's conservative political damage stuck; as historian Jan Doolittle describes, by 1930, around the time Noyes and the ANA had joined the Women's Joint Congressional Committee, it "had lost most of its congressional and public support and began a gradual descent into political obscurity until its ultimate demise in 1970."[5] Again, we see how the War Department needed and supported some facets of women's advancement – in nursing, specifically – insomuch as it suited the government's aims and prerogatives; but that support would evaporate when it confronted a more robust level of political activism on the part of women's groups. The committee nevertheless made some important gains during the 1930s, helped by a growing appetite for New Deal national reforms. One success in this period was the enactment of Title 5 of the Social Security Act, which provided grants to states for maternal and child health programs. A longtime struggle by women's groups for labor protections also led to passage of the Fair Labor Standards Act in 1938.[6] During Noyes's tenure, the group hosted receptions for women members of Congress, including one in May 1933, attended by Florence P. Kahn (the first Jewish woman to serve in Congress), Edith Nourse Rogers, Mary T. Norton, Virginia Jenckes and Kathryn O'Laughlin McCarthy.[7] More women were gaining ground in Congress, following Jeanette Rankin's lead.

Clara Noyes was becoming an even more active political voice, and she did so as chief of the world's largest organized body of professional women, the ANA, which had more than 30,000 members by 1922,[8] her last year as president (though she continued to have an influential role in the organization, including as its delegate to the Women's Joint Congressional Committee). As Noyes wrote in an unpublished 1934 article about nursing's role in the Women's Joint Congressional Committee, the ANA "has adopted a policy – to restrict its activities to those federal measures concerning general welfare, health and education, and such matter as pertain to nurses – making it possible for the American Nurses' Association representative to serve it with intelligence." Again, we see her exhibiting trademark pragmatism and restraint when it came to women's causes, applying her political voice to issues almost exclusively affecting the practice of nursing and its professional concerns. Among the bills of interest to the ANA was the Sheppard-

Towner measure in 1921, providing funding for maternity and child care. Another focus, says Noyes, was "reclassification of nurses" in government hospitals, "from the sub-professional to the professional grade."[9] Noyes testified before Congress on this issue, citing the difficulty maintaining a roster of nurses. Many were discouraged by the lack of opportunities for advancement within the government. Noyes also testified in support of a new government agency being proposed in the expanding pre-New Deal nation-state: the Department of Education. "Through the results of research and distribution of findings, which may be conducted under such a department, all educational work, including schools of nursing, will ultimately be greatly benefited," Noyes said in her remarks to Congress.[10]

Though engaged in major women's issues of her time, it is unclear, however, to what degree Noyes's efforts on behalf of these political causes were strictly defined by a conviction about her career and its practical purpose in public life; or whether her voice for women's causes also reflected a broader temperament about the status of women generally. Regardless of this orientation, Clara Noyes led several important advocacy positions drawn from her observations of wartime nursing. These efforts had a profound impact on the elevation of women's roles and public recognition – at least in the context of nursing and, at most, marking important historical efforts to achieve fairness for women.

The first of these major advocacy positions inveighed against military rules stating that nurses would lose their pay if captured as prisoners of war. In September 1918, Noyes issued her first salvo against the ruling in her newly appointed capacity as ANA president. Her approach, in filing a protest with both the Treasury Department and Surgeon General Gorgas, revealed an astute ability to wade complex political waters. The Red Cross, we know, was designed as an organization of professed neutrality, except in the case of wartime, when the neutrality clause was suspended in deference to the imperative of national interest. Ironically, as the neutrality clause was suspended, Red Cross leaders seemingly had to adopt a neutral stance of their own when they confronted unfair policies – even those policies that undermined the Red Cross' ability to serve the nation-state in time of war, as Noyes's arguments over the pay issue would claim. Thus, Clara Noyes was compelled to use her status under the ANA – not the American Red Cross – to protest the wartime pay issue.

The pay issue was largely a theoretical win, as there is no recorded instance of nurses ever being held captive in the First World War.[11] Even though most nurses served far from the lines of battle – only in rarer instances did they operate at the field units closer to the theaters of war – the potential ramifications for women being held captive was nevertheless an eventuality that nurse leaders in the war effort did not want to risk. Their advocacy sent a strong message on the value of women's work, and status, in a newly enlarged role during wartime.

Clara Noyes's decision to choose her ANA pulpit was shrewd; but, perhaps equally wise, was the way she tempered her arguments. She couched them in more "conservative" terms, similar to the ways in which some nurse leaders relied on "safer" appeals to prod support of the suffrage movement (i.e., by arguing that the right to vote would allow women to influence moral and public safety causes, as well as purely professional interests, like nurse registration laws and positions on boards of health). On suffrage, particularly, "nurses argued that the vote was essential because as women they were power-less in their professional and personal life without it," Sandra Beth Lewenson writes.[12] Suffrage was, for many nurses, a case of professional need if not also personal interest. This balance between professional and personal differed for various women, though the difference may not matter when the aim for a specific outcome was uni-fied.

As press reports during this episode show, Clara Noyes's primary argument against the government's un-fair pay rule was that it harmed the war effort. The ruling "could not help but be destructive of nursing enroll-ment," she said in remarks reported by the *Washington Post*, which noted that the military's policy "has aroused a storm of protest, not only by the heads of the nurse's organizations, but by the public in general."[13] In reality, if loss of pay might have stopped women from enrolling, perhaps a far greater stymieing effect were the rumors of atrocities to women, especially sexual violence or mutila-tion on the part of the enemy, which Red Cross leaders continually confronted early on.

Sociological studies have explored the phenomenon of political "salesmanship" in efforts to win over particu-lar segments of the public or government leaders. As scholars Rob Willer and Matthew Feinberg recently wrote in the *New York Times*, the "rule of salesmanship ... also applies in political debate – i.e., you should frame your position in terms of the moral values of the person you're trying to convince."[14] This strategy applied in the messaging of nurses on the more moderate wing of women's rights advocacy, like Clara Noyes in her use of "patriotic salesmanship."

The pay win was a morale boost and a landmark pol-icy change recognizing women's rights and privileges in the military context. And the ANA was wise in its use of a compelling patriotic point rather than a social-justice point to achieve this win. The government's position was plain wrong; but in a conservative political environment of patriotism and national interest, Noyes and others recognized that a practical claim about "hindered enrollment" was more persuasive in terms of "salesmanship" than lodging a social-justice protest. Clara Noyes understood the War Department's anxieties about the need for nurses, especially in the war's climax. In August of 1918, army officials requested an additional 2,312 nurses, as the Spanish Flu epidemic raged and major enemy advances led to a surge in war wounded.[15] These anxieties and personnel needs offered a point of leverage for her claim about hindered enrollment. As Clara Noyes wrote in the *American Journal of Nursing*, about the Treasury Department's change of heart:

> Although we hope that the word "enemy" will soon be relegated to the background, with other war terms, nurses in service will be interested to know that Comptroller Warwick has reversed his decision that members of the Army Nurse Corps who have been taken prisoner by the Germans, were not entitled to salary. The decision, as first rendered by the Comptroller, at a time when the Surgeon General was calling for thousands of nurses for the military establishment, dealt a serious blow to enrollment. The Red Cross announced immediately that it would provide all nurses who were captured by the enemy, with food, clothing and, if necessary,

money for living expenses. It is now a matter of congratulation that the armistice was signed before the Red Cross was called upon to perform this unhappy function.[16]

With the American Red Cross's "immediate announcement" of funding for nurses – though deemed as an "unhappy function"– it appears that the American Red Cross also used, quite craftily, the stimulus of American charitable giving as a potential lever for shaming the government about its deaf political ear when it came to supporting nurses' sacrifices, even though the American Red Cross wasn't officially involved in fighting the unfair pay issue.

At nearly the same time that Clara Noyes and others protested the government's pay position, the Red Cross Nursing Service was collecting reports from nurses overseas who were expressing another form of mistreatment: Their authority was questioned by military officials and enlisted men. Under established standards, a clear hierarchy had existed in civilian hospitals, and women relied on it in their work. But that established hierarchy bumped up against ideologies of hyper male privilege in the context of a military campaign. Under the civilian hospital's long-devised chain of command, surgeons were at the top. But in the middle ranks were a chief nurse who oversaw the work of ward nurses. Below them were the orderlies. Except, in the case of war, the orderly was often an unranked enlisted man, conscripted for army service and imbued with prerogatives of male privilege that couldn't help but be amplified in the masculine context of battle. This isn't to say that the traditional hospital hierarchy was any less male-autocratic, but the hurried deployment of hospital units for war service overlapped with a separately defined military rank schedule that was incompatible, at best, in recognizing the division of authority across the entire field of medical relief. As reports of recalcitrant male orderlies rolled into national headquarters, the Red Cross Nursing Service was attuned to a threat that jeopardized hard-fought practical standards for the authority of nurses in assuring the safety and hygienic needs of the patient care zone. Like the arguments for pay during captivity, Clara Noyes and others seeking to address chain-of-command issues in the Army Nurse Corps again relied on patriotic terms. "Approximately 15,000 nurses are in the service with the army and navy," Clara Noyes argued. "They have gone quietly and without blare of trumpets, and are willing to accept hardships in order that our men and boys may not suffer for the want of skilled nursing. Will you not give those who are in the service and about to enroll the assurance that the government is ready to protect their statutory rights?"[17]

On this issue, nurses had a strong ally: former President Taft.

Because this question had a military command dimension, Taft and the nursing profession employed a uniquely military strategy for codifying the authority of nurses during wartime, by seeking the insignia of rank. In early 1918, a new National Committee on Rank for Nurses was assembled, with Taft as chairman. "I have been nursed from death to life by Army nurses in Army hospitals," the former president said of his experiences at a hospital in the Philippines. "And I know from personal observation just what their problem is with the disobedient hospital orderly. Rank is the remedy and rank they should have."[18]

But it was more than just "disobedient hospital order-lies." The officer class was also inconsistent about the authority of nurses, in part due to vague regulations. Those regulations, issued in the summer of 1917, stated that army nurses "are to be regarded as having authority in matters pertaining to their professional duties (the care of the sick and wounded) in and about the military hospitals next after the officers of the Medical Department and are at all times to be obeyed accordingly."[19] But without defined rank, these regulations were open to a vast array of interpretations.

Clara Noyes agreed to serve on the committee as vice chair with Taft, again representing the ANA. This ANA affiliation reflected the more political nature of the rank campaign, ill-suited as it was for official or uniform Red Cross endorsement. The Red Cross ostensibly kept at arms-length from this hot political issue. But it was increasingly difficult to maintain neutrality, as officers from all levels of the relief organization began separating into different camps. General Merritte Ireland of the executive committee was himself on record opposing rank, while nurse leaders within the Red Cross used the pulpit of related nursing organizations to push the cause. The War Department was opposed, but Surgeon General Gorgas was supportive. Press reports quoted one unnamed army officer as saying of the nurses: "Under shot and shell when the well-being of the wounded was in question, they have shown a magnificent disregard of personal safety and have ever been the last to seek cover ... They ought to have recognized status."[20]

Joining Taft and Noyes on the committee for rank were presidents of the three national nursing organizations and Helen Hoy Greeley, who served as counsel and perhaps one of the campaign's most articulate advocates.

"Few of the orderlies have read the orders giving a nurse authority," Greeley explained. "It is military psychology that if they see on her shoulder the bars that they have been taught to respect they will not question her right to command them."[21]

The campaign did not end until well after the armistice was signed – and, quite fittingly, at about the same time that states were ratifying another women's rights measure: the Nineteenth Amendment for women's suffrage. Nurses were already returning home from the war front as nursing leaders continued to press their case for public support on the rank question, paving the way for the utility of military rank in future conflicts. Indeed, the *American Journal of Nursing* and other forums seemed keenly aware that the rank campaign was sowing the seeds for the use of rank at a later time. "I believe that the women of the country must demand that their experience in this war shall not be duplicated," wrote Greeley in the *Journal*, saying of possible future conflicts: "Gentlemen, we want to do our part in this, but not as before."[22] The slow-going nature of the campaign – especially due to opposition from the conservative War Department – made it an increasingly uphill battle. Even some nurses were reluctant to support the cause, especially those nurses already relieved of duty overseas who saw little benefit in fighting for rank's future efficacy. Some other nurses were dissuaded by doctors who told them rank was unnecessary. Many physicians feared that rank would lead to insubordination in the patient care arena. "We occasionally hear that nurses themselves do not want rank," Noyes said during the hotly contested debate. "There may be nurses that do not want rank, there were many women that did not want suffrage, but that is no argument against it," again linking professional concerns for nursing with larger causes on behalf of women – two causes (rank and suffrage) which would eventually coincide in achieving their intended outcomes. "This is just one step onward, and if we do not progress, if we do not develop, what is the use of living at all?"[23] It was clearly a very personal issue of conviction, existential even, as Clara Noyes and allies ramped up calls for nurse advocacy. Noyes sent an impassioned appeal to state nursing organizations asking them to pledge money and provide testimony supporting the need for rank: "That the Army Nurse Corps is to-day an integral part of the Regular Army is due to the vision and labor of those who served amid unspeakable disorganization in the Spanish-American War," she wrote, conjuring the early period of wartime nursing. She adds:

> When they came home, they faced opposition, prejudice and unbelief … They stopped short of asking rank for the army nurse because they were weary and because they hoped it would come naturally, without struggle. To-day they regret their optimism. They realize that whom the gods reward they first make work. Experience is a good teacher. She instructs us that rank is essential to the most efficient functioning of the Army Nurse Corps, not only, but to the dignity of our womanhood.[24]

Nurses like Gertrude Bowling, who served valiantly in a shock team unit, cited the usefulness of rank as she recalled her experiences during the Meuse-Argonne offensives. "At times the congestion was great. The dead sometimes waited three and four on the ward with the living, because the stretcher bearers were too busy carrying the wounded and the dead could wait. It was here and in some of the other hospitals ... that we often felt that the authority of rank might have given us a freer hand in organizing the work."[25] The *New York Tribune* quoted another unnamed nurse who faced chain-of-command issues as she directed an orderly to disinfect medical equipment. "Returning from a short period off duty I found that my precious solution had been emptied out. Upon inquiry as to what became of it I was asked by what authority I was interfering with the care of utensils. No recital of army regulations would have been necessary if I had had a title and a bar on my shoulders."[26]

While the nursing profession and committee acted quickly, the slow machinery of Congress resulted in a delayed victory. Not unlike the issue of nurses' pay during captivity, which was more a matter of principle than practical application, the rank victory was preempted by the much larger victory of the Germans' surrender. Clearly the two campaigns – fair pay and rank – were seen as linked. One principled win for nurses was being used as justification for the other. As one press report noted about the pay issue: "The Treasury Department ruling [reversing its policy on pay for captured nurses] is being used to induce members of Congress to support the Lewis-Raker bill, which provides relative military rank for nurses."[27]

It wasn't until May 1920, more than a year after the armistice, that both houses of Congress passed the rank measure, with President Wilson signing it into law on June 4.[28] It provided "relative rank," not "actual rank," conferring symbolic status, an insignia of authority, and other benefits – except without equal pay or the pension benefits extended to regularly commissioned officers. The superintendent of the Army Nurse Corps would have the rank of major, assistant superintendents would be captains, chief nurses would be first lieutenants and nurses would be second lieutenants. "The lowest commission given a medical officer in the army is that of first lieutenant, and any first lieutenant in the Medical Corps will outrank the major of the Army Nurse Corps," explained one description of the rank schedules.[29]

A few months later, Tennessee became the thirty-sixth state to ratify the Nineteenth Amendment for women's suffrage, meeting the threshold for certification of the amendment in late August of 1920.

On the then-settled question of rank, Clara Noyes told delegates at the 1922 convention of the ANA, in Seattle, that: "It is almost too early to state whether it is as successful as its advocates hoped. We have heard some rumors that it is not, but I at least have not spoken to any member of the Army Nurse Corps who would wish to give it up. Furthermore, it is reasonable to believe that its full value could hardly be determined in time of peace."[30]

And so, while her father, Enoch, served as a captain in the Civil War, commanding 100 men in Company C of the 26th Connecticut Regiment during a 49-day siege in Louisiana, Clara Noyes rose to national prominence in her effort to muster 20,000 nurses for duty in World War I, later paving the way for women to achieve the rank of second lieutenant and higher, for the first time, in recognition of their service to country.

1411 29th Street NW in Georgetown, Clara Noyes's last home.
Photo taken by the author.

FORGET YOURSELF

Seeking refuge from the demands of Red Cross headquarters, Clara Noyes found serenity in a quiet, private, home life. She made her place on M Street Northwest during her early years at the Red Cross, and, later, at 1411 Twenty-Ninth Street NW, a squat two-story home typical of the Colonial Revival and Federalist architecture lining the proud streets of early twentieth-century Georgetown. This house, which she would inhabit for the rest of her life, was a nearly two-mile drive to American Red Cross headquarters. Her friends later recalled Noyes's home as "a real refuge" where "close friends and friends' friends whom she so graciously welcomed therein enjoyed a rare privilege."[1]

The home had a small terrace garden, which Noyes cherished as a retreat, dining at night in "that sweet secluded bit of out of doors,"[2] welcoming the sight of an errant bird perched in her yard on sultry summer evenings. Her capacious knowledge for detail made her an expert at bird identification, no doubt cultivating this skill as a child in the wilderness of Mount Ararat where many of the same species could be spotted amid the brush. "Her knowledge of birds was indeed remarkable in one who had been most of her life a city dweller," recalled some of her former classmates at Johns Hopkins,[3] perhaps forgetting Noyes's early life in rural Maryland as a farm girl surrounded by nature. Her retreat on Twenty-Ninth Street must have provided a welcome balance to the frenetic thrum of Washington, DC, Red Cross headquarters, and the breakneck flurry of trans-Atlantic cables she sent and received from nurses in far-reaching corners of the globe. Alice Fitzgerald remarked about Noyes's "Washington flat" that "comfort, order, consideration surrounded her guests," as Noyes "used to thrill at the visits paid to her terrace garden by some humming birds and other feathered friends."[4]

While Clara Noyes was guarded, cool, aloof, patrician in demeanor, those who knew her privately saw different shades of her personality. Pursuing solitude outside the city, she drove to Mount Vernon along the Potomac, "taking herself and her friends out of the city and into the quiet loveliness of the woods."[5] Solitude was prized. But it also came at the cost of loneliness and sacrifice, which seemed part and parcel to the entirety of her service as a nurse.

Like Jane Delano and others of her professional coterie, Clara Noyes would never marry. Many aspects of her personal life are unknown, friends and peers having passed decades ago, but it is clear that her strict work ethic held for her a somewhat ascetic view. Noyes was consumed with her prolific writing, as well as professional leadership roles at virtually every nationwide nursing association, from the NLNE during her time at Bellevue, to the ANA, to her role as editor of the influential *American Journal of Nursing*, and, of course, in demanding work at the American Red Cross. Perhaps her personal qualities or simply her drive for professional achievement led Noyes to trade a life of intimacy for one of global impact. In a widely published interview on her work, in 1921, Noyes's ethic as a nurse leader is plainly stated in the two-word headline "Forget Yourself."[6]

"What natural qualifications must the girl who would study nursing have?" she said, repeating the reporter's question in this telling profile. "Well – in the first place I should tell her that it is a very lonely life, very lonely ... If she wants to go on I would ask her if she could live weeks without ever thinking in terms of herself and her family. Next I'd like to know something of her attitude of mind – how serious it is. And she must have administrative ability."[7] While Clara Noyes was a champion of nurse training, her worldview seemed to envision a certain set of basic qualities upon which an intelligent woman with the right affinities could build up a skill set for nursing. "The public scarcely realizes how big a factor nurses are in the life of both the ailing and the well," she remarks in the "Forget Yourself" article, chronicling the self-sacrificing work of nurses in service to people in need, far from home. "Just consider the influence of our nurses who work among the Mohamedan women, among the Albanians who for 700 years have been under Turkish control. We have a mother's club in Albania, and in Athens we have a baby clinic which has cared for 700 babies." She adds: "At first these women, especially the Mohammedans who had never been in a public meeting, regarded us with suspicion. They couldn't understand an unselfish interest in their babies; they couldn't accept our home hygiene. But we've won them over. Their babies are healthier. Their homes are more comfortable – and they regard America and the Red Cross nurse as very much a factor in their betterment." Beyond the health and welfare of the American public, Clara Noyes saw in the nurse's selfless work a larger diplomacy role – one that women were uniquely able to carve out for themselves in an otherwise restricted realm of public life, leadership and policy development. At least within the context of nursing, women oversaw a preserve of global impact and, indeed, empowerment. It was through women's work that minds could change, and lives improved. This definition of women's work, albeit a defined one, created a context and a sphere for change. Nurse leaders like Noyes leveraged a *de facto* value placed upon their shoulders by global disasters and the crisis of war. They drew every last drop from this domain of influence.

After being awarded the prestigious Nightingale Award in 1923, Clara Noyes explained how she achieved her status through the route of nursing, with a modest remark: Nursing, she said, was "the one thing the world most needs that a woman can do."[8] Similar to her activism on pay fairness and rank, Clara Noyes would many times strike a moderate posture, ever aware of her culture's attitude toward women. She clearly saw, or at least knew the benefit of reinforcing, that a woman's influence was gender-defined. Her advocacy for women often found recourse not in the rhetoric of social equality or justice, but in leveraging fairness for women by highlighting the prerogatives of domestic preparedness and patriotic appeals on behalf of the nation-state. The nation needed nurses, virtually all of them women. But the recognition of women's value was in many ways confined by the nation's impulses, not by proclaiming the inherent equality of women. Just as she had traded a life of domestic intimacy for autonomy in the one profession that tolerated it, her appeals for women's status and, at times, social justice, were tempered by her acknowledgement of the limits placed on women in professional and public life. Those limits were moveable – and she strived to move them – but her advocacy for women almost exclusively drew from within these shifting limits. She was the rare example of an autonomous woman who would never marry, owned a house and a car, came and went as she pleased. This was only possible because she had applied her intellect and innate executive abilities within the now-enlarged, but still defined, limits of a woman's one professional domain of influence: as a nurse. Had she lived in a different, later period of history, she may have been embraced within the broader fold of executive leadership, like Francis Perkins, who became secretary of labor under Franklin Delano Roosevelt, and the first woman in a presidential cabinet.

Nevertheless, she rose to the top of her profession in the limited executive ladder of her time for women. While Cora Sutton Castle's *Statistical Study of Eminent Women* counted only a handful of names in its ranks of nineteenth and twentieth-century women of influence – and only two "nurses," Florence Nightingale and Clara Barton – Clara Noyes would eventually gain entry into Robert McHenry's encyclopedia of *Famous American Women: A Biographical Dictionary from Colonial Times to the Present* in the 1980s.[9]

Throughout her rise, Noyes was nevertheless greeted with male chauvinism as she asserted her authority, often scornfully, at the American Red Cross Nursing Service. "Miss Noyes declared her position in forthright fashion, fought to maintain it, and if rebuffed held aloof in outraged indignity," writes historian Portia Kernodle. "In moments of impatience, men at the Red Cross staff referred to her as an old maid," revealing a particular brand of chauvinism targeted against an unmarried woman, forever a maiden.[10]

But her executive skills as a nurse were needed, especially after the death of her mentor Jane Delano. That experience, working under Delano's wing, made her a natural successor; and so, by the spring and summer of 1919, the National Committee of the American Red Cross looked to Clara Noyes as the next leader of its flagship nursing division. But Noyes, who was seven years junior to Jane Delano, would possess very distinct leadership differences from her predecessor, again as related by Kernodle. "Miss Noyes, a little younger than Miss Delano, represented the spirit of the nursing profession in its period of growing self-consciousness; and she spoke a different language. Sensitive to any slight of nurses and nursing, proud of the accomplishments of the profession, watchful of its standards, jealous of its prestige, she was one of the women who ably piloted it through the stress of expansion to maturity, stability and power."[11]

Noyes's "jealousy" of nursing's prestige made her quite a warrior in defending the profession from any slight or attempt to diminish its status; her tenacity also continued to be a target of chauvinism from male-dominated medical authorities. When Charles H. Mayo, namesake of the Mayo Clinic, suggested that the nation's nursing shortage could be alleviated by developing a lower rung of less-trained "sub-nurses," Noyes fired off a response that was printed in the same popular women's magazine that had published Dr. Mayo's article: "If sub-nurses, why not sub-doctors?" she pondered. "How would the doctors like it if we were to advocate sub-doctors with modified education to take the place of full-graduate doctors at smaller fees?"[12] The broader physician community fired back, republishing and commenting on her remarks in trade journals. On the question of sub-doctors, the *Medical Standard* countered: "We are really astonished that so intelligent a woman should advance so specious an argument." The physician, its editors argued forcefully, assumes the "entire responsibility for the case which is entrusted to his care ... The nurse, no matter how well trained or vouched for, never carries this kind or degree of responsibility. Her responsibility moves chiefly toward the doctor, and is limited to an intelligent and skillful carrying out of the doctor's instructions."[13] Again, Clara Noyes found herself greeted by patriarchal attitudes of male privilege. Having guarded and fought reflexively against a perceived attack on her profession, she ran up against the paternalistic medical establishment in its influential trade journals.

One can understand the protectionist view of nurse leaders, like Noyes, who fought back tenaciously against any incursion from the outside into what had become a sacred professional sphere worthy of staunch protection.

As with the midwife debates, scope of practice and turf battles continued to rub raw wounds. But Kernodle sheds further light on the origins of Clara Noyes's rigid, somewhat autocratic leadership style, as well as her zealous regard for the nursing profession and its training standards. It appears likely that these attitudes were rooted in Noyes's early executive experiences as superintendent of nursing schools. Regardless of origin, clearly this temperament was a source of friction in the transitional period of the American Red Cross Nursing Division, further contrasting Noyes from her predecessor's more collaborative style. "Even those who liked her knew that they would incur her displeasure if they failed at any single moment to measure up to her exacting standards," Kernodle elaborates. "Her habits were those of one who for many years had held a position of authority in which she received deference and absolute obedience. Used to dealing with student nurses in the manner of nurse administrators of the old school, she might keep a member of her staff standing before her desk ungreeted while she read a letter."[14] Here Kernodle conjures the image of a military general seated at his desk, task-oriented to the point of allowing no interference from the order or priority of executive duties. Much like the military, the American Red Cross at this point had, indeed, created a hierarchical governance structure. This included a central committee with individual bureaus housed at national headquarters. From this center of power, regional divisions, committees and local chapters took instruction. With organizational activities emanating in pyramid form, the arrangement was not unlike the military structure.

Perhaps no other woman was more responsible for this hierarchy than Mabel Boardman. She is remembered

for her fervent work to bring more rigidity and account-
ability to the organization. Boardman's tenure was distinct from the management style of American Red Cross
founder Clara Barton, whom Boardman criticized for being too loose with financial record-keeping, as newcom-
ers to the American Red Cross sought to incorporate
standardized executive practices, with oversight from
organizations like the Russell Sage Foundation. Indeed, it
was Boardman who led efforts to oust Barton from the
very organization she founded, packed away from the
public eye as a "skeleton in the closet."[15] Through the
lens of history, it is tempting to see these early American
Red Cross leaders as outsized figures on a continuum of
temperamental extremes between visionary, communal
figures, on one hand, to the more rigidly autocratic, on
the other, whether it is Clara Barton, Jane Delano, Mabel
Boardman or Clara Noyes.

Perhaps it was also Clara Noyes's Civil War captain
father, Enoch, or the strictness of her Maryland upbringing at Mount Ararat farm, or simply the leadership style
nurtured in her own nursing education ("in the manner
of nurse administrators of the old school") which inspired an autocratic leadership style. Some evidence suggests that this ethic may have been spirited (at least in
part) from the culture of Johns Hopkins School of Nursing. The historical record of Johns Hopkins refers to a
"small notebook" that "affords a glimpse of the organization and content" of Lavinia Dock's first classes there,
when Clara Noyes was a student. Dock, a product of the
Bellevue Training School later led by Noyes, left behind
notes which offer a telling statement on the ethic of forg-
ing young nurse professionals: "The nurse is a soldier.
Absolute and unquestioning obedience to a superior officer is the fundamental idea of the military system in or-

der that responsibility may be rightly placed ... There is a necessity for drill in producing quickness, skill and quiet. Criticisms are not accusations. Strictness and exactness produce better nurses."[16] In many ways, Clara Noyes may have taken this ethic to heart, reared on the Dock curriculum and mingling with the coterie of early nursing leaders who shared certain professional views and value systems.

Nurse management educators today have identified broader principles of leadership management styles, breaking them down into a set of types. The American Association of Nurse Assessment Coordination, for instance, describes five classes of nursing leadership, including the "authoritarian or autocratic leadership style," where a leader makes "all decisions without considering input from staff." Exclusionary and vertical in its approach, this management style does have plusses in certain contexts, perhaps fitting for wartime or crisis nursing: "The positive side of this style is that it works perfectly in emergencies or chaotic situations where there is little time for discussion."[17]

These temperamental differences drew other battles from within the nursing community, particularly Noyes's friction with leaders from the National Organization for Public Health Nursing (NOPHN). The organization began as an affiliation of the ANA but later broke off independently when the ANA reorganized under its articles of incorporation in Washington, DC.[18] The NOPHN's rocky relationship with the American Red Cross was rooted in the Red Cross' expansion into public health nursing during the war – and the NOPHN's worry that the Red Cross was drawing experienced public health nurses away from community health work into wartime service overseas at a time when resources were scarce and when public health nursing was growing to meet long-neglected needs.[19] As nursing scholar M. Louise Fitzpatrick notes in her history of the NOPHN, the antagonism of its leadership was aimed at both Jane Delano and Clara Noyes, with particular friction between NOPHN Secretary Ella Crandall and Noyes. Fitzpatrick quotes a 1919 letter from Crandall where she fumes: "I believe that the Red Cross power in the field of public health nursing will be an actual menace. I believe that even if Miss Delano and Miss Noyes were removed ... the ruthless arbitrariness governing the Red Cross would still be entrenched." Fitzpatrick goes on to chronicle a specific feeling of acrimony between Crandall and Noyes: "The attitude of Clara Noyes ... was especially distressing to Miss Crandall. Whether there was a personality conflict between the two women and either actual or unfounded reason for dislike of Miss Noyes, there was no question that Miss Crandall distrusted her."[20] American Red Cross work in public health nursing was, indeed, growing. Noyes reported in December 1920 that its Public Health Nursing Services increased from 155 to 817 personnel, operating under working agreements with Boards of Health in 35 states. In one community, almost 200 tonsil and adenoid operations were performed on children, through the initiative of one Red Cross Chapter and its public health nursing program, Noyes described anecdotally.[21]

Portia Kernodle mentions other personality conflicts within the Red Cross itself, specifically over the use of volunteer nurses' aides, which Mabel Boardman considered an area of prided development. Even Mabel Boardman, herself a rigid leader, was not immune to Noyes's autocratic bent. Their conflict appears, again, driven by Noyes's zealous regard for the hard-fought status of professional nursing. Boardman sought to expand the nurses' aide service during the Great Depression, when staffing was needed in hospitals and in volunteer work through local chapters. She "came out openly and strongly for a development of this corps, defied Miss Noyes, and did everything in her power to make the Health Aids a flourishing program," writes Kernodle in a subchapter titled "Noyes vs. Boardman." As Kernodle elaborates: "Miss Noyes seems to have opened the attack" after reading a report showing considerable increases in the health aid corps. "Her tart query was how there could be an increase when she had authorized no new corps in the past year." Noyes pushed to reign in Boardman's pet program:

> The real point is that Miss Noyes was a nurse and Miss Boardman was not. Miss Noyes believed, with many other members of her profession, that nursing care should be given only by professional workers. She knew that some hospitals would be only too willing to get free service from volunteer amateurs, even to the detriment of their professional nursing staff and possibly of their patients. She knew that the nursing profession had been seriously affected by the depression – that many nurses were unemployed. She did not want to encourage the training of workers who would compete with women who must make their living by nursing.[22]

Before she replaced Jane Delano, Noyes's work was largely technocratic in nature. Her administrative duties involved marshalling nurse forces, approving enrollment applications, standardizing surgical dressings, and coordinating with field nurses on strict organizational needs that required efficiency and exactness: two attributes she clearly excelled at, in part due to her autocratic tendencies, her "precision and dispatch." Beyond these technocratic duties, Clara Noyes's real area of visionary impact, as many have noted, was in the sphere of nurse education and practice, where she had the strongest voice of influence. Noyes especially shined in her work to export American principles of nurse education to foreign nations after the spasm of war, just as she had brought the Nightingale standards to the early New England nursing schools. In Europe, she endeavored to engage both local and national stakeholder institutions in developing a self-sustaining nurse education infrastructure.

If the post-war relief effort and her ascendancy to Jane Delano's office constituted a second act, this second act was perhaps Clara Noyes's finest performance. It was a duty in which she was most capable to lead, and it brought her into a mode of leadership that required increasing collaboration – with heads of state, nursing leaders in other countries, as well as international Red Cross societies in Poland, Bulgaria, Czechoslovakia and other nations. These collaborations were not without conflict. But Noyes showed herself equable to the cause of partnership, at least in the cherished domain of nursing education. Her efforts advanced the cause of professional nursing in countries that requested American Red Cross help to repair the countries' underdeveloped nursing infrastructure and training programs, by then in a state of crisis following war.

Clara Noyes Red Cross publicity photo. *Photo courtesy of the Harris and Ewing Collection of the Library of Congress.*

'GREETED BY COURTS AND KINGS': AN OVERSEAS MISSION

"The signing of the armistice brought a change to the Red Cross Bureau of Field Nursing Service, similar in nature to that of the military establishment," Noyes wrote in February 1919, drawing an important parallel. "The Department of Nursing, which had recruited and assigned to the military establishment over 21,000 graduate nurses, completely reversed its machinery, almost over night, and took up at once the equally difficult problems of readjustment and peace,"[1] reestablishing its motto of "neutrality, humanity, service."[2]

Much of this activity involved post-war relief work in Europe, which fell to aid organizations like the American Red Cross. The U.S. government and military establishment – war-weary, battle-scarred and reluctant to have entered the conflict to begin with – did not persist in its interventionist orientation. As the *History of American Red Cross Nursing* pointed out: "A strong feeling existed on the part of many individuals in the United States, even though they were sympathetic, that the countries of Europe should assume the question of rehabilitation for themselves."[3] The Red Cross nevertheless overcame this view, using surplus funds from its wartime chest for peacetime uses and a continued overseas presence.

Other private, charitable commissions had already sprung up during and after the war, including Herbert Hoover's ambitious Commission for the Relief of Belgium, which fed over nine million people a day in Belgium and Northern France when the regions were racked by war-time famine. Hoover's work made him a star in the arena of international relief, later compelling President Calvin Coolidge to tap him for organizational work with the American Red Cross, notably during the Mississippi Flood of 1927 when Hoover was Commerce Secretary. This intersection with charitable causes helped buoy Hoover's later rise to the presidency.

In her August 1920 passport application, Clara Noyes is described as 5 foot 6. Age 52. High forehead. Blue eyes. Fair complexion. Oval face. On it, she listed her intentions to travel to France and the British Isles for a period of four months, for Red Cross work; but she was later drawn much deeper into the continent on a peacetime inspection tour of the Red Cross's international nursing program, assessing the needs for more permanent nursing institutions in war-ravaged Europe. That September, Noyes headed overseas to join colleague Helen Scott Hay, who was chief nurse for the American Red Cross Commission for Europe. As the 1921 Annual Report of the American Red Cross put it, her tour had three basic purposes: "to make a general inspection of Red Cross Nursing Activities, in order to determine the character and scope of the work now being performed by Red Cross nurses; to study the Schools of Nursing, which had already been established in various countries, with the cooperation of the American Red Cross [and] to advise upon those under consideration; and to review the nursing needs of the proposed health units."[4]

Noyes was especially eager to see Prague's new nursing school, which was already being developed under the banner of the League of Red Cross Societies. By the time of her 1920 tour of Europe, the number of American Red Cross nurses stationed overseas had dropped to 150, and Noyes was anxious to visit "in order to judge the character of the work our nurses are doing."[5] In addition to inspection detail, she also came with a gift: The ANA and

Greeted By Courts and Kings 173

allied organizations had raised $50,000 to fund a Florence Nightingale School for Nurses in Bordeaux, France. The school would also function as an official memorial to American nurses who died in service alongside their French sisters. Noyes was instrumental in the planning work to install a more modern nursing school facility there, along the lines of the Nightingale models that had taken root in the U.S.

Requests were already coming in from governments and groups in Poland, Czechoslovakia, Bulgaria and Turkey seeking American Red Cross help to either build new nursing programs or to strengthen programs that had already existed in these nations. A request from the Queen of Bulgaria, in particular, had reached the American Red Cross as early as 1913. Arrangements were made for Helen Scott Hay to sail in August of 1914 for purposes of beginning the project. "She had proceeded as far as the port of New York and was all ready to sail when like an exploding bomb came the news of the outbreak of World War and Her Majesty cabled that all negotiations would have to be broken off," Noyes wrote in a history of the Bulgaria program.[6]

The general plan was to organize a committee of stakeholders in each country, engaging government agencies, universities, and the nation's own Red Cross Society for governance purposes. Once a suitable facility was identified, connected to a training hospital, a faculty of American nurses would run the host country's nursing programs while a contingent of nurses from that nation would be placed in American or English schools for a two-year course in graduate nursing, supported by scholarships.[7] But to get the European nursing schools started, American nurses were responsible for developing the foreign school's curriculum and training – a task that would eventually be handed off to native-born peers trained in nursing skills at U.S. or English teaching hospitals.[8] This exchange of authority and sponsorship was important. The Red Cross couldn't maintain a robust presence in Europe forever, and the host nations needed to do their part to assume duties. As the 1921 Annual Report of the Red Cross put it: "The duty of the nurse would be but half done if she were to leave no permanent structure upon her withdrawal."[9] As Noyes later remarked to an audience in Los Angeles, all of the European work was designed on a "fifty-fifty" basis, "by which the local authorities furnished the premises, undertook the maintenance and provided securities to aid in the work" of the American Red Cross to help develop strong nursing programs in Europe.[10]

As Noyes made plans to set sail in late September, her assistant, Ida F. Butler, took the helm of the Nursing Division in National Headquarters, just as Noyes had done nearly two years prior when Jane Delano left on her fateful tour.

Clara Noyes (center) with a group of American nurses at Warsaw.
Photo courtesy of the Library of Congress.

Greeted By Courts and Kings 175

Noyes's Europe sojourn included stops in Warsaw, Vienna, Belgrade, Turkey, Athens, Florence, parts of Albania and Montenegro, and Prague, capital of the new Czech nation-state, whose leaders were among the more eager, and involved, proponents of European nursing work. There, she spent the day with President Tomáš Masaryk and his daughter, Dr. Alice Masaryk, both of whom sought Noyes's counsel in developing improved nurse training programs in the new Republic of Czechoslovakia. Arriving at the Czech capital, Noyes was motored to the president's summer home twenty miles into the country. "During our conference I found that the Czechs are determined to create a proper nursing system, together with certain other central educational features under the Czech Red Cross, later to be transferred to the Government," Noyes recalled,[11] crediting the Masaryks for "crystallizing" public support for a Nightingale-based school of nursing in their country.[12] Noyes's visit was a unique opportunity to see the evolution of a nation firsthand. A unified sense of public spirit appeared to be backing the nascent Czech state: "The people seem to move as one person," she observed of the Czech capital, "inspired by a common thought and purpose: to make Czechoslovakia an independent nation of independent thought and action." In the city, she visited a facility for crippled children and one for prisoners. But while the country was imbued with a "common thought and purpose," it was also racked by poverty, malnutrition and famine. "The people look anemic, especially the children," she said, noting the lack of nutritional staples like milk, butter and eggs.[13]

The prime minister's daughter, Dr. Alice Masaryk, took an active role in shaping the country's medical development work. But to oversee nursing services specifically at the Czech school, American Red Cross nursing officials had also identified within their vast enrollment records a Czech-American nurse, fluent in the native language, who fit the role for Prague duty at the state hospital for training. Noyes gave this initial survey of the facility: "Equipment was almost primitive, the tea kitchens and lavatories antiquated and inadequate, and little or no provision made for hot water supply. An occasional portable bath tub was seen." One small cake of soap was issued to the entire ward each week, "while the shortage of bed linen and blankets, to say nothing of the limited diet of patients and nurses, were pitiful," she observed.[14] At the hospital wards, the students and graduate nurses "looked pale and anemic and it seemed marvelous that upon so meager a diet they were able to drag through a day's work." Supplies were scarce, modern amenities of a nursing program were non-existent, but nutritional concerns prevailed, as Noyes ordered an allowance of 18,000 additional francs to supplement the food supply until the Czechoslovakian Red Cross was able to take over this responsibility.[15] Despite these grave conditions, sixteen students graduated from the first nursing class in 1921, with total enrollment at sixty-six pupils.[16]

When their train reached the Polish border for inspection, Noyes and Hay happened upon a group of American nurses in a heated discussion with customs officials. The nurses were on route from Paris to Warsaw for assignment in one of the health units there. The imbroglio had to do with customs officials insisting that the nurses' heavy "regulation" boots be weighed and taxed. "After a voluble argument in German, Miss Hay succeeded in getting them to see the light and the shoes were admitted to Poland free of duty."[17]

With so much cross-border activity engaged by the

Greeted By Courts and Kings 177

American Red Cross, it seemed inevitable that Noyes and Hay would casually run into a group of young women under their charge – in this case, at the Polish border.

Visiting Poland in October, Noyes conferred with local authorities in Krakow who were seeking American Red Cross help to build a local school, along the lines of the Czech model. Krakow wasn't originally on their travel itinerary, but Noyes and Hay came to the city because a railroad strike had prevented them from reaching Warsaw immediately. They toured a tuberculosis clinic, a day nursery and food distribution center, noting that a nourishing diet was "hopelessly beyond the reach" of most tuberculosis patients. "To send patients home lacking both food and clothing, knowing beyond doubt that there was not a possibility of their obtaining either the one or the other, has been one of the heartbreaking tasks ... in that 'Zone of Horror.'"[18]

By rail they traveled to Posen (also written as Poznan) in an American Red Cross car which was "rather a glorified caboose." They visited Kornik, a village fifteen miles away, where two Polish-speaking American nurses were stationed. There Noyes and Hay met Count Zamoysa, who had been exiled from his home for thirty-four years and had "just been able to return to his ancestral estate, following the German evacuation," Noyes said. "He recited with great glee a story of the Red Cross nurses' rowing a boat around the moat, something that had not stirred the placidity of those historic waters for many a year."[19] The country was racked by famine and war's ravages, but, like the stride of citizens in post-revolution Prague, a bit of hope, no matter how infinitesimal, was fanning the waters of war-torn Poland.

But the ravages of war were a constant reminder inveighing against these small ripples of hope. In Warsaw,

Noyes witnessed "five miles of freight cars filled with war orphans, children for whom no one was responsible and who would have perished but for the help of the American Red Cross."[20] A plan for the development of a Polish school of nursing was advanced, including facilities, uniforms, textbooks, allowances, affiliation with district hospitals for practical training and a governance structure. Having fought for supportive nurse practice regulations at the ANA, Noyes called for a program of government registration for Polish nurses and nurse practice acts, knowing full well that hard-fought licensure and professional standards were safeguards against efforts to weaken the status of nurses. "No doubt the suggestions which had already been made, in addition to the plan submitted by Miss Noyes and her associates, seemed a radical one," Red Cross historians write. "Time was needed for the Polish committee to digest it."[21]

A school in Posen (Poznan) opened in November 1921, incorporating a two-year course of training under the direction of Ita MacDonnell, an American nurse.[22] The Warsaw school also opened that same year, with an anonymous pledge of $10,000 annually over three years from an American nurse.[23] Letters of application came from 125 girls, the first being from the daughter of a Polish countess who was too young and was withdrawn until the following year.[24] Its first class had a registration of twenty-six students. "For the formal opening of the school," on October 19, "it was of course necessary to have the house blessed, following the Polish custom," said Noyes. "It was very much an occasion and all the leading citizens of Warsaw attended, the Cardinal himself officiating."[25]

Noyes also met with nursing students in Sofia, Bulgaria, where Hay had already begun work on a nursing school in 1915 even as war was raging. But the political situation at that time made the school's outcomes less decisive than the American Red Cross work in Czechoslovakia or Poland. Noyes and Hay would have audiences with King Boris III, who had assumed the throne in 1918 and was receptive. Noyes described him as "a tall, dark, rather delicate young man" who called the Red Cross plan for instruction a possibility of "new life for Bulgaria," adding: "It is my most earnest hope that the best facilities of Bulgaria will permit their daughters to take up the study of nursing."[26] But the Acting Prime Minister, Noyes explained, "was wholly non-committal" about availing his country of American Red Cross nursing education. Noyes and Hay waited several days in Sofia to gain a definitive decision on the future course of nursing there. Without a commitment, they submitted a recommendation before departing back to the U.S. just before January 1921 – "That we assist the Bulgarian government as far as possible in the resumption of a school of nurses, providing the Bulgarian government itself is ready to do its full part, financially and otherwise."[27] Noyes sketched out a plan for Red Cross support of salaries for two American nurses, "and at least partial maintenance for not less than two years." The plan was bogged down by delays, procrastination and economic woes, at a time when "the lev was selling ninety to a dollar."[28]

Europe wasn't the only region calling for American Red Cross nursing help. Back in the Western Hemisphere, the Haitian government requested four American Red Cross nurses to serve the country in early 1920. Plans had previously been made to establish a nursing school there, but were later withdrawn. A renewed effort in the early 1920s was led by Vashti Bartlett, whom Noyes had first recruited to the Red Cross in her early days with a "Macedonian Call." Having joined the American Red Cross for wartime administrative work, Bartlett would yet further fulfill Noyes's missionary plea in the Caribbean and other overseas work throughout her career.

All of these efforts – whether in Bulgaria, Poland, Czechoslovakia and, even, France – brushed up against cultural views and customs that complicated American Red Cross work with host nations. Noyes later remarked: "Until the principle that actual work with one's hands is dignified and honorable and uplifting ... where autocratic forms of government prevailing for centuries have developed sharp class lines, modern schools of nursing or other democratic systems of education will make but slow progress."[29] The view of nursing in foreign lands resembled some of the early American preconceptions about nursing. In America's pre-Nightingale period, leading up to the Civil War, nursing was the domain for "drifters" and poorly trained social outcasts. Noyes, one of the first generation to benefit from a new trajectory in the profession of graduate trained nurses, brought this contemporary spirit with her to Europe, as did the nurses she and others recruited to lay a foundation for training work. But she often confronted the same cultural attitudes about nursing that had prevailed in the colonial, antebellum and immediate post-bellum period of United States history.

When Noyes left Europe at year's end 1920 (her final report was filed with a date of December 30), she had made some important gains, but had not yet secured commitments from the political establishments in Greece and Bulgaria. In Athens, she described that "no better work has been done in Europe" than the Infant Welfare station established there by the Red Cross, but she was less enthusiastic about a Red Cross-sponsored nursing school in the city, noting in her final report that "nothing [was] done about this as all interested actors in the case had gone out of the country with the Venezelos Government. It is felt most emphatically, however, that ARC money can much more consistently be spent elsewhere."[30]

The "last word" from Sofia," she wrote, "is to the effect that the Ministry feels it is unwise to act before the return of the Prime Minister who is expected back about January 21st, but that it is confidentially expected, after this date, the plan for the resuming of the school will be agreed and the necessary passed."[31]

Her general recommendations to Col. Robert E. Olds, commissioner of the American Red Cross in Europe, called for the appointment of a supervising nurse for all public health activities in Europe and the development of different health, public health, nursing and relief units. A plan was also devised for child health centers and a regime of educational work to bring nursing principles to the public and help native personnel "carry-on" after the withdrawal of American nurses.[32] "The European countries, with the exception of a few of the more advanced, are conspicuously lacking in nursing personnel," summed up the 1921 Annual Report of the American Red Cross. "The establishment of these schools of nursing is among the most constructive and cumulatively valuable contributions the American Red Cross Nursing Service has made to Europe."[33]

Examining Noyes's work – firmly established as it was in the domain of nursing – one finds little distinction from the activities of public diplomacy inherent to the duties of an American Service Officer under today's State Department. She met with heads of state and other stakeholders to change attitudes about hard-fought American cultural principles (in nursing but also in the role of women), and she sought arrangements to develop humanitarian institutions of goodwill through programmatic endeavors.

Meanwhile, as Noyes was surveying American Red Cross nursing work across allied Europe, American nurses elsewhere around the globe were observing the more menacing side of geopolitical and factional struggles in the immediate post-war period, including genocide. Accounts from nurses like Blanche Knox, stationed in the Caucuses after the armistice, add to the historical record of atrocities and violence that held various regions in grip as national and cultural boundaries underwent a painful realignment. "At Alexandropol ... the people were dying of starvation, dysentery, and typhus – 200 a day, requiring twenty carts to carry out the dead," wrote Knox in her report back to American Red Cross headquarters. "Part of the town had been blown up by the Turks when they left last December. The streets swarmed with refugees, over 60,000 of them, and I never imagined such desolation and misery – living skeletons walking or crawling on the filthy, muddy cobblestones, many of them blind with hunger. All of those who could see went with their eyes glued to the ground hoping to find a morsel of food."[34] As with their previous wartime experiences, women in service during the post-war period witnessed gruesome acts of inhumanity, contributing vividly to the historical record.

But in other cases, this unique window into world affairs brought political trouble for nurses. Anna Tittman, a Red Cross nurse from Illinois, had one of the bleakest overseas assignments, with the American Expeditionary Forces in Siberia. There, the U.S. found itself pulled into two simultaneous crises: a Russian Civil War and the need for war-time strategic placement of manpower. Returning home from Russia, Tittman was interviewed by local press in Springfield, Illinois. Her politically charged comments later got picked up for wider distribution by the wire services: "I have been told on good authority that a revolution is believed to be pending in Japan," she said. "Spreading all over Siberia is the menace of the Jap ... It is growing stronger and stronger throughout all Europe."[35]

Noyes was overseas, and unable to deal with the publicity problem. Back home, the Acting Director of Nursing, Ida F. Butler, wrote Tittman at her Springfield address, clipping the news article along with a comment from Dr. F.P. Keppel, vice chairman at Red Cross headquarters, calling Tittman's remarks "the kind of thing we have to be very careful about."[36]

"With Miss Noyes away, I felt that I must call your attention to the danger of publicity, unless we know all its pitfalls and are equipped to deal with them,"[37] Butler gently chided. Tittman expressed her regrets, stating that she assumed any ban on expressing political opinions was only in effect during her service period. "I, frankly, did not give the matter any thought and had I done so, I probably should not have made the mistake," Tittman replied. "I only talked to the reporter under the greatest pressure," she said. "I feel very sad to have had this unfortunate matter come as the conclusion to my very trying and difficult service in Siberia."[38] Butler appeared satisfied enough by Tittman's explanation: "There will be no ill results from it," adding: "I think Dr. Keppel's feeling was that just at the time of our roll call, it was well for us not to be quoted in any of the political issues of this country or any other."[39] As the American Red Cross was about to engage in another call for donations, a few careless words from one of its nurses was potentially damaging to the campaign for funding of relief work. In Siberia, there was no country estate for nurses to fan the waters of a moat as Clara Noyes observed in Poland: just cold, hard labor amid Russian frontier fighting, as American Red Cross nurses tended to the wounds of civilians and combatants alike. In letters to Noyes from Siberia, Tittman was considerably more charitable about the Red Cross's relief work there, in contrast to her press comments, noting how the various nationalities she served "exemplified the true principles of Red Cross neutrality," as nurses in Siberia cared for a Korean, two Japanese, a Russian priest, a British officer, as well as "soldiers of all the factions involved in the fight; railroad men; innocent bystanders; and even an American sailor."[40] The hinterlands of Siberia had drawn forces from all over the globe in a chaotic, multi-purpose and, at times, cross-purpose campaign.

As Noyes explained in November 1919, more than 150 nurses were still stationed at Red Cross hospitals in Vladivostok, Russian Island, Omsk, Tumen, Novo-Nikolaevsk, and the Engineers' Hospital connected to work on the Trans-Siberian Railway following the war. A campaign was underway there to battle typhus, which, the winter prior, had killed 10,000 people in the region. A train of seventeen cars was sent to the region with bathing and delousing facilities, "which can be rushed to the point where the plague is most severe," Noyes wrote about the efforts.[41]

Tittman was appointed chief nurse to the Eastern Division's Commission to Siberia in about March of 1919, as the American mission was becoming extraordinarily complex. "Difficulty of communication, danger from the

Bolsheviki, the great distances which separate the isolated groups of Americans from each other, and the presence of the dread typhus, have made the work of the Siberian Commission a gallant and persistent fight against almost incalculable odds," Noyes said.[42]

The purpose of the U.S. military campaign in Siberia – which had overlapped the European War, the armistice and the Russian Civil War – was multifold. In March of 1918, the Bolsheviks had signed a treaty with Germany, and U.S. forces feared that some of the military supplies and resources stored in Siberia would fall into enemy hands. Meanwhile, the Bolsheviks had detained a unit of Czechoslovakian troops as the Czechs attempted a return to the Western Front, where the allies needed their support. Given the complex political dynamics, the campaign in Siberia was multinational, with Allied forces, Bolsheviks, the Chinese military (seeking to protect business interests in the region), and the Japanese all drawn into the region. President Wilson had specifically urged the Japanese to join in the effort, ostensibly in alignment with western goals, a request that at first met with reluctance. Despite this reluctance, the Japanese committed a far larger force to the region than expected, surprising American allies.[43] The island nation, it seems, was driven by an ulterior strategy to buffer eastern Russia from Bolshevik control.[44]

This intense political and relief environment may have prompted Tittman's remarks to the press, as newspapers were eager for some word of activities on the ground in Siberia, especially where the strategic goals were complex or nebulous. Skepticism was rising in America about U.S. engagement overseas in the post-war period, whether in Siberia or elsewhere. Noyes and others at the American Red Cross addressed this criticism, aimed at the organization's still-expansive mission, at a time when the nation was weary of any further interventionism. "I realize," Noyes told colleagues at a May 1921 Red Cross chapter in Philadelphia, "that we cannot furnish nurses forever to Europe, anymore than we can furnish money forever to Europe."[45] But the humanitarian need was enormous. She and her nurses saw it firsthand on their travels and duties, from famine-stricken Prague to genocide-racked Turkey. "We must for a time try to feed and clothe these people until they have a chance to rehabilitate themselves and they have not been able as yet to do this."[46]

By July 1922, she found herself still answering criticisms about U.S. interventionism overseas. She was compelled to explain that new Red Cross chapter donations, needed for domestic activities, were not being sent abroad.[47] The American Red Cross was still drawing on surplus funds it had amassed during wartime, not new monies. She stressed the progress that came from intervention, including in Czechoslovakia, where graduates at Prague's nurse training school had taken charge of twenty child welfare stations, freeing up American nurses to return home. Post-war intervention, she contended, was a necessary antecedent to eventual American withdrawal.

American nurses left behind important cultural gains as they began to draw down their overseas work. "In our school in Constantinople, that part of the world where women have been so subjugated and suppressed, Turkish women are coming out of their seclusion and taking courses as nurses," Noyes told skeptics.[48] She referred to the streams of Russian refugees in that part of the world, "suffering in filth and heat and rags and presenting a terrific problem to the people of the various countries to which they went – countries already appalled by the care of their own suffering people." Nevertheless, by the summer of 1922, she acknowledged, "It has seemed right and proper to turn over to the people of Europe the responsibility of caring for their own, and the American Red Cross is withdrawing as rapidly as possible from the work which it organized and carried on."[49]

The Bordeaux school in France is one concrete tribute to this general program of overseas relief and reconstruction work. By the time of Noyes's 1920 Europe tour, the hospital connected to it had been in operation for nearly sixty years with the express purpose of caring for foreign officers, including American servicemen. For nurses, the hospital held special status as a marker of America's alliance with the French. Eighteen years after it was organized, the school there had begun adopting American standards of nursing education, counting twenty-six pupils on its roster. Much of this early development work was overseen by Dr. Anna Hamilton; but more work was needed to turn the nursing school into a true Nightingale model. Early in the post-war period, the ANA and other groups raised funds for the school, as a gift to their French sisters. During the planning stages, it was decided that the school would also be a fitting memorial to the 296 American nurses who died in service during World War I, many of these deaths occurring in France.

Plans called for an inscription at the front and back entrances of the new nursing school identifying it as the "American Nurses' Memorial." The modern facility would house single bedrooms, a large assembly hall, and demonstration and lecture rooms. "The plot of ground which contains sixteen acres, is most admirably situated," Noyes reported on her first visit to the site in the early 1920s. "There are beautiful gardens including forty fruit trees and an old French manor house," an inspiring location for a tribute to American nurses' aid in the allied cause.[50]

The Bordeaux school was not only an important recognition of nurses' sacrifice, but the funding campaign showed how the three American nursing organizations continued to work in close collaboration, stemming from their first major cooperative work assisting nurses at the Red Cross's Bureau of Information. The joint committee of the ANA, NLNE and NOPHN sent letters and distributed leaflets to state nursing organizations and training schools to get every registered nurse to contribute at least one dollar to the campaign, even sending follow-up letters when a certain division of the country had not "given its quota."[51]

Eventually raising $50,000 to fund the endeavor, American nurses attended a dedication ceremony for the new facility and memorial on May 12, 1922, the 102nd anniversary of Florence Nightingale's birth. Clara Noyes was unable to attend, but an ANA representative, Sophie C. Nelson, went on Noyes's behalf to deliver the key in a grand, widely publicized ceremony.[52] The school and memorial opened on June 25, 1931, finalizing an important chapter in American nursing's engagement with European allies. Noyes, so instrumental in the fundraising and development effort, was again unable to attend the opening ceremonies, but she sent a message read by Elnora Thompson who had by then assumed the presidency of the ANA. "Why did the nurses of America go so far afield to commemorate in a suitable manner the life and service of those valiant young women – for the majority were in the first flush of womanhood?" Noyes wrote in her prepared remarks for the occasion. To an-

Greeted By Courts and Kings 189

swer this question, she stressed the humanitarianism that had compelled so many Americans to offer aid to their European fellows, even in the post-war period of disengagement; it seemed fitting for the nurses of America to do the same, by offering a memorial and the gift of a new nursing school in Bordeaux. Noyes answered her first rhetorical question with another: "Everyone in America was then adopting something – ruined villages, orphaned children, or demolished churches – why not," she reasoned, "ask the American nurses to adopt the Florence Nightingale School and build for it a suitable home" in Bordeaux? [53]

French and American nurses found themselves working in league with one another throughout the war; even at the start of the conflict, the need for a stronger nursing program was evident in America's allied country. As authors of the *History of American Red Cross Nursing* remarked, "It may readily be appreciated that in a modern system of nursing, the French nation was far behind the United States, where practically every town over ten thousand population possessed, at the time of the United States' entry into the war, a hospital maintaining a professional school for nurses founded on the Nightingale System."[54]

The school made important inroads for French nursing. Its Assistant Director, Marguerite Cornet-Auquier, later told reporters in 1934: "The war did much to improve the rating of nurses in France. Before then, almost anyone could be a nurse, and consequently the profession suffered. Today the standards are almost as high as in the United States," adding: "Our requirements are growing stricter every year." Clara Noyes remained head of the school's governing unit via an advisory committee.[55]

Clara Noyes continued to follow-up on the status of nursing education efforts globally well beyond her initial Europe tour. In 1926, she revisited Sofia, Bulgaria where her efforts had previously been stymied by political inaction. As vividly described in the *American Journal of Nursing*, her travels in 1926 took her, by train, past cornfields, tiny houses, oxcarts and "orchards of plum trees laden with the most luscious fruit."[56] There, she and colleagues inspected the American Red Cross-affiliated nursing school, which was finally beginning to bear fruit of its own. Even though she had left Bulgaria in 1920 without firm government commitments, training school work was later resumed under the direction of American Red Cross nurse Rachel Torrance, beginning in 1922 with a school in Sofia.[57] As Noyes recalled in a history of the Bulgaria effort, Torrance was greeted to her assignment with a "picturesque old Bulgarian custom observed for centuries when a bride is welcomed into her new home; a loaf of bread and a dish of salt were given to the American directress with instructions to carry them later into her new dwelling place – in this case her room."[58] Nursing, with its personal sacrifices, was yet again reinforced as a stand-in at the expense of matrimony, the work akin to women in a "religious order."

Four years later, the Sofia school had thirty students, led by a supervisory group of four graduate nurses overseeing a two-year course. Little by little, the school was growing; yet, as with other Red Cross work to foster nursing programs, the Sofia school met with cultural barriers. As Noyes explained: "Bulgarian traditions resembled those of other European countries. Public opinion was against women entering a field regarded more or less as one relegated to the servant group and one, moreover, which interfered with the usual system of early marriage – from time immemorial wifehood has been looked upon as the only sphere of dignity a woman could occupy."[59] Just as nursing was a stand-in for matrimony, it also interfered with cultural views and values assigning women to marital roles.

Remarking about her work in Bulgaria, as with other overseas endeavors, Noyes expressed near astonishment at the fulfillment of her "Macedonian Call." Developments "happened so fast and furiously from the 9th of July until the 9th of September when I sailed from Constantinople," she said of her follow-up visit to Europe, "I can hardly appreciate that it was really I who was doing these things."[60]

As with the Red Cross work in Turkey and the Middle East, cultural attitudes were changing, bit-by-bit, at least in terms of satisfying public health needs. By 1926, two Bulgarian nurses had completed courses and practical training at Columbia University, as part of the American Red Cross exchange program. "In a year or two," Noyes wrote, "it is hoped they will be able to relieve the American nurses and continue the direction of the school under native auspices."[61]

But even with all of these important inroads, Red Cross management work from afar was not without conflict. The American Red Cross kept a tight withdrawal timetable that ran into the intransigence of host states' Red Cross societies, and personnel issues. Among the difficulties, the fledgling Warsaw school had to move at least a portion of its physical location as the Polish Railroad system was being extended through the property of the nurses' quarters. The engineers "said that both buildings could be saved but now they say that number one, our largest building will be destroyed," wrote the school's American director Helen L. Bridge to Clara Noyes in June 1923.[62]

Internally, American Red Cross officials expressed frank concerns about Bridge's work. Her anxious letters back to Red Cross headquarters described a range of difficulties at the school and conflicts with doctors on the wards as the Polish Red Cross seemed to drag its feet in taking over the nursing program consistent with America's plans for withdrawal. In a cover note appended to Bridge's letters, one Red Cross vice chairman told Noyes: "I fancy that Miss B. is rather difficult at times – perhaps a little aggressive – and the Polish doctors' self-importance was subjected to too severe a strain."[63]

Operating on a limited budget, Bridge ended up using her own funds to cover basic necessities like coal to heat the nurses' quarters, prompting American Red Cross officials to note that "Miss Bridge has all along shown herself too ready to act on her own responsibility ... instead of insisting that Polish agencies involved do their share before expenditures are made."[64] The American Red Cross kept its finances tight – and the withdrawal schedule on target – to ensure that the Polish Red Cross would take over in due time. Any meddling with the financial equation – even righteously so – threatened this eager plan for European sponsorship of the American-built programs.

Noyes's own frustration with Polish authorities bubbled up in reports from a follow-up trip to Warsaw in 1923. She expressed her prior reservations about the current location of the school, by then facing demolition. "Even if the buildings can be found, a move will prove a serious interruption," she wrote. "I was, therefore, obliged to leave Warsaw without settling the future location of the school."

Regarding the Polish Red Cross, Noyes did not mince words:

> A contract signed by all, including the Polish Red Cross, covered two years, expires January 1st, after which time the Polish Red Cross states that it cannot continue financial support ... it was a matter of great surprise that they regarded their contract purely from the technical viewpoint and seemed to recognize no moral obligation.[65]

Noyes learned that Polish authorities intended to organize their own school for Red Cross nurses. "Where they would get the money, the equipment, the trained direction, did not seem to occur to them," she wrote of the Polish Red Cross' plans after the withdrawal of American staff.[66] She added: "It seems incredible that after all the American Red Cross has done for the Polish Red Cross, the money and supplies that we have given that country, that they should break down at the critical point in the life of this school," especially since it was the Polish Red Cross that asked for help in the first place. "Had we for one moment thought that they would withdraw the Hospital and the buildings at the end of two years, we would not have connected our School with that institution."[67]

Her assessment of the Polish Red Cross even extended to other nations: "I have little faith in the stability of European Red Crosses," she remarked in another letter from this period, pointedly noting the European organizations' reliance on government funds and "an amateurish trend in all their activities, especially their Nursing Services."[68]

Bridge stayed on at the Warsaw school until 1928. The directorship was passed to Zofia Szlenkier who led the school until December 1936, when it was taken over by an early graduate, Jadwiga Romanowska. Germans occupied the school during the Second World War. "At the end of October 1944, the new government did not allow the school for further activity, although the director started searching the possibilities of its reactivation immediately," explained Helena Witkiewicz, Chair of the Warsaw Nursing School Graduates' Circle in a history of the school. It appears that the Minister of Health proposed another school in Gdansk, which opened in 1945, though its students received certificates under the Warsaw name. The school later returned to its Warsaw location, with financing from the Rockefeller Foundation and the Polish Government.[69]

Noyes wrestled with similar management issues from afar at the Prague school where the work met with death and illness. One of the Czech nurses sent to America for training died just before returning to her homeland. A second nurse had "rather of a breakdown, due largely I think to over work, lack of knowledge of the English language, etc.," Noyes reported in an exchange of letters with Helen Scott Hay.[70] Both tragedies led to further delays in American withdrawal, all predicated on the return of American-trained Czech nurses back to Prague. "Fate seems to have been against us," Noyes wrote, "for out of the three nurses brought to this country two have given out physically. One cannot help but feel that the starvation diet upon which they were living, together with the change, was perhaps too much for them."[71]

The two personnel losses required extra time for replacement nurses. Noyes pressed for a reapportionment of existing fund balances to keep the program operating. Her plan received blessings from Red Cross Vice Chairman Ernest Bicknell in order to keep the school afloat past the planned March 31, 1923 withdrawal date.[72] "Any other plan would, I believe, jeopardize the future of the School, too seriously, and would lay us open to some criticism for having 'pulled out the props' too soon," Noyes wrote.[73]

An update from Prague's Marie Bernatzikova was published in the May 1948 *American Journal of Nursing*. In a touching gesture of thanks to American nurses, Bernatzikova referred to Prague's nursing students as the "Forget-Me-Nots," referencing the bright blue uniforms made from material donated by the American Red Cross. The report offered a hopeful note, tinged with hardship and the menace wrought by a second world war on a still-struggling program. "Progress is being made. The right attitude toward nursing, said to be another casualty of the war, is being gradually restored." Nevertheless, for the 35 students in the first-year course, scarcities remained. "There is one practice bed with insufficient equipment and instruments for teaching nursing techniques. Crowding is another problem. At Prague the dining room is also used for class instruction, and several times each day there is a little 'migration' when it changes functions." [74]

While the First World War helped sow the seeds and plant roots for European nursing programs, a second global catastrophe in the 1940s had frosted those efforts, as did the Cold War era of disengagement. The Red Cross School in Sofia, for instance, existed until about 1950. In 1940, its director Krustanka Pachedjieva was replaced by Zafira Majdrakova "because of her contacts to America," explained scholar Kristina Popova in a recent e-mail exchange. When the Communist Party came to power in the mid-1940s, a new director was appointed: Sophia Basheva, wife of a party activist and, later, foreign minister. Meanwhile a new school at the Health Ministry opened at another location in Sofia, at Jordanka Filareto-va Street, where it exists today. After 1950, some staff from the Red Cross school joined the new one, which is regarded as part of the "institutional tradition of the Red Cross School," Popova explains, but the school is no longer sponsored by the Red Cross. It later became a medical college and, today, the nursing program is part of the Medical University of Sofia.[75]

All of these complications notwithstanding, Clara Noyes began racking up a series of awards, medals and citations related to her overseas nursing work during the 1920s and 1930s: An honorary cross from the Latvian Red Cross in 1934; the Saunders Medal awarded to a member of the ANA "for distinguished service in the cause of nursing" in 1933; the Medaille d'Honneur de L'Hygiene Publique of the French Government in 1928, as well as La Medaille de la Reconnaissance Francaise for her work connected to the Bordeaux School and American Nurses Memorial; an honorary cross from the Bulgarian Red Cross in 1925; an honorary cross from the French Red Cross Society in 1926; and an American Legion Post named in her honor in Palo Alto, California, whose members were all women. Her biggest honor was the Florence Nightingale Award, in 1923, which is presented to a nurse in each of twelve countries.

Clara Noyes's post-war work revolved around culti-vating roots for nursing education internationally, but the American Red Cross Nursing Service found itself tested again by a new period of cataclysms on the domestic front. 1927 proved a particularly destructive year, caused not by the raining bullet fire of man but by an indomitable series of tornadoes, hurricanes and, most dramatically, pummeling cloudbursts above the raging Mississippi Valley.

'ALL I DO IS PRESS A BUTTON AND THINGS HAPPEN': MISSISSIPPI FLOOD OF 1927

T he years 1926 and 1927 were especially violent in terms of natural disasters. As Clara Noyes wrote in December 1926, as part of her regular column in the *American Journal of Nursing*, "Disaster has succeeded disaster in one or other parts of the world since early September." These were both domestic and global: hurricanes in Florida; flooding in the Midwest, Mexico and the Bahamas; and earthquakes as far as the Red Cross's reach in the Middle East. There, "the American Red Cross nurses figure in the stories of courage and endurance that light up the otherwise somber reports of Armenian suffering." A series of tremors in the region around Leninakan "opened the land in yawning fissures from which fountains of hot sulfuric water, sand and silt gushed forth," killing 350 people.[1] Near the base of Turkey's Mount Ararat, the Red Cross's Near East Division was in service to the largest orphanage in the world, housing more than 20,000 children.[2] Born at Maryland's Mount Ararat, Clara Noyes found her work connected to a modern-era disaster at the base of Noah's high peak of the same name, where biblical flood waters, ages ago, had decimated life and property, and where natural disasters continued to plague the region.

Little did Noyes or others realize that these events would be subsumed by another massive flood of near-biblical proportions in the heart of America.

The Mississippi Flood of 1927 is one of the most destructive river floods in American history, engulfing parts of ten states: Arkansas, Illinois, Kentucky, Louisiana, Mississippi, Missouri, Tennessee, Texas, Oklahoma and Kansas. Of all the domestic calamities that year, the Mississippi flood was the biggest, dwarfing overflows along the Susquehanna basin that drowned the tiny town of Port Deposit in Clara Noyes's youth.

The American Red Cross garnered significant press coverage for its response efforts to the flood, both positive and critical, including a major wire story profiling Clara Noyes, not only for the flood work but also her office's hub of administrative efforts overseeing American Red Cross work globally. "The broad desk at which Miss Noyes sits is a keyboard contacting nurses in all corners of this country and nursing organizations in a score of countries abroad," the Associated Press (AP) wrote, citing correspondences with a Red Cross nurse in the Philippines "who tells of riding through swamps to isolated parts of the islands upon the only conveyance that is suitable for such a trip – a water buffalo."[3]

When the AP asked Clara Noyes "how it was done and if she wasn't awfully busy" – as she "handled the affair" of deploying nurses to the Mississippi flood – she quips: "Why no, not any busier than usual. All I do is press a button and things happen."[4]

Here Noyes keeps her trademark cool demeanor in response to a chauvinistic question. (Would a man have been asked how he was able to manage being "awfully busy" in his executive work?) Noyes attempts to disarm the question by suggesting that she grips the proverbial levers of power. A mere keystroke from her finger sets events in motion. Yet her response also succeeds in ironically understating the enormity of her work. If we assume a whiff of irony ("all I do is press a button and things happen"), Noyes manages to have it two ways:

communicating her power by hinting, rhetorically, that she is also understating the extreme difficulty of that work.

But the chauvinism is most explicit at the end of the article, as it ran in certain editions, revealing the media's apparent sense of novelty in reporting on a woman's executive-level position: "These buttons that the women are pressing now! And to remember back to a not distant day when all that women were supposed to know was how to sew them on!"[5] Not all editions of the article ran this way, but many did, and it is unclear whether this statement was tacked on as a newsroom editor's afterthought or if included in the reporter's original copy.

Despite the ironic quip about her important work, Clara Noyes's writings about the Mississippi flood response elsewhere were anything but glib as she conveys the enormous task of nurses under her charge. In the October 1927 edition of the *American Journal of Nursing*, she offers up this gripping account of the flood:

> Refugees had been streaming into the camps – and at the peak of the disaster the Red Cross was maintaining 138 camps with a population of 600,000 homeless – as fast as the levees broke inundating homes and farmlands. Each boatload increased the burden which the nurses carried ... literally tons of quinine were administered in an effort to prevent malaria and thousands were inoculated daily against smallpox and typhoid with the result that a possible, serious epidemic was forestalled ... Nurses were assigned to camps

and in addition frequently went from house to house in boats, caring for those who were marooned on second and third stories. One nurse went her rounds in hip boots! Another reported that she wore out her hypodermic needles during the rush of inoculations and not being able to secure more, immediately, kept her eyes alert for the first grindstone that appeared above the water, salvaged it, and sharpened them to continue her work. Alone, they presided at childbirths on levees and in box cars![6]

This account reads very much like warfare. The steely resolve of nurses, described here, seems little different from that of the field soldiers fighting battles in Europe a mere ten years prior – and, of course, little different from the nurses who tended to those soldiers' war wounds as they dropped from fatigue at operating tables. No doubt the experience of deploying nurses for military service helped inform the American Red Cross Nursing Service strategy domestically.

But unlike war, the crisis of 1927 was caused not by men or nations but torrential rains in the upper and lower Mississippi Valley. Unremitting rainfall turned farmland and towns into a muddy slurry that ravaged life and property. The sloggy mass of water rose to the tops of trees and the upper floors of homes. More than forty thousand buildings were destroyed. Hundreds of thousands of livestock were killed, their massive, bloated carcasses adrift.[7] More than 162,000 families were flooded from their homes. Crop and farm losses amounted to $124,648,545. [8]

Distinct from the swift blow of tornados or hurricanes, which can leave physical injury, the public health toll of the rising Mississippi was different. A region already host to yellow fever, typhoid, smallpox and an underdeveloped public health program had turned into an incubator for disease as refugees huddled in the top floors of homes or streamed into refugee camps throughout the delta. There, hundreds of thousands of people crammed into makeshift medical and relief facilities. Some larger camps held well over twenty thousand people each.[9] "In the destruction of property, the menace to public health and the paralyzing of economic and social life, the Mississippi Valley flood stands as the greatest disaster this country has ever suffered," wrote the American Red Cross in its report on the flood. "It ranks, in fact, well among the great natural catastrophes of the world's history."[10] Even, perhaps, a runner-up to Noah's flood.

Realizing the public health threat, the Red Cross engaged in an ambitious campaign to immunize as many people as possible in the crowded camps. Traveling nurses took to the oars in relief boats, reaching stranded populations to administer inoculations. Over 200,000 barrels of crude oil were shipped to the affected region, the viscous slop poured out to insulate stagnant pools of water from breeding mosquitoes and malaria.[11]

The American Red Cross found itself again ushered into a role that institutions in other Red Cross societies internationally had not carved out: one of civilian relief in times of natural disaster. A decade after mobilizing 20,000 nurses to war, Clara Noyes again oversaw a major nurse relief operation, this time with approximately four hundred nurses deployed from local chapters to assist with inoculations, keeping refugee camps hygienic, and attending at births in makeshift hospitals, be it a converted schoolhouse, a Red Cross tent, or a railroad boxcar. The compatibility between war and natural-disaster relief did not go unrecognized. As one news report noted, "It was relief work in a peace-time catastrophe, but it resembled war in the mingling of science and rough-and-ready measures with which it was carried on."[12] The great concentration of human life in crowded refugee camps demanded sanitary zones, quarantine units, and makeshift medical wards, not unlike the tented military cantonments that sprung up amid farm fields and buildings where the Spanish Flu pandemic of 1918 and other diseases had spread like wildfire. Nurses and other relief workers found themselves again operating in a ravaged landscape, with major supply points cut off; the need for mass mobilization of human capital and supplies; and a swirling stream of desperation and loss. Except this time, unlike the war, the camps and medical units resonated with the wails of children, and women in labor. At one of the largest camp hospitals, a converted school building, fifty babies were delivered.[13]

Further connecting the war with peacetime disaster relief, Red Cross officials had picked the right woman to take charge of the nursing field work: I. Malinde Havey. A decorated war nursing veteran, Havey earned the Royal Red Cross, First Class British as Assistant Chief Nurse of Base Hospital No. 36 at Compeigne where "she served under fire."[14]

Nearly 250 Americans perished from the flood. Like the war, few of these deaths were from physical injuries directly related to the flood or drowning. Most stemmed from disease during the early stages of the disaster.[15] It is unclear if these death tolls, however, accounted for some of the more egregious instances of "relief" work, where hunger overtook ill-equipped and ill-treated segregated camps in Greenville, Mississippi and other locations. As in prior episodes, the color line prevailed in relief work down South. Havey, in remarks republished by Noyes in the *American Journal of Nursing*, describes two hospitals in Lafayette, Louisiana: "One for white and one for colored patients." The hospital for black refugees was located at the Paul Breaux school "which includes several buildings surrounded by lovely huge live oaks," Havey reported. "A number of colored nurses are on duty in the hospital and were so proud to exhibit their various wards, all of which were in perfect order."[16] Despite this "orderly" assessment conveyed to the *Journal's* nursing audiences, it appears that conditions at segregated Lafayette were actually among the more chaotic, based on the full versions of Havey's internal memos.

Lafayette "continues to have its troubles," Havey wrote in one narrative report on the nursing response. "Measles have been on the steady increase. The families themselves are unwilling to report cases of illness which makes it necessary to keep a vigilant watch over the tent inhabitants."[17] Many of the families were reluctant to report outbreaks for fear of separation from their children. As Havey elaborates:

> One child reported ill by a resident in an adjoining tent could not be found anywhere. After a thorough search the nurse finally discovered the child under a bed rolled up in a blanket, thoroughly broken out with a measles rash … It seems that the families are loathe [*sic.*] to having

members of the family removed to either the hospital or into isolation.[18]

On another occasion, Havey reported how "Lafayette has been troublesome from the beginning," noting a high turnover of personnel and other concerns. "Although Lafayette is heavily staffed, the need there is great. Just yesterday, diphtheria again broke out with a number of exposures due to late diagnosis. Extra nurses were provided and with adequate isolation we hope that no further cases will develop."[19] The medical work at Lafayette was complicated by the presence of 6,000 refugees and a hospital census of 76 per day. Many were already ill when the flood came and "were brought to the camp from sick beds," revealing the already precarious community health needs in the region.[20] Louisiana was one of the last areas to emerge from the flood. Of eighteen camps still operating by mid-July, twelve were in Louisiana, three in Arkansas and three in Mississippi, a substantial drop from the 136 camps at the height of the operations.[21]

But the flood unearthed an even more sinister side of relief work, particularly where the intersection of race, class and natural disaster is concerned – and Louisiana was at the center of the crisis. Not only had the governor infamously approved the dynamiting of levees in less politically-favored communities downriver, to save business interests in New Orleans,[22] but the relief work itself was subject to racial inequity, outright exploitation and abuses throughout the valley, especially in Greenville, Mississippi. As John M. Barry chronicles in *Rising Tide: The Great Mississippi Flood of 1927 and How it Changed America*, curfews were imposed on black refugees, as local authorities in Greenville forced black men to work, at gunpoint, repairing the damaged levees. Commerce Secretary Herbert Hoover, having distinguished himself in the war-time Belgian Commission for famine relief, was tapped by President Calvin Coolidge to coordinate much of the Red Cross relief work. Public outcries from his mishandling of the Greenville situation cost Hoover an estimated fifteen percent of the black vote, although he won the 1928 presidency in a landslide, having inoculated criticism in "mainstream" public quarters.[23] "The truth was harsh enough," says Barry. "Only one camp would generate enough criticism to bring intense political pressure on Hoover – the camp on the levee in Greenville."[24] As Barry sums it up succinctly, "The levee camp became a slave camp."[25]

The black press was all over the story. Hoover and others frantically engaged in damage control, sending a flurry of fact-finding telegrams to local authorities and engaging with officials like Walter White, secretary of the NAACP, who had written a particularly stinging exposé of the flood response for *The Nation*. In correspondence to White, Herbert Hoover asserted: "The outstanding fact remains that only three lives have been lost (none colored) since the national organization initiated its action on April 20th." Most deaths occurred before the Red Cross got involved, as other reports maintained. He added, defensively: "In fact, I am informed on all sides that the colored people have been provided with better and more ample food than they normally receive."[26] However, at least one *Chicago Defender* report indicated that a white national guardsman shot one refugee, Marshall Dunbar, in the stomach "when he attempted to take food and clothing into a relief camp occupied by members of our race."[27] An even larger stack of accounts detailed other abuses that shock the conscience.

Greenville wasn't the only sore spot. Some of the more egregious abuses included rehabilitation work under the direction of Katherine Monroe in Arkansas who left the distribution of food, seed and feed for stock "entirely in the hands of plantation owners." These owners allegedly charged refugees for supplies furnished by the Red Cross in an attempt to hasten their return back to share-cropping work.[28] As *The Crisis* reported, plantation managers in Mississippi were also pressing refugees back to work, arriving at camps "coming after their negro tenants," as early as May, "while boat-loads of refugees were still coming in to Vicksburg."[29]

To inoculate criticism, Herbert Hoover organized a Colored Advisory Committee to travel the region, make inspections, report conditions from the ground, and issue recommendations. When the committee members entered the camp at Sicily Island, Louisiana without forewarning, inspectors found half a dozen "white subordinates and militia men, the latter with rifles" at the camp headquarters "lounging." A white man working the commissary approached the black inspectors, who weren't dressed like refugees, laughing: "You boys don't need anything here, not with all those clothes you have got on. What do you want us to give you?" The inspectors presented their letter, which the relief worker read "and then flew into rage," fuming: "What in the Hell do you think of this?"[30] The Colored Advisory Committee found iron and wooden cots in each tent for white refugees but not a single government cot for any of the black refugees, which, by then, accounted for ninety percent of inhabitants at the camp.[31]

Greenville clearly outshined other camps in its abuses and inequities. At the emergency hospital, "the committee was most unfavorably impressed with the unsanitary conditions ... refugees could not secure supplies without an order from a white person."[32] Black men reported "carrying their belongings on their shoulders, leading their wives and children to points of safety," only to be "held up at the point of guns, made to drop their belongings, leave their families and form into squads to work on the protection levee."[33] The inspectors were told that a "squad of Negro workers was brought to the levee for work by a white overseer, who had a large revolver strapped to his side as though he were in charge of criminals."[34] A group of black men circulated leaflets looking for volunteers to work the levees to prevent the "embarrassment of conscription."[35] Similar conditions were found at Vicksburg, where about twenty-five male refugees were "corralled in their attempt to leave the camp, to avoid being drafted for work on the river front, and severely whipped by National Guardsmen."[36]

The Red Cross frantically wired local authorities to determine the validity of charges being made in the black press, by the NAACP and other quarters. In some cases, local authorities replied that restrictions on the movement of refugees were for public health reasons at a time when the Mississippi Board of Health had ordered that all refugees get inoculated against typhoid fever.[37] But this couldn't explain away the more forceful abuses.

Clearly the Red Cross was aware of the political ramifications on the election (specifically, Hoover's involvement). Even though the Hoover-appointed Colored Advisory Committee had already tendered its report of conditions on the ground, the Red Cross was sensitive to the timing of the final document. One official wrote in a letter marked "confidential" that Red Cross Chairman John Barton Payne "decided that because we were approaching the political campaign it would be better to postpone the printing of the report until after the election inasmuch as it dealt to a considerable extent with the work of one of the presidential candidates." The report, by then already months old, was delayed in printing to accommodate modifications to a document that "seemed to us to invite unwarranted criticism of the Red Cross."[38]

The report also failed to catch up with the progression of the crisis. By the time the Red Cross received the report, refugees were already moving out of the camps. "Our camps are practically closed up," wrote one reconstruction officer in June 1927. "The camp at Vicksburg is practically closed as far as the negro population is concerned, there being less than fifty refugees there today."[39]

Though the American Red Cross was a massive organization with central authority in Washington, its structure had relied on a system of somewhat autonomous local chapters. This structure had summarily failed in Greenville, and other communities, under the aegis of local control. No doubt the color line in hospital wards (described from Havey's field notes) was a region-wide phenomenon and certainly in force during the war-time Red Cross medical relief work nationally; but local circumstances and cultures in places like Greenville would cast an even darker shadow on the American Red Cross history of disaster response. It appears that higher-up officials at American Red Cross headquarters were quick to blame many of the abuses on local issues, either to insulate the relief agency itself or Hoover. The Colored Advisory Committee's report was notably used for political cover, as its findings were spun to cast judgment on local authorities. "In those camps where unfair treatment was meted out, the commission placed the blame squarely on the shoulders of the communities where the camps were located," explained a "special press release" in the Red Cross central files, dated June 14, 1927. "Red Cross activities are based upon county units which are active or in form in times of peace as well as disaster, and the final word and contact with the refugees is in its hands."[40]

The Colored Advisory Committee said little about the nursing work specifically. The starkest abuses seemed to center on the distribution of supplies and the use of relief articles as a way to force unpaid work on the levees. In the committee's one point of explicit critique on the medical work, inspectors were "surprised to find that, apparently, no special precautions were taken in any of the camps visited to prevent the spread of venereal disease."[41] In Baton Rouge, "The American Red Cross nurses entered upon their duties of vaccination, care of minor illnesses and injuries, and education and guidance of the refugees with thorough interest in the work, expedition of its demands and cheerfulness in its fulfillment."[42]

Distinct from the Spanish Flu crisis, black nurses played a significant role in the response. Of the 383 nurses who reported for duty, 329 were white and 54 African-American.[43] It is not known, at least from internal reports, whether their involvement had a more sympathetic effect on the treatment of refugees when it came to nursing work in black communities disproportionately affected by the flood, or whether the nature of nursing work was itself immune to the abuses engendered by other aspects of the relief operation. Criticisms appear to have fallen squarely on other quarters of the campaign, enough to overshadow some of the good humanitarianism accomplished by nurses and others devoted to the cause of helping flood victims.

Clara Noyes' headstone at Duck River Cemetery in Old Lyme, Connecticut. *Photo taken by the author.*

'QUIETLY, QUICKLY, WITH HER HAND STILL AT THE WHEEL'

From long-brewing resentment of defeat in World War I, the 1930s saw the emergence of a new political and nationalistic force: German fascism. By 1933, Adolph Hitler had risen as Germany's chancellor, buoyed by animosity over the Treaty of Versailles, coupled with a sinister program of anti-Semitism. "Historians have looked back upon the mid-thirties with some vexation," explains Hitler historian Joachim C. Fest. "This was the period in which

213

Hitler repeated, on the plane of foreign policy, those same practices of overwhelming his opponents that had yielded him such easy triumphs at home. And he applied them in the same effortless manner and with no less success."[1] Within a month of Hitler's rise, Jane Delano's distant cousin was sworn in as president of the United States – Franklin Delano Roosevelt – cruising to victory past the incumbent Herbert Hoover who had risen to the nation's highest office, in part, by the distinction of his work coordinating American Red Cross relief activities during the Mississippi Flood, even in the face of stinging criticism from the black press. But Hoover had not been up to meeting the challenge of another crisis, the Great Depression, as the economy crumbled and jobs vanished. While 1927 was a year of floods, America's heartland in the early 1930s was baked in drying dust (the "dirty thirties," as it was called). Economic woe also invaded the world of nursing. As the unemployment picture became worse, some of the smaller nurse training organizations evaporated like the Dust Bowl and hospitals began cutting back on nurses' hours. The private-duty field similarly took a hit. Personal wealth dried up and families could no longer afford to pay for private, in-home care. The American Red Cross maintained its public health nursing programs, especially its "Town and Country Service" to assist largely rural areas lacking public health resources to battle disease and malnutrition. But the federal government was also stepping in at unprecedented levels, distinct from the past.

Indeed, U.S. government money was not spent in relief *during* the Mississippi Flood of 1927. This absence of government support drew criticism from several quarters as the 1930s gave rise to a stronger appetite for government domestic intervention. During the 1927 crisis, President Coolidge declined to even visit the flood zone. "Taking center stage, Coolidge feared, would feed demands for a greater federal role in dealing with the calamity," explains Rutgers University historian David Greenberg, drawing parallels between government absence in the 1927 flood and the Hurricane Katrina response of President George W. Bush in 2005. As Greenberg puts it, Coolidge feared that direct government involvement would set a "dangerous precedent – and, he knew, might imperil the budget surpluses he had worked hard to achieve." Coolidge's tepid response drew criticism from localities hard hit by the flooding. Only later, in 1928, did Congress eventually pass a bill – reluctantly signed into law by Coolidge – assuming government financial responsibility for the flood and paving the way for further intervention in disaster support. "FDR and, for that matter, Coolidge, held office at a time when public sentiment was building behind the idea that a strong state in a wealthy nation could – and should – alleviate human suffering," says Greenberg. He argues that this trend toward public support in domestic response set the stage for expanded federal involvement during the Roosevelt era.[2]

Roosevelt's New Deal reforms included the Federal Emergency Relief Act and the Civil Works Administration, which employed more than 10,000 nurses in community health programs, further changing the role of the American Red Cross, as government involvement had now entered into the space of public health nursing formerly occupied, mostly, by private organizations.[3] Having enrolled, credentialed, equipped and prepared nurses for World War I service, having taken a lead role in postwar health and relief work in the early interwar years, and having been the primary relief organization for domestic tragedies like the Mississippi Flood of 1927, the American Red Cross was finding itself in a changing relationship to the New Deal expansion of the nation-state.

In one of her final articles for the *American Journal of Nursing*, Noyes described back-to-back tornadoes in Greensboro, Georgia and Tupelo, Mississippi. Red Cross relief services were joined by Workers Progress Administration (WPA) crews who labored with the railroad companies to lay tracks for temporary shelter. "Throughout both the flood and tornado areas, the directors of the WPA workers cordially cooperated with the Red Cross,"[4] wrote Noyes about this new level of government partnership. The "Chinese Boxes" of Red Cross and government alignment, previously described by Portia Kernodle, were yet again shifting their fit.

Nursing's gain of "relative rank" – pursued aggressively by Clara Noyes and her peers during the First World War – would eventually lead to full-commission status for nurses during World War II, starting in 1942 with the granting of "relative" rank, as before, but pay and allowances "approximately equal to those male commissioned officers without dependents." This was later changed in 1944 to temporary commissions with "full pay and privileges of the grades from second lieutenant through colonel," and extended for the duration of the Second World War "plus six months."[5] It was during this period that the American Red Cross began carving out a new wartime role, establishing, in 1941, its Red Cross Blood Donor Service to supply the United States military.[6]

While America's New Deal nation-state was expanding, Hitler's Germany was making grandiose motions of its own, withdrawing from the League of Nations and, on

January 13, 1935, reassuming control of the Saarland region, which had been partitioned off under the Treaty of Versailles. Soon, Hitler was reinstating a mandatory draft, pursuing an army of 550,000.[7] In March, he sent forces to occupy the Rhineland, a stark violation of the peace treaties. He also began courting Benito Mussolini and pursuing alliances with England and Japan in an effort to box-in Soviet Russia.[8] In the summer of 1936, Berlin hosted the storied Nazi Olympics, which brought the world's eye to Germany. Hitler used the events to great political advantage, even as American track-and-field great Jesse Owens, a black man, swept four gold medals at the games, posing a direct challenge to Hitler's white-supremacist ideologies. Hitler was already beginning to hatch his Four-Year plan for war.[9]

As these events unfolded, Clara Noyes pressed forward with her work in the late 1920s and early 1930s, maintaining contact with nurse training school work overseas, managing nurses' response in the Great Depression and continuing to lead nursing efforts amid domestic tragedies, even as the American Red Cross mission was changing. Noyes also kept in touch with European nurses now running their countries' programs. In a 1935 letter to nurses running the Bulgarian school, Noyes referred to Sofia's institution as "a daughter" of the American Red Cross, revealing a continued sense of stewardship over the nursing programs and the young graduates that Noyes and others had helped nurture even as the schools were taken over by native auspices. "This paternalistic discourse in the communication was supported by the both sides," writes Bulgarian scholar Kristina Popova, citing letters in the Bulgaria State Archives. Neneva Sendova took over the school's directorship until 1934, when Krustanka Pachedjieva began leading the program. To her, Noyes wrote: "I am anxious to maintain the connection between your school and the American Red Cross on a warm and cordial basis," passing along copies of the *American Journal of Nursing*,[10] and extending – across borders – the culture of collegiality and mentorship that fostered the rise of early nursing leaders in the U.S. Sendova replied with ongoing status updates, telling Noyes about the nurses' work responding to a typhoid outbreak in Brazigovo, Bulgaria, where one-eighth of the town's tiny population became ill.[11] By the late 1930s, the Sofia School for Nurses "became a stable institution," writes Popova.[12]

Back home, Clara Noyes's own niece had followed in her aunt's footsteps. Mary Hubbard Noyes was among 57 nurses to graduate from the Hartford Hospital Training School program in June 1932. The former ANA president and Red Cross Nursing Service director again stood before an audience of young graduates to offer some remarks and wisdom drawn from a long career in nursing leadership. Those remarks reflected a country still in the grip of depression, a new crisis again reaching into the profession of nursing. Citing figures from the ANA's Grading Committee on Nursing, Noyes revealed the toll of an oversaturated market. In Connecticut, there was one nurse for every 248 people, at a time when 25,000 nurses were graduating annually. "What has caused this situation?" Clara Noyes said in her address at Hartford. "Briefly, as soon as the student in the ward demonstrated her usefulness, she became a financial asset to the hospital. Unconscious exploitation began, and schools multiplied." Flashing forward to present conditions, "The financial 'bubble' burst, with the inevitable result that hundreds of nurses were and are without employment."[13] Too many nurses were graduating, and schools were not distributed "proportionately" throughout the country. "It is not particularly pleasant to hear about unemployment and depression," she told graduates about to enter the workforce. "But, as unpleasant as it may be, facts must be faced as they are." Despite these hardships, she noted a few "bright spots" and opportunities for advanced training as well as affiliation with organizational nursing. She also told graduates to "adopt hobbies and ride them hard, especially those that will bring returns in general satisfaction and mental and moral stimulation, even if there is little return in gold and silver." Look to the future, she said, as the profession may produce "another Nightingale who will help lead nursing through its present difficulties and perplexing problems to a land of promise."[14]

"With this challenge to these young graduates," she said, "I wish God-speed."[15]

On June 3, 1936, Noyes was making her usual commute to Red Cross headquarters, this time with a companion, another niece, the young Lucy Noyes, daughter of her youngest brother, Charles Reginald Noyes. According to Clara Noyes's nephew James Noyes, in a 2015 interview, James's sister Lucy lived with their aunt Clara. His family was poor, and his aunt was very generous to her nieces and nephews, ensuring that the young Lucy had a good education in the Washington, DC schools, living with aunt Clara during this period at 1411 Twenty-Ninth Street NW.[16]

James, in his nineties at the time of the interview, had also been visiting aunt Clara in June of 1936, though only for a brief period to learn a little bit more about Washington, DC and tour the city where his aunt lived and worked. He recalls that aunt Clara had just purchased a brand-new 1936 Chevy and, on June 3, was driving his sister Lucy to work so that Lucy could later take the vehicle and pick up her siblings to tour around Washington in aunt Clara's car.[17]

On the drive that June morning, just a block away from reaching Red Cross headquarters, Clara Noyes suddenly collapsed at the wheel. Her Red Cross labors, having turned her "gray hair a snowy white," gave way to a sudden heart attack amid morning traffic; her niece, "Miss Lucy Lay Noyes, riding with her," acted quickly during the tragic moment and "prevented a collision by pulling up the emergency break," as her aunt lay slumped at the steering column.[18] Lucy had jumped from the back seat to take hold of the brake. "A taxi happened to be passing, and the driver took the stricken woman to the Emergency Hospital, nearby. She had scarcely been laid on the bed in the hospital when she breathed her last." She never recovered consciousness after "clasping her hand to her breast" at the wheel of her car.[19]

At Emergency Hospital, on Tenth Street, near D Street NW,[20] Clara Noyes was pronounced dead, not far from Fords Theater and a block from Peterson House where President Lincoln took his final breaths. Her brother, Charles Reginald Noyes (Lucy and James's father), left Old Lyme at once upon the news, heading to Washington.[21]

Like her predecessor, Jane Delano, Clara Noyes died in the line of duty on the brink of her twentieth anniversary at the American Red Cross. Her death from cardiac arrest came as a surprise to Red Cross colleagues who recalled how "her mind" had been "clear and keen as ever, her spirit happy and buoyant, and seemingly she was in the prime of health and filled with energy and ambition."[22]

To the very end, Clara Noyes was engaged in her life's work "driving her car to her duties in Washington." And even her death, like much of her work in life, involved a crisis that would have been even bigger had it not been for the quick thinking of someone by her side, acting in the most urgent of moments, in this case her young niece Lucy. Clara Noyes had pressed 20,000 nurses into wartime disaster work; and, in her time of death, her quick-thinking niece had similarly warded off disaster, preventing the hand of death from taking more than one life.

Echoing remarks about Jane Delano's death, Clara Noyes's friend, colleague and former superintendent at Johns Hopkins noted the parallels between Noyes's duty and her demise quite elegantly in the *Johns Hopkins Nurses Alumnae Magazine*: "It was in keeping with her whole life that she would have gone from us quietly, quickly, with her hand still at the wheel."[23]

The first memorial service, at the Georgetown Presbyterian Church, was "a bower of flowers,"[24] attended by a guard of honor of Red Cross nurses, members of the Central Committee and the Nursing Service. Clara Noyes's body was then brought to Old Lyme by federal express for services at the parish founded by her kin, the Reverend Moses Noyes, at the Old Lyme Congregational Church. Pall bearers at the Old Lyme service included her cousins Col. Kendall Banning, Waldo L. Banning, John E. Noyes and George Chadwick, as well as her nephew Harry E. Noyes, and Thomas R. Ball, a congressman representing that part of Connecticut.[25] "The service in Lyme was beautiful and it was very gratifying that so many of the nurses from Boston, New York,

Rhode Island and Connecticut attended," wrote Ida A. Butler, who succeeded Noyes as Acting Director of the Nursing Service. "It was a perfect day, the kind that Miss Noyes used to call 'a Lyme day.'"[26] Noyes was interred a few days later at Duck River Cemetery, a plot that includes her father, Enoch; her mother, Laura Lay Banning Noyes; and several generations of Noyeses. Her headstone engraving at Duck River Cemetery sums up Clara Noyes's achievements in two sentences: "Director of American Red Cross Nursing Service, 1916 to 1936. Selected and Assigned Twenty Thousand Red Cross Nurses to Service During World War." As the *British Journal of Nursing* noted in its remembrance, Clara Noyes "sleeps in the spot that was dear to her throughout life."[27]

With words that seemed to reverberate from the great beyond, the July 1936 edition of the *American Journal of Nursing* ran Clara Noyes's regular column, "The Department of Red Cross Nursing," with the following editor's note spanning the top two columns:

> In all the years during which Miss Noyes was editor of this department of the Journal, the fifth of the month preceding publication was the date on which her "copy" was due. Not once, in that period, was her material ever late, in fact it was usually received in the Journal office in advance of the date specified. Word of Miss Noyes' death came to us on June 3, 1936. It was characteristic of her that the manuscript for the July Department of Red Cross Nursing, which follows, had been sent to the editor of the Journal well before that

date, so that it was on the press on the day she died.[28]

"We like to remember that she knew of our appreciation of her dependability,"[29] the *Journal* added plainly.

Even in the echoes of death, she would commission her work – in this case her written report to the *Journal* – with promptness and exactitude, "precision and dispatch."

The *Journal* would also run a longer editorial, with reflections from those who knew her closely. "Consistently loyal to the highest ideals in nursing, Miss Noyes was a staunch friend and, on occasion, could be a redoubtable opponent."[30] Her friend Alice Fitzgerald – who served in France during the war and had a hand in many of the same nursing school development activities overseas as Noyes – remembered Noyes as "a rare combination of head and heart ... a great nurse, a good friend and a charming lady."[31]

Her alma mater ran a special section of its alumnae magazine with remembrances from friends and colleagues. It included poetic verses written by Louise P. Yale, class of 1916, who was among the very generation that Clara Noyes enrolled for duty. The Hopkins-trained Yale, a Kansas City native, served in the Red Cross Nursing Service during the war where she reported to Base Hospital Camp Lee in Petersburg, Virginia,[32] and later at U.S. Army Base Hospital No. 117.[33] Yale's poem, printed in full as an epigram of this book, makes a clear connection between Noyes, a first-generation professional nurse trained on the Nightingale system, and "The Lady with a Lamp," Nightingale, herself. It is a touching tribute, in

Romanticist verse, from one Red Cross nurse to another. Yale writes:

Yea – Once in the long history of the race
There stood the "Lady with a Lamp,"
Strong and kind of face.

At that bright lamp eternal-rayed,
Multitudes have lighted
Little candles of skilled aid.

One who but now has laid aside human frame,
So trimmed and fed her bit of flame.

The verses proceed to conjure "barren hills" and "teeming towns" as well as "foreign lands" where "valiant bands, Seek to bind up wounds of wars" – where the name "Clara Noyes brought courage, cheer and poise."

Greeted by courts and kings,
Busied with a great task and all it brings,
From near and far,
Yet ever the warm friend,
Constant as any star.

The Red Cross Chairman, Admiral Cary T. Grayson, remarked of Noyes that "In the Red Cross, her name will be enshrined with the names of Florence Nightingale and Jane Delano,"[34] forming into words the visual trinity of nurse leaders displayed on that iconic postcard from 1918, bearing the images of women leading the early nursing profession. Again, conspicuously absent from this panel of leaders, both on the postcard and in Admiral Grayson's remarks, was the actual founder of the

American Red Cross, Clara Barton, by then deemed an "amateur nurse," having been pushed away from the organization she founded, but a hallmark figure nevertheless.

The "marble palace," national headquarters, went dark on the afternoon of June 5 in Noyes's remembrance.[35] American Red Cross officials drafted a resolution stating that "The sudden death of Clara Dutton Noyes ... took from the American Red Cross Nursing Service, and from the nursing profession throughout the world, one of the most commanding and influential personalities of her generation. It was, in large part, Miss Noyes's genius for organization that gave the American Red Cross Nursing Service worldwide renown from the moment this country entered the Great War ... Miss Noyes's death brought personal loss to thousands of nurses who had been strengthened by her courageous loyalty to well-established ideals of service."[36] As a legacy to Noyes's contributions in nursing, a scholarship was adopted in her name to provide a year of training to an American nurse and a nurse from overseas, both attending the Nightingale Foundation in London. Its first recipients in 1938 were Lena Alma Koller of Texas and Chen Shuiyuin, a nurse from the Red Cross Hospital in Shanghai.[37]

Clara Noyes's life was one of unique alignment with political movements, humanitarian crises and professional trends in nursing. A product of Civil War parentage, she came into life during a period of post-bellum, Progressive-Era changes, on the very dawn of key women's suffrage organizational work in the year of her birth: 1869.

She entered adolescence and adulthood just as the nurse training movement was taking hold, opening up opportunities to her and her peers – first-generation graduates of the Nightingale system – where intelligent, administrative-minded women were whisked into executive roles at the many new nursing programs that had cropped up in the late 1800s.

She came of age and prominence in nursing as the nation entered a world war. That war demanded action from young women and leadership from an elder generation of nurses who had fostered educational advances in the superintendent seats of institutions like Bellevue Hospital.

She gained experience in disaster nursing and reconstruction work on a global stage, which put her in good stead as natural calamities like the Mississippi Flood of 1927 placed demands yet again on veteran nurses, and as flood waters gave way to the Dust Bowl work of Red Cross nursing to face the indigent-care and relief crisis during a time of drought and economic collapse.

As if those demands were enough to fill a lifetime of service – and surely they were – her heart gave out just before the world would yet again press nurses into a global battle, collapsing at the wheel, in the summer of 1936, at virtually the exact moment that Germany was reemerging as a combatant foe drawing America into another Great War.

NOTES

EPIGRAM

[1] Louise P. Yale, "Clara D. Noyes," poem as printed in the *Johns Hopkins Nurses Alumnae Magazine* 35, no. 3 (July 1936): 157-158. Courtesy and with permission of the Alan Mason Chesney Medical Archives of The Johns Hopkins Medical Institutions, Baltimore.

PROLOGUE

[1] Clara D. Noyes, "The Red Cross," *American Journal of Nursing* 20, no. 5 (February 1920): 395-396.

[2] Roger L. Noyes, "Home Care Emergency Response: Hurricane Sandy Lessons Learned and Actions Taken," *Caring Magazine* (June 2013): 11.

[3] Richard Knox, "Home Health Care Proves Resilient In Face Of Sandy Destruction," *National Public Radio*, November 2, 2012, accessed October 13, 2015, http://www.npr.org/sections/health-shots/2012/11/02/164207669/home-health-care-proves-resilient-in-face-of-sandy-destruction.

[4] "Woman Heads Red Cross Aid: World-Wide Activities Center at Desk of Miss Clara D. Noyes," *Milwaukee Journal*, September 7, 1927.

[5] Ibid.

[6] As stated in a June 11, 2013 press release from the Home Care Association of New York State (HCA) entitled "HCA Seeks Passage of Bills Supporting Home Care's Role in Medicaid Redesign": "Transportation issues were among the biggest obstacles for home care personnel seeking to reach vulnerable patients at home during and after Hurricane Sandy ... HCA urges the Senate and Assembly to pass 'essential personnel' legislation to support home care providers in their important emergency response role," accessed October 13, 2015, http://hca-nys.org/wp-con-tent/uploads/2015/03/PRHCA2013SessionPriorities.pdf.

[7] "The American Medical And Surgical History of the War," *Army and Navy Register* 64, no. 1999 (November 9, 1918): 528.

[8] Irises 1932, by Cooley's Gardens; Henry G. Gilbert Nursery and Seed Trade Catalog Collection: 11.

[9] Ibid.

CHAPTER ONE

[1] William McDonald, ed. *The Obits: Annual 2012* (New York: Workman Publishing Company, 2011), Introduction.

[2] "Miss Clara Noyes of Red Cross Dead," *New York Times*, June 4, 1936.

[3] Genesis 8:4 (Revised Standard Version).

[4] Walter Buck, owner of Mount Ararat Farm in 2009, speculates as follows: "When the Susquehanna flooded at Port Deposit, people would come up here on the hill. Mt. Ararat was the name they chose because of the high ground." Rick Barton, "Cecil County Farmer: Mt. Ararat," *Cecil Soil Magazine*, March/April 2009, accessed November 13, 2015, http://www.bluetoad.com/article/Cecil+County+Farmer%3A+Mt+Ararat/117972/0/article.html.

[5] Col. Henry E. Noyes and Harriette E. Noyes, *Genealogical Record of Some Noyes Descendants, Volume II* (1904; repr. Salem MA: Higgins Book Company, 2015), 26.

[6] Some Noyeses even suggested raising funds for a "Noyes Association" to embark on an expedition of Turkey's Mount Ararat for evidence of their connection to Noah; Ibid, 28.

[7] Ibid, 28.

[8] For a detailed account of the siege, see Edward Cunningham, *The Port Hudson Campaign: 1862-1863* (Baton Rouge, LA: Louisiana State University Press, 1963).

[9] "Lest We Forget," Lymeline.com, May 27, 2013, accessed October 1, 2015, http://lymeline.net/2013/05/lest-we-forget/.

[10] Maryland. Cecil County. Deed of Sale. Folio 242, no. 7, April 23, 1864. Cecil County Circuit Court Land Records.

[11] "A Big Walnut Tree," *New York Times*, January 28, 1894.

[12] Col. Henry E. Noyes et al., *Genealogical Record of Some Noyes Descendants, Volume II*, 27.

[13] Genesis 5:21-24 (Revised Standard Version).

[14] Maryland. Cecil County. Deed of Sale. Folio 519, no. 2, May 23, 1898. Cecil County Circuit Court Land Records.

[15] "Maryland Brevities," *The Evening Times* (Washington, DC), November 7, 1898.

[16] "News of the State: Events of Interest Here and There Yesterday and Today," *The News* (Frederick, MD), May 29, 1902.

[17] "Discredited by Mother: Mrs. Noyes Does Not Believe Daughter Eloped with Davidson," *Washington Post*, May 25, 1905.

[18] Yale University, *Leaders in Nursing* (1924), Clara Noyes Biofile, The Alan Mason Chesney Medical Archives of the Johns Hopkins Medical Institutions, Baltimore.

[19] Susan Zeiger, *In Uncle Sam's Service: Women Workers with the American Expeditionary Force, 1917-1919* (Ithaca, NY: Cornell University Press, 1999), 48.

[20] Nina Silber, *Daughters of the Union: Northern Women Fight for the Civil War* (Cambridge, MA: Harvard University Press, 2005), 28-29.

CHAPTER TWO

[1] Susan M. Reverby, *Ordered to Care: The Dilemma of American Nursing, 1850-1945* (Cambridge: Cambridge University Press, 1987), 47.

[2] Ibid.

[3] Ibid, 124.

230 Clara D. Noyes

[4] Ibid, 24.

[5] Ibid, 124.

[6] Susan M. Poslusny, "Feminist Friendship: Isabel Hampton Robb, Lavinia Lloyd Dock and Mary Adelaide Nutting," *The Journal of Nursing Scholarship* 21, no. 2 (June 1989): 64.

[7] Ibid.

[8] Susan M. Reverby, *Ordered to Care*, 77.

[9] George Coulson to Johns Hopkins School of Nursing, 11 January 1894. "Clara Noyes, JHH SON Student Records," box 2, folder 14, 1894, Alan Mason Chesney Medical Archives of the Johns Hopkins Medical Institutions, Baltimore.

[10] Clara D. Noyes to Superintendent of Nurses at Johns Hopkins Hospital, 27 January 1894. "Clara Noyes, JHH SON Student Records," box 2, folder 14, 1894, Alan Mason Chesney Medical Archives of the Johns Hopkins Medical Institutions, Baltimore.

[11] Ibid.

[12] Mary O'Neil Mundinger, *A Path to Nursing Excellence: The Columbia Experience* (New York: Springer Publishing Company, 2014), 9.

[13] David J. Hacker, Libra Hilde, and James Holland Jones, "The Effect of the Civil War on Southern Marriage Patterns," *Journal of Southern History* 76, no. 1 (February 2010): 39-70.

[14] Clara D. Noyes to Superintendent of Nurses at Johns Hopkins Hospital, 27 January 1894.

[15] Ethel Johns and Blanche Pfefferkorn, *The Johns Hopkins School of Nursing: 1889-1949* (Baltimore: Johns Hopkins Press, 1954), 108.

[16] Ibid, 197.

[17] "World War Red Cross Nursing Director Visitor During Illinois Convention Here," *Peoria Journal Transcript* (Peoria, IL), October 14, 1934.

[18] Ethel Johns et al., *The Johns Hopkins School of Nursing*, 8.

[19] Ibid, 22.

[20] Edith Moriarty, "With the Women of Today," *The Charlotte News*, June 4, 1922.

[21] Ethel Johns et al., *The Johns Hopkins School of Nursing*, 59.

[22] Ibid, 80.

[23] Ibid, 110-111.

[24] "Extracted from letters from Miss Hay to Miss Noyes, May 4, 1922" and "Ans. By Miss Noyes, May 20, 1922." Records of the American National Red Cross 1917–1934, Record Group 200, folder 958.52, "Commission to Czecho-Slovakia, W.W. I, Prague School of Nursing, July 1922-Dec. 1926."

[25] Ethel Johns et al., *The Johns Hopkins School of Nursing*, 135-136.

[26] *Johns Hopkins Nurses Alumnae Magazine* 35, no. 3 (July 1936): 158.

[27] Anna C. Jammé, "Recollections," *Johns Hopkins Nurses Alumnae Magazine* 36, no. 1 (January 1937): 13.

[28] A vaccine wasn't developed until 1896 or used widely in the United States until 1909. "Vaccination against typhoid fever is now an established procedure," wrote L.H. Webb in the New *Charlotte Medical Journal* in 1917. "Its use began in 1896" when scientists "demonstrated that persons injected with killed typhoid bacilli develop the same antibodies in their bodies as found in the recovered cases of typhoid." He adds: "Typhoid vaccination was started voluntarily in the United States Army in 1909." L.H. Webb, "Vaccine in Typhoid Therapy," *The Charlotte Medical Journal: A Southern Journal of Medicine and Surgery* 76, no. 1 (July 1917): 12.

[29] Anna C. Jammé, "Recollections," 14.

[30] Ibid.

[31] Ibid.

[32] Ibid.

[33] "Miss Clara D. Noyes, National Red Cross Nursing Head Dies," press release from the American Red Cross News Service (June 3, 1936), private collection of James Noyes, Old Lyme, CT.

[34] Anna C. Jammé, "Recollections," 14.

[35] Clara D. Noyes to Miss Dick, undated letter (probably from 1908, according to a note in the file). "Correspondence, Class of 1896." Alan Mason Chesney Medical Archives of the Johns Hopkins Medical Institutions, Baltimore.

[36] Ibid.

[37] Anna C. Jammé, "Recollections," 14.

[38] Sandra Beth Lewenson, *Taking Charge: Nursing, Suffrage and Feminism in America: 1873-1970* (New York: National League for Nursing Press, 1996), 88.

[39] Ibid.

CHAPTER THREE

[1] "Ex-Mayor Davidson Weds: Baltimorean Marries the Nurse with Whom He Eloped in This City," *New York Times*, November 16, 1905.

[2] "Former Mayor and a Trained Nurse Elope," *San Francisco Call*, May 24, 1905.

[3] Ibid.

[4] "Mrs. Davidson Free: Court Grants Her Divorce and $50,000 Alimony," *Washington Post*, November 11, 1905.

[5] Susan Gelfand Malka, *Daring To Care: American Nursing and Second-Wave Feminism* (Chicago: University of Illinois Press, 2007), 14.

[6] Reverby, *Ordered to Care*, 97.

[7] Ibid, 104.

[8] "Discredited by Mother: Mrs. Noyes Does Not Believe Daughter Eloped with Davidson," *Washington Post*, May 25, 1905.

[9] "Ex-Mayor Davidson Weds," *New York Times*, November 16, 1905.

[10] "Davidson Remarried: Former Mayor of Baltimore Weds Nurse with Whom He Eloped," *Washington Post*, November 16, 1905.

[11] Clara D. Noyes to Miss Dick, undated letter probably from 1908 (according to a note in the file), "Correspondence, Class of 1896." Alan Mason Chesney Medical Archives of the Johns Hopkins Medical Institutions, Baltimore.

[12] Ibid.

[13] *Johns Hopkins Nurses Alumnae Magazine* 1, no. 1 (December 1901): 22.

[14] Clara D. Noyes to Georgiana Ross, 7 July 1907. "Class of 1896, Correspondence." Alan Mason Chesney Medical Archives of the Johns Hopkins Medical Institutions, Baltimore.

[15] Ibid.

[16] Ibid.

[17] Clara D. Noyes to Georgiana Ross, 21 July 1908. "Class of 1896, Correspondence." Alan Mason Chesney Medical Archives of the Johns Hopkins Medical Institutions, Baltimore.

[18] H.P. Coile, M.D., "The Hydrotherapy of Typhoid Fever, and Improved Bath Apparatus for its Successful Implementation," *Transactions of the Seventieth Annual Session of the Tennessee State Medical Association, Nashville, 1903* (Nashville: Southern Publishing Association, 1903): 173.

[19] Clara D. Noyes, "A Modern Laundry," *American Journal of Nursing* 8, no. 7 (April 1908): 513-519.

[20] Ibid.

Chapter Four

[1] *Bellevue and Allied Hospitals Ninth Annual Report 1910* (New York: Lecouver Press Company, 1910), see pages V and 25.

[2] New York State Census, s.v., "Noes, Carrie D. [*sic.*], Head of Nurses Residence," Election District No. 4, Ward No. 21, New York City.

[3] "No Conservation of Life of Child: Midwife not recognized," *Huntington Herald* (Huntington, IN), September 30, 1912.

[4] Laura E. Ettinger, *Nurse-Midwifery: The Birth of a New American Profession* (Columbus, OH: Ohio State University Press, 2006), 13.

[5] The series, which included 20 titles on subjects from tuberculosis to venereal disease, nutrition and heart health, sold 750,000 copies. United States Public Health Service, *The Health Officer* 1, no. 9 (January 1937).

[6] "No Conservation of Life of Child: Midwife not recognized," *Huntington Herald* (Huntington, IN), September 30, 1912.

[7] Ibid.

[8] Ettinger, *Nurse-Midwifery*, 13.

[9] Judith Pence Rooks, *Midwifery and Childbirth in America*, (Philadelphia: Temple University Press, 1997), 27.

[10] Katy Dawley, "Origins of Nurse-Midwifery in the United States and its Expansion in the 1940s," *Journal of Midwifery & Women's Health* 48, no. 2 (March/April 2003): 86-87.

[11] J. Whitridge Williams, "Medical Education and the Midwife Problem in the United States," *Journal of the American Medical Association* 58, no. 1 (January 6, 1912): 7.

[12] Charles Edward Ziegler, "The Elimination of the Midwife," *Journal of the American Medical Association* 60, no. 1 (January 4, 1913): 32.

[13] Clara D. Noyes, "The Midwifery Problem," *American Journal of Nursing* 12, no. 6 (March 1912): 466-468.

[14] Ettinger, *Nurse-Midwifery*, 13.

[15] W.E.B Du Bois, *The Souls of Black Folk* (1903, repr., New York: Bantam Books, 1989), 1-2.

[16] Katy Dawley, "Origins of Nurse-Midwifery in the United States and its Expansion in the 1940s": 86.

[17] Clara D. Noyes, "The Midwifery Problem": 466-467.

[18] Ibid, 469.

[19] U.S. National Library of Medicine, "Certified Nurse-midwife: History of the Profession," *MedlinePlus*, accessed October 13, 2015, https://www.nlm.nih.gov/medlineplus/ency/article/002000.htm.

[20] Clara D. Noyes, "The Midwifery Problem": 470.

[21] Clara D. Noyes, "Training of Midwives in Relation to the Prevention of Infant Mortality," *American Journal of*

Obstetrics and Diseases of Women and Children (New York: William Wood and Company, 1912), 1053-1056.

[22] Ibid.

[23] Ibid.

[24] "Report of the Section of Nursing and Social Work of the American Association for the Study and Prevention of Infant Mortality," *American Journal of Nursing* 12, no. 4 (January 1912): 333.

[25] Clara D. Noyes, "Training of Midwives in Relation to the Prevention of Infant Mortality," 1053-1056.

[26] Clara D. Noyes, "Training School for Midwives at Bellevue and Allied Hospitals," *American Journal of Nursing* 12, no. 5 (February 1912): 417.

[27] Ibid.

[28] See Ettinger, *Nurse-Midwifery*, Notes to Chapter 1, footnote 41, p. 205.

[29] Ettinger, *Nurse-Midwifery*, 11-12.

[30] Rose Tyndall and Mary Murphy, *A History of the Bellevue School for Midwives: 1911-1936*, series 1, box 2, Bellevue Hospital School of Nursing Alumnae Association Records, 1873-2009 (MC19), Bellevue Alumnae Center for Nursing History, Foundation of New York State Nurses, Guilderland, NY: table 6, p. 251, "Summary Table of Official Records: Number of Applications Submitted; Number of Students Accepted, Withdrawals, Graduated – 1911-1936."

[31] J. Clifton Edgar, "Why the Midwife?" *The American Journal of Obstetrics and Diseases of Women and Children* 78, no. 1 (July 1918): 242-243.

[32] Ibid, 243.

[33] Ibid, 244-245.

[34] Ibid, 254.

[35] "Nurses in Convention Condemn Kitchen Duty," *Chicago Daily Tribune*, June 5, 1912.

[36] "Scarcity of Nurses: Hospitals Have Trouble in Recruiting Training Classes," *New York Tribune*, May 18, 1912.

[37] Ibid.

[38] Robert V. Piemonte, *A History of the National League of Nursing Education 1912-1932: Great Awakening in Nursing Education*. Dissertation Submitted for the Degree of Doctor of Education in Teachers College, Columbia University (1976), 35.

[39] Ibid, 41-42.

[40] Ibid, 55.

[41] Ibid, 127-128.

[42] Sarah Slavin, ed., *U.S. Women's Interest Groups: Institutional Profiles* (Westport, CT: Greenwood Publishing Group, 1995), 383.

[43] Robert V. Piemonte, *A History of the National League of Nursing Education*, 2.

[44] See Portia Kernodle, *The Red Cross Nurse In Action* (New York: Harper and Brothers, 1949), 354-359, for a chapter on "Noyes vs. Boardman" regarding Clara Noyes's opposition to Red Cross official Mabel Boardman's attempts to expand the Red Cross's volunteer aid

programs, which Boardman referred to as her "Ladies of Saint Filomena" program.

[45] Virtually all official documents and reports indicate 1869 as Clara Noyes's birth year; however, her gravestone lists 1866 as her birth year. The vast majority of sources mention 1869.

[46] These women "were determined to challenge Republican plans for Reconstruction because the party so obviously refused to support woman suffrage," according to Ellen Carol Dubois, *Feminism and Suffrage: The Emergence of an Independent Women's Movement in America, 1848-1869* (Ithaca, NY: Cornell University Press, 1978), 163.

[47] Writes Dubois: Republican suffragists "believed that the woman suffrage movement had no alternative but to continue to solicit the help of Republicans. They came to this conclusion because they considered the party the most powerful force in postwar politics." Ellen Carol Dubois, *Feminism and Suffrage*, 163.

[48] As Dubois records, any attempt at unity had crumbled during the convention of the Equal Rights Association where "the conflict between its abolitionist and feminist priorities [were] too deep to be reconciled by a campaign for the Sixteenth Amendment." The 1869 convention "ended something old," she explains, "leading almost immediately to the formation of a new national reform organization, the National Woman Suffrage Association." Ellen Carol Dubois, *Feminism and Suffrage*, 187-189.

[49] Ibid.

[50] As Sandra Beth Lewenson notes, the *American Journal of Nursing* first registered the debate on suffrage in 1906 with a letter from the National American Woman Suf-

frage Association (142). Other letters followed, including columns by Lavinia Dock on the issue, though the *Journal* maintained a neutral stance on suffrage, as emphasized in an editorial in September 1908 (150). It wasn't until the ANA's 1912 convention that nurses supported a suffrage resolution (187). During Clara Noyes's presidency at the NLNE, it, too, passed a resolution supporting the Susan B. Anthony Amendment at the NLNE's 1915 conference in San Francisco (197). Sandra Beth Lewenson, *Taking Charge: Nursing, Suffrage and Feminism in America: 1873-1970* (New York: National League for Nursing Press, 1996), 142-197.

51 Susan Rimby, *Mira Lloyd Dock and the Progressive Era Conservation Movement* (University Park, PA: Pennsylvania State University Press, 2012), 130-131. See also Barbara Sicherman and Carol Hurd Green, eds., *Notable American Women: The Modern Period: a Biographical Dictionary* (Cambridge, MA: The Belknap Press of Harvard University Press, 1980), 197.

52 "Address of President Clara D. Noyes: Proceeding of the Twenty-first Annual Convention of the NLNE, 1915," Nettie Birnbach and Sandra Beth Lewenson, eds., *Legacy of Leadership: Presidential Addresses from the Superintendents' Society and the National League of Nursing Education, 1894-1952* (New York: National League for Nursing Press, 1993), 123.

53 "Address of President Clara D. Noyes: Proceeding of the Twenty-second Annual Convention of the NLNE, 1916," Nettie Birnbach and Sandra Beth Lewenson, eds., *Legacy of Leadership*, 128.

[54] Lewenson, *Taking Charge: Nursing, Suffrage and Feminism in America: 1873-1970*, 168-170.

[55] Clara D. Noyes to M. Adelaide Nutting, 8 April 1917. New York Nursing Archives, Teacher's College.

[56] "Address of President Clara D. Noyes: Proceedings of the Twenty-first Annual Convention of the NLNE, 1915," Nettie Birnbach and Sandra Beth Lewenson, eds., *Legacy of Leadership*, 121-122.

[57] Ibid.

CHAPTER FIVE

[1] Clare Coss, ed., *Lillian D. Wald, Progressive Activist* (New York: Feminist Press of the City University of New York, 1989), 71. See also "Win Their Diplomas," *Washington Post*, June 9, 1913, for a record of Senetta Anderson graduating from M Street High School in Washington, DC.

[2] Clara D. Noyes to Lillian Wald, 14 August 1914, Lillian Wald Papers, Rare Book and Manuscript Library, Columbia University in the City of New York.

[3] Ibid.

[4] Ibid.

[5] Ibid.

[6] Ibid.

[7] Lewenson, *Taking Charge*, 95.

[8] Lillian Wald to Clara D. Noyes, 13 August 1914, Lillian Wald Papers, Rare Book and Manuscript Library, Columbia University in the City of New York.

[9] Ibid.

[10] Lillian Wald to Chapin Brinsmead, 18 August 1914, Lillian Wald Papers, Rare Book and Manuscript Library, Columbia University in the City of New York.

[11] 1930 United States Census, s.v., "Nelon [sic], Senetta B.," Precinct 2, District of Columbia, Washington, April 13 to 15, 1930.

[12] District of Columbia, Select Marriages, 1830-1921. Salt Lake City, Utah: FamilySearch, 2013. FHL Film Number: 2051925, Reference ID: 93377. The Neloms' recent marriage is also mentioned in a wedding announcement for another couple, whose wedding the Neloms attended, on October 3, 1919, according to the article "Miss Olive Boggess Marries," *Chicago Defender*, October 4, 1919.

[13] "Declaration of Rights of the Negro Peoples of the World," *The Philosophy and Opinions of Marcus Garvey, Or, Africa for Africans*, Amy Jacques Garvey, ed. (Dover, MA: The Majority Press, 1986), 135-143.

[14] "157 Pass 1st Bi-Racial Examination," *Washington Post*, July 14, 1954.

[15] Electronic Army Serial Number Merged File, ca. 1938-1946 (Enlistment Records). National Archives and Records Administration, box 0021, film reel no. 1.21#.

[16] "College Grads in Negro WAC Band, Chorus," *Chicago Defender*, December 4, 1943.

[17] Sherrie Tucker writes: "The black WACs at Fort Des Moines, Iowa, were barred from membership in the official (white) WAC band, so they formed their own. Although not officially authorized, the band patterned itself after the established WAC band in instrumentation and repertoire ... In June 1944, the army granted them a band rating. However, a month later, after they played well-received concerts and a parade for the thirty-fourth annual NAACP conference in Chicago, the army stripped their band rating, and members of the WAC band were demoted and reassigned to other duties." Sherrie Tucker, *Swing Shift: "All-Girl" Bands of the 1940s* (Durham, NC: Duke University Press, 2000), 253.

[18] "WAC Band Gets Final Okeh By War Department," *Chicago Defender*, September 2, 1944.

[19] Ralph Ellison, *Invisible Man* (1952, repr., New York: Vintage Books, 1990), 8.

CHAPTER SIX

[1] Cora Sutton Castle, "A Statistical Study of Eminent Women," repr. from the *Archives of Psychology* 4, no. 27 (New York: August 1913): 2.

[2] Robert D. McFadden, "Ex-Rep. Jeanette Rankin Dies; First Woman in Congress, 92," *New York Times*, May 20, 1973.

[3] Kimberly Jensen, *Mobilizing Minerva: American Women in the First World War* (Urbana, IL: University of Illinois Press, 2008), 17.

[4] Providing a counterargument to this syllogism was Carrie Chapman Catt, in her publication *The Ballot and the Bullet*, "an unassailable rebuttal of the claim that each ballot must be defended by a bullet." Carrie Chapman Catt, *The Ballot and the Bullet* (New York: Published for the National American Woman Suffrage Association, 1897), 7-9.

[5] Lavinia L. Dock, Sarah Pickett, and Clara D. Noyes, *History of American Red Cross Nursing* (New York: Macmillan Company, 1922): See chapter on the "Mercy Ship," 139-228.

[6] Ibid.

[7] Writes Norma Smith in *Jeanette Rankin: America's Conscience*: "Hardest to bear was the thought that [Rankin's] vote had hurt the suffrage movement. In New York some suffragists canceled a coming reception and a number of speaking engagements they had arranged for her." Smith quotes Carrie Chapman Catt as follows: "'Miss Rankin was not voting for the suffragists of the nation – she represents Montana.' Privately she wrote, 'Our Congress Lady is a sure enough joker. Whatever she has done or will do ... she loses us a million votes.'" Norma Smith, *Jeanette Rankin: America's Conscience* (Helena, MT: Montana Historical Society Press, 2002), 113.

[8] Rankin sought to have her name attached to the legislation, "though Republicans on the Committee did not agree and Chairman [John E.] Raker's name was attached." Raker, Chairman of the Suffrage Committee, nevertheless shared with Rankin a role in the floor debate when the suffrage bill passed the House that year. "Suf-

frage Wins in the House Without One Vote to Spare; Democrats Divided on Issue," *New York Tribune*, January 11, 1918.

[9] Clara D. Noyes, "Address to the Graduating Class of 1917," *Johns Hopkins Nurses Alumnae Magazine* 16, no. 3 (August 1917): 100-106.

[10] Ibid.

[11] "Pacifists in Suffrage Ranks Object to Preparedness Plan," *Brooklyn Daily Eagle*, February 21, 1917.

[12] Ibid.

[13] Jensen, *Mobilizing Minerva*, 17.

[14] Dock et al., *History of American Red Cross Nursing*, 689.

CHAPTER SEVEN

[1] See Michael Zwerdling, *Postcards of Nursing: A Worldwide Tribute* (Philadelphia: Lippincott Williams & Wilkins, 2003). In his cover notes, Zwerdling provides the following explanation of the postcard which is in circulation on commerce websites like *ebay.com*: "Clara D. Noyes, and Jane Delano superimposed on a Photograph of F. Nightingale. Among other accomplishments, Ms. Noyes was Director of the Red Cross Nursing service during World War I and Ms. Delano was the Superintendent of the Army Nurse Corps during the same period. U.S., 1918."

[2] In a radio address on the anniversary of Nightingale's birth, Clara Noyes offered this connection between Nightingale and the Red Cross movement: "While we

cannot say that she was the originator of the Red Cross idea, it has been said that her work in Crimea gave Henri Durant his inspiration to create a great movement for the relief of human suffering." Radio Address by Miss Clara Noyes, National Director of Nursing Service, American Red Cross: "Anniversary of Florence Nightingale's Birth Adopted as National Hospital Day." Press release from the American Red Cross News Service (May 12, 1921), private collection of James Noyes, Old Lyme, CT.

3 Dock et al., *History of American Red Cross Nursing*, 343.

4 Anne Tjomsland, M.D., *Bellevue in France: Anecdotal History of Base Hospital No. 1* (New York: Froben Press, 1941), 17.

5 Ibid.

6 Dock, et al., *History of American Red Cross Nursing*, 505.

7 Records of the American National Red Cross, 1881-2008, Series: Historical Nurse Files, 1916-1959. Folder: Clara D. Noyes, Red Cross Badge No. 6215.

8 Ibid.

9 Jane Delano to Clara D. Noyes, 7 June 1916. Records of the American National Red Cross, 1881-2008, Series: Historical Nurse Files, 1916-1959. Folder: Clara D. Noyes, Red Cross Badge No. 6215.

10 Ibid.

11 Ibid.

12 Ibid.

13 Ibid.

[14] Dock, et al., *History of American Red Cross Nursing*, 233.

[15] Ibid.

[16] Ibid, 235.

[17] Nettie Birnbach et al., *Legacy of Leadership*, 125-126.

[18] Dock, et al., *History of American Red Cross Nursing*, 232.

[19] Delano, *Franklin Delano and the Delano Influence*, 34.

[20] "Bellevue Gives Another Official," *American Red Cross Magazine* 11, no. 1 (1916): 355.

[21] "Miss Clara Noyes of Red Cross Dead," *New York Times*, June 4, 1936.

[22] Francis Cooke married the sister of Philippe de la Noye's mother, according to William Grant Cook's *William Grant Cook, his ancestors and descendants* (Chicago: Privately Published, 1942): 11.

[23] Dock, et al., *History of American Red Cross Nursing*, 542.

[24] Ibid, 501.

[25] Ibid, 235.

[26] "To Guide Red Cross Nurses: Head of the Bellevue School is Made Superintendent," *New York Times*, August 1, 1916.

[27] William Howard Taft to Maj. Gen. Murray, 30 June 1916. Records of the American National Red Cross, 1881-2008, Series: Historical Nurse Files, 1916-1959. Folder: Clara D. Noyes, Red Cross Badge No. 6215.

[28] Julia Irwin, *Making The World Safe: The American Red Cross and a Nation's Humanitarian Awakening* (Oxford: Oxford University Press, 2013), 49.

[29] The first big wartime drive brought in a whopping $114 million followed by a second drive of $169 million. "Nearly overnight, the [American Red Cross] had become the nation's leading charitable institution," writes historian Marian Moser Jones, *American Red Cross from Clara Barton to the New Deal* (Baltimore: Johns Hopkins University Press, 2013), 163-164.

[30] Ibid, 157.

[31] Kernodle, *The Red Cross Nurse in Action*, 35.

[32] Dock, et al., *History of American Red Cross Nursing*, 550.

[33] Ibid, 547.

[34] Ibid, 550.

[35] Mary T. Sarnecky, *A History of the U.S. Army Nurse Corps* (Philadelphia: University of Pennsylvania Press, 1999), 100.

[36] Dock, et al., *History of American Red Cross Nursing*, 574.

[37] "Red Cross Plans Base Hospitals: Miss Clara Noyes Reveals Fact in Address to Women's Section of Navy League," *The Washington Times*, March 7, 1917.

[38] Clara D. Noyes, "Department of Red Cross Nursing," *American Journal of Nursing* 25, no. 5 (May 1925).

[39] "Red Cross Plans Base Hospitals: Miss Clara Noyes Reveals Fact in Address to Women's Section of Navy League," *Washington Times*, March 7, 1917.

[40] "Itinerary of Miss Noyes' Tour, 1917-18." Records of the American National Red Cross, 1881-2008, Series: Historical Nurse Files, 1916-1959. Folder: Clara D. Noyes, Red Cross Badge No. 6215.

[41] "Old Lyme: Red Cross Work Described," *The Day* (New London, CT), September 5, 1917.

[42] Ibid.

[43] Clara D. Noyes, "The Red Cross." *American Journal of Nursing* 17, no. 7 (April 1917): 622.

[44] "Old Lyme: Red Cross Work Described," *The Day* (New London, CT), September 5, 1917.

[45] Anna C. Jammé, "Recollections," 15.

[46] Dock et al., *History of American Red Cross Nursing*, 237.

[47] Acts 16: 6-10 (Revised Standard Version).

[48] Noyes was apparently fond of this phrase "Macedonian Call," referencing it on other occasions, including in a January 23, 1923 letter to Ernest Bicknell, Red Cross Vice Chairman for Insular and Foreign Operations, describing a potential donation for scholarships related to the Prague School of Nursing.

[49] Dock et al., *History of American Red Cross Nursing*, 388.

[50] Clara D. Noyes, "Service of Women in Time of War," *Twenty-Third Annual Convention of the American Nurses Association, Held at Philadelphia, PA, April 26 to May 2, 1917* (Baltimore: Williams & Wilkins Company, 1917), 235-236.

[51] Ibid.

[52] H.E.C Bryant, "Secretary Daniels Will Review Red Cross Parade in New York," *News and Observer* (Raleigh, NC), October 3, 1917.

[53] Kernodle, *The Red Cross Nurse in Action*, 133.

[54] Clara D., Noyes, "Sailing of the Units," *American Journal of Nursing* 17, no. 11 (August 1917): 1096.

[55] Dock et al., *History of American Red Cross Nursing*, 423.

[56] American Red Cross, *The American National Red Cross Annual Report for the Fiscal Year Ended June 30, 1918* (Washington, DC: American Red Cross, 1918), 94.

[57] Ibid, 93.

[58] Ibid, 93-94.

[59] Meta Rutter Pennock, ed., *Makers of Nursing History* (New York: Lakeside Publishing Company, 1940), 50.

[60] Dock et al., *History of American Red Cross Nursing*, 442.

[61] Clara D. Noyes, "Address to the Graduating Class of 1917," 100-106.

[62] Irwin, *Making The World Safe*, 35-36.

[63] Clara D. Noyes, "Address to the Graduating Class of 1917," 100-106.

[64] Elizabeth Brown Pryor, *Clara Barton: Professional Angel* (University of Pennsylvania Press, 1987), 341.

[65] Dock et al., *History of American Red Cross Nursing*, 298.

[66] Ibid.

[67] Ibid.

[68] Ibid.

[69] "Clara D. Noyes," editorial, *Wilkes-Barre Record* (Wilkes-Barre, PA), June 9, 1936.

[70] Dock et al., *History of American Red Cross Nursing*, 390-391.

[71] Clara D. Noyes, "Department of Red Cross Nursing," *American Journal of Nursing* 18, no. 4 (January 1918): 317-321.

[72] Lewenson, *Taking Charge*, 94.

[73] Andrea Patterson, "'Black Nurses in the Great War' Fighting for and with the American Military in the Struggle for Civil Rights," *Canadian Journal of History* 47.3 (2012).

[74] Ibid.

[75] Ibid.

[76] Dock, et al., *History of American Red Cross Nursing*, 405.

[77] Ibid.

[78] Ibid, 408.

[79] William Keylor, "The Long-forgotten Racial Attitudes and Policies of Woodrow Wilson," *Professor Voices*, Boston University, March 4, 2013, accessed October 13, 2015, http://www.bu.edu/professorvoices/2013/03/04/the-long-forgotten-racial-attitudes-and-policies-of-woodrow-wilson/.

[80] National Association of Colored Graduate Nurses records, 1908-1958, Schomburg Center for Research in Black Culture of the New York Public Library, SC Micro R-6565.

[81] Ibid.

[82] Ibid.

[83] Ibid.

[84] Ibid.

[85] Ibid.

[86] "Use Red Cross Nurses As Lure: Girls Promised Positions as Nurses Fall Victims to Bad Men," *Washington Post*, June 23, 1918.

[87] See Records of the American National Red Cross 1917–1934, Record Group 200, folder 109.1, "Nurses – Charged with Immorality 1917-1918," and folder 109.1, "Nurses – Brutal Treatment By Germans."

[88] Alexander B. Bielaski, Chief of the United States Department of Justice, to Charles Magee, Secretary of American National Red Cross, 13 April 1917. Records of the American National Red Cross 1917–1934, Record Group 200, folder 109.1, "Sabotage – World War #1."

[89] Alexander B. Bielaski, Chief of the United States Department of Justice, to Charles Magee, Secretary of American National Red Cross, 5 July 1916. Records of the American National Red Cross 1917–1934, Record Group 200, folder 109.1, "Sabotage – World War #1."

[90] Department of Justice Report, "Re: Eleanor Von Boehmer, German Neutrality Matter," completed by Agent Arthur T. Bagley, 24 June 1916. Records of the American National Red Cross 1917–1934, Record Group 200, folder 109.1, "Sabotage – World War #1."

[91] Miss Bartlett to Jane Delano, 18 February 1918, subject "Execution of nurse, at Camp Sevier, Greenville, S.C." Records of the American National Red Cross 1917–1934, Record Group 200, folder 109.1, "Sabotage – World War #1."

[92] Clara D. Noyes to Frederick Daw [sic.], 12 July 1918. Records of the American National Red Cross 1917–1934, Record Group 200, folder 109.1, "Nurses – Brutal Treatment By Germans."

[93] Frederick Dorr to Clara D. Noyes, 15 July 1918. Records of the American National Red Cross 1917–1934, Record Group 200, folder 109.1, "Nurses – Brutal Treatment By Germans." The letter indicates that it was "dict. by Frederick Dorr. Wrote [sic.] by Mrs. Dorr."

[94] Jane Delano to Miss Alice Meggison of Haverhill, MA, 15 May 1918. Records of the American National Red Cross 1917–1934, Record Group 200, folder 109.1, "Nurses – Charged with Immorality 1917-1918."

[95] "Nurses Defended Against Sen. Watson; Col. James R Church, Medical Corps, Quotes Records on Immorality Charges: Article by Gen. Winter, who investigated slanderous report, re-issued here." Records of the American National Red Cross 1917–1934, Record Group 200, folder 109.1, "Nurses – Charged with Immorality 1917-1918."

[96] Jane Delano to Surgeon General William Gorgas, 15 February 1918. Records of the American National Red Cross 1917–1934, Record Group 200, folder 109.1, "Nurses – Charged with Immorality 1917-1918."

[97] "National Investigation of Slander Against Red Cross," *Los Angeles Times*, January 6, 1918.

[98] Susan M. Poslusny, "Feminist Friendship," 65-55.

[99] Lyndia Flanagan, *One Strong Voice: The Story of the American Nurses' Association* (Kansas City: American Nurses' Association, 1973), Appendix I, 610-612.

[100] Ibid.

[101] Ibid, 612.

[102] *The Story of the American Journal of Nursing,* 4th revision, March 1950, 27.

[103] Flanagan, *One Strong Voice,* 61-65.

[104] Ibid.

[105] *Twenty-fourth Annual Report of the National League of Nursing Education: 1918.* (Baltimore: Williams & Wilkins Company, 1919), 251.

[106] National Association of Colored Graduate Nurses records, 1908-1958, Schomburg Center for Research in Black Culture of the New York Public Library, SC Micro R-6565.

[107] Ibid.

[108] Mabel Keaton Staupers, *No Time For Prejudice: A Story of the Integration of Negroes in Nursing in the United States* (New York: Macmillan Company, 1961), 123.

[109] Ibid, 15.

[110] Ibid, 16.

CHAPTER EIGHT

[1] Dock et al., *History of American Red Cross Nursing,* 451.

[2] Ibid, 611.

[3] Sarnecky, *A History of the U.S. Army Nurse Corps,* 101.

[4] Ibid, 104.

[5] Ibid, 105.

[6] Ibid, 111.

[7] "History In Brief of Base Hospital No. 18," *Johns Hopkins Nurses Alumnae Magazine* 18, no. 2 (May 1919): 57.

[8] Bessie Baker, "An Outline of The Work of Our Nursing Unit," *Johns Hopkins Nurses Alumnae Magazine* 18, no. 2 (May 1919): 58-59.

[9] Gertrude Bowling, "Side-Lights on Life With a Shock Team," *Johns Hopkins Nurses Alumnae Magazine* 18, no. 2 (May 1919): 63.

[10] Ibid, 64.

[11] Ibid, 66.

[12] Pauline Stock, "Experiences With A 'Shock Team'," *Johns Hopkins Nurses Alumnae Magazine* 18, no. 2 (May 1919): 70-73.

[13] Dock et al., *History of American Red Cross Nursing*, 611.

[14] Clara D. Noyes, "For Extraordinary Heroism," *American Journal of Nursing* 19, no. 7 (April 1919): 531-535.

[15] Ibid.

[16] Clara D. Noyes, "The Red Cross," *American Journal of Nursing* 20, no. 5 (February 1920): 395-396.

[17] Ibid.

[18] Ibid.

[19] Ibid.

[20] Dock et al., *History of American Red Cross Nursing*, 515.

[21] Ibid, 517.

[22] "Only Third of Nurses Ready Used in Camps," *Chicago Daily Tribune*, January 26, 1918.

[23] Ibid.

[24] Ibid.

CHAPTER NINE

[1] Agnes Von Kurowsky to Clara D. Noyes, 2 January 1918. Records of the American National Red Cross, 1881-2008, Series: Historical Nurse Files, 1916-1959, File Unit: Stanfield, Mrs. Agnes H. (Wm. C).

[2] See "Bureau of Investigation: Detection of Violations of Federal Laws," *Annual Report of the Attorney General of the United States for the Year 1917* (Washington, DC: Government Printing Office, 1917), 82.

[3] Clara D. Noyes to Agnes Von Kurowsky, 5 January 1918. Records of the American National Red Cross, 1881-2008 Series: Historical Nurse Files, ca. 1916-ca. 1959 File, Unit: Stanfield, Mrs. Agnes H. (Wm. C).

[4] Dock et al., *History of American Red Cross Nursing*, 322.

[5] Bernice Kert, *The Hemingway Women* (New York: Norton, 1983), 51.

[6] Ernest Hemingway, *A Farewell To Arms: The Hemingway Library Edition* (1929; repr., New York: Scribner, 2012), 16.

[7] Jean Shulman, "They Were Giants In Those Days," *Nursing Matters Past and Present*, a publication of the

American Red Cross National Nursing Committee, 18th edition (Spring 2015): 6-7.

[8] Kert, *The Hemingway Women*, 58.

[9] K.C. Melhorn to Clara D. Noyes, 28 November 1928. Records of the American National Red Cross, 1881-2008 Series: Historical Nurse Files, ca. 1916-ca. 1959 File, Unit: Stanfield, Mrs. Agnes H. (Wm. C).

[10] National Director of the Nursing Service to Dr. K. C. Melhorn, 19 December 1928. Records of the American National Red Cross, 1881-2008. Series: Historical Nurse Files, ca. 1916-ca. 1959. File Unit: Stanfield, Mrs. Agnes H. (Wm. C).

[11] National Director of the Nursing Service to Agnes Stanfield, 5 December 1928. Records of the American National Red Cross, 1881-2008. Series: Historical Nurse Files, ca. 1916-ca. 1959. File Unit: Stanfield, Mrs. Agnes H. (Wm. C).

[12] Agnes Garner to Clara D. Noyes, 21 November 1929. Records of the American National Red Cross, 1881-2008. Series: Historical Nurse Files, ca. 1916-ca. 1959. File Unit: Stanfield, Mrs. Agnes H. (Wm. C).

CHAPTER TEN

[1] Michael C. LeMay, *Doctors at the Borders: Immigration and the Rise of Public Health* (Santa Barbara, CA: Prager, 2015), 66.

[2] Sandra Opdycke, *The Flu Epidemic of 1918: America's Experience in the Global Health Crisis* (New York: Routledge, 2014), 2-3.

[3] Records of the American National Red Cross 1917–1934, Record Group 200, folder 803.08, "Epidemics, Influenza, Reports and Statistics."

[4] Opdycke, *The Flu Epidemic of 1918*, 46.

[5] Records of the American National Red Cross 1917–1934, Record Group 200, folder 803.08, "Epidemics, Influenza, Reports and Statistics."

[6] Opdycke, *The Flu Epidemic of 1918*, Introduction, xiv.

[7] Arlene W. Keeling, "'A Most Alarming Situation': Responding to the 1918 Influenza Epidemic in Alaska," *Windows in Time*, University of Virginia School of Nursing 21, no. 2 (October 2013): 6.

[8] Opdycke, *The Flu Epidemic of 1918*, 35.

[9] Arlene W. Keeling, "'Alert to the Necessities of the Emergency': U.S. Nursing During the 1918 Influenza Pandemic," *Public Health Report*, 2010; 125 (Suppl 3): 105-112.

[10] Ibid.

[11] Red Cross Acting Vice Chairman to Secretary of the Navy Josephus Daniels, 30 September 1918. Records of the American National Red Cross 1917–1934, Record Group 200, folder 803.08, "Epidemics, Influenza, Reports and Statistics."

[12] General Letter No. 1, Subject: "Request from Surgeon General Blue, U.S.P.H.S," Frank Persons to all Division

Managers, 3 October 1918. Records of the American National Red Cross 1917–1934, Record Group 200, folder 803, "Epidemics – Influenza, 1918, Divisions."

[13] Report: "The Influenza Epidemic." Records of the American National Red Cross 1917–1934, Record Group 200, folder 803, "Epidemics, Influenza."

[14] Ibid.

[15] "Woman Heads Red Cross Aid: World-Wide Activities Center at Desk of Miss Clara D. Noyes," *Milwaukee Journal*, September 7, 1927.

[16] Indeed, the American Red Cross had long proven its robust domestic service role, in its early history under Clara Barton, who rendered service not only to the Civil War wounded, but, notably, in response to the Johnstown flood of 1889, in Pennsylvania, securing the American Red Cross's "place as an iconic American disaster-relief organization," according to Marian Moser Jones, *American Red Cross from Clara Barton to the New Deal*, 47.

[17] "Reports from Camps on Influenza Show a Total of 144,095 Cases," *The Official U.S. Bulletin*, October 7, 1918: 3.

[18] Records of the American National Red Cross 1917–1934, Record Group 200, folder 803.08 "Epidemics, Influenza, Reports and Statistics."

[19] Ibid.

[20] Ibid.

[21] Ibid.

[22] Opdycke, *The Flu Epidemic of 1918*, 27.

[23] Dock et al., *History of American Red Cross Nursing*: "Appendix to List of American Red Cross Nurses Who Died in War Service or as a Result of Disability Contracted Therein."

[24] A memo with extracts of quotes attributed to Red Cross War Council Member George B. Case and Charles Scott, Jr., Vice Chairman of the American Red Cross in Charge of Finance, 13 January 1919. Records of the American National Red Cross 1917–1934, Record Group 200, folder 803.3, "Epidemics, Influenza, Personnel."

[25] A memo with extracts of quotes attributed to Red Cross Vice Chairman Willoughby G. Walling and Frederick C. Monroe, General Manager at Red Cross, 28 January 1919. Records of the American National Red Cross 1917–1934, Record Group 200, folder 803.3, "Epidemics, Influenza, Personnel."

[26] Jeffrey Taubenberger, "The Origin and Virulence of the 1918 'Spanish' Influenza Virus," *Proceedings of the American Philosophical Society* 150, no. 1 (March 2006): 86-112.

[27] Ibid.

[28] Keeling, "'A Most Alarming Situation,'" 10.

[29] Clara D. Noyes to Lillian White, 3 June 1919. Records of the American National Red Cross 1917–1934, Record Group 200, folder 803.11, "Epidemics, Influenza, Alaska."

[30] Lillian White to Clara D. Noyes, 26 July 1919. Records of the American National Red Cross 1917–1934, Record Group 200, folder 803.11, "Epidemics, Influenza, Alaska."

[31] Clara D. Noyes to Lillian White, 12 June 1919. Records of the American National Red Cross 1917–1934, Record Group 200, folder 803.11, "Epidemics, Influenza, Alaska."

[32] Undated and untitled report. Records of the American National Red Cross 1917–1934, Record Group 200, folder 803.11, "Epidemics, Influenza, Alaska."

[33] Ibid.

[34] Dock et al., *History of American Red Cross Nursing*, 980.

[35] Alice Fitzgerald, "Clara D. Noyes – An Appreciation," *The Trained Nurse and Hospital Review* 97, no. 1 (July 1936): 21.

[36] Dock et al., *History of American Red Cross Nursing*, 981.

[37] Stanley Sandler, ed., *Ground Warfare, An International Encyclopedia, Volume I A-G* (Santa Barbara, CA: ABC-CLIO, 2002), 566.

[38] Heather Jones, *Violence Against Prisoners of War in the First World War: Britain, France and Germany, 1914-1920* (Cambridge: Cambridge University Press, 2011), 273.

[39] American Red Cross, *The American National Red Cross Annual Report for the Fiscal Year Ended June 30, 1918* (Washington, DC: American Red Cross, 1918), 91-93.

[40] Dock et al., *History of American Red Cross Nursing*, 981.

CHAPTER ELEVEN

[1] "Miss Noyes to Inspect Red Cross Work Abroad," *The Red Cross Bulletin* 4, no. 39 (September 20, 1920), 8.

[2] Dock et al., *History of American Red Cross Nursing*, 1000.

[3] Ibid, 1001.

[4] See Records of the American National Red Cross, 1881-2008, Series: Historical Nurse Files, 1916-1959, Jane A. Delano files: 301, folder labeled "Delano, Jane, April 1-23, 1919," for a series of telegrams from Carrie Hall, Nurses Bureau, Paris.

[5] "Army Nurses Honor Memory of Chief," *New York Tribune*, May 9, 1919.

[6] Sarnecky, *A History of the U.S. Army Nurse Corps*, 122.

[7] Clara D. Noyes to The American National Red Cross, undated correspondence. Records of the American National Red Cross, 1881-2008, Series: Historical Nurse Files, 1916-1959. Jane A. Delano files: 301, folder labeled "Delano, Jane, April 1-23, 1919."

[8] Anna C. Jammé to Clara Noyes, 19 April 1919. Records of the American National Red Cross, 1881-2008, Series: Historical Nurse Files, 1916-1959. Jane A. Delano files: 301, folder labeled "Delano, Jane, April 1-23, 1919."

[9] Laboratory Hospital Center, Savenay France (May 12, 1919). Death Certification, signed by Lt. Col. J.S. Coulter. Series: Historical Nurse Files, 1916-1959. Jane A. Delano files: 301, folder labeled "Delano, Jane, April 1-23, 1919."

[10] "Army Nurses Honor Memory of Chief," *New York Tribune*, May 9, 1919.

[11] Dock, et al., *History of American Red Cross Nursing*, 1006.

[12] Ibid, 1013.

[13] Clara D. Noyes to Susan Francis, 28 December 1918. The American Nurses Association Collection, Howard Gotlieb Archival Research Center at Boston University, N 87, box 180, folder 7.

[14] Susan Francis to Clara D. Noyes, 2 January 1919. The American Nurses Association Collection, Howard Gotlieb Archival Research Center at Boston University, N 87, box 180, folder 7.

[15] Dock, et al., *History of American Red Cross Nursing*, 1019.

[16] Flanagan, *One Strong Voice*, 72-73.

[17] Ibid, 72.

[18] "Editorial Comment," *Pacific Coast Journal of Nursing* 27, no. 8 (August 1922): 475.

[19] Clara D. Noyes, "Department of Red Cross Nursing: The Fifth Annual Roll Call," *American Journal of Nursing* 22, no. 1 (October 1921), 34.

[20] Dock, et al., *History of American Red Cross Nursing*, 1037.

[21] Flanagan, *One Strong Voice*, 421.

[22] Ibid, 423-424.

[23] "Tells of Red Cross Work: Prominent Executive Talks to Luncheon Guests," *Los Angeles Times*, July 9, 1922.

[24] Clara D. Noyes, "Department of Red Cross Nursing: Nursing Ex-Service Men," *American Journal of Nursing* 21, no. 11 (August 1921): 801.

[25] "Speeches Through Radiotelephone Inspire New York Crowds," *Electrical Review* (May 31, 1919), 895-896.

[26] Ibid.

[27] Ibid.

[28] Ibid.

[29] Ibid.

[30] "Mrs. M'Adoo Lauds Women in the War: President's Daughter, Speaking for Loan, Praises Heroism of Red Cross Nurses, *New York Times*, April 24, 1919.

CHAPTER TWELVE

[1] Clara D. Noyes, "Subnurses? Why Not Subdoctors?" republished in the *Indianapolis Medical Journal* 24, no. 21 (December 1921): 315-16. Originally published in *Pictorial Review*, no. 28 (December 1921).

[2] "Official Program, National Convention of the Women's Party, Washington, DC, February 15-18, 1921," *Suffragist* 9, no. 1 (January to February 1921): 342.

[3] Jan Wilson Doolittle, *Women's Joint Congressional Committee and the Politics of Materialism, 1920-30* (Champaign, IL: University of Illinois Press, 2007), 1.

[4] Carrie Chapman Catt, "Poison Propaganda," *The Woman Citizen*, no. 14 (May 31, 1924), 32-33.

[5] Doolittle, *Women's Joint Congressional Committee and the Politics of Materialism, 1920-30*, 1.

[6] Ibid, 173.

[7] "Happenings of Interest in Washington Society Circles," *Washington Post*, May 18, 1933.

[8] "Attends Seattle Meeting: Miss Clara Noyes Leaves for Conclave of Registered Nurses," *Washington Post*, June 17, 1922.

[9] Clara D. Noyes, "American Nurses' Association: Federal Legislative Measures and the American Nurses' Association." The American Nurses Association Collection, Howard Gotlieb Archival Research Center at Boston University, N 87, box 328, Folder 13.

[10] "Proposed Department of Education: Hearing Before the Committee on Education, House of Representatives, Seventieth Congress, First Session on H.R. 7. April 25, 26, 27, 28 and May 2, 1928." (Washington, DC: Government Printing Office, 1928), 62-63.

[11] The first nurses to be captured by enemy forces overseas were a group of nurses held in Japanese internment camps during World War II in battles on the Philippine Islands in Bataan and Corregidor in late 1941 and 1942. See Elizabeth M. Norman, *We Band of Angels: The Untold Story of American Nurses Trapped on Bataan by the Japanese* (New York: Random House, 1999).

[12] Lewenson, *Taking Charge*, 139.

[13] "Protest Loss of Pay: Army Nurses in Captivity Off Rolls, Comptroller Says," *Washington Post*, September 2, 1918.

[14] Robb Willer and Matthew Feinberg, "The Key to Political Persuasion" *New York Times*, November 15, 2015.

[15] Dock, et al., *History of American Red Cross Nursing*, 510.

[16] "Care of Nurses Taken By the Enemy," *American Journal of Nursing* 19, no. 5 (February 1919): 372-373.

[17] "Protest Loss of Pay: Army Nurses in Captivity Off Rolls, Comptroller Says," *Washington Post*: September 2, 1918.

[18] "The American Medical And Surgical History of the War," *Army and Navy Register* 64, no. 1999 (November 9, 1918), 528.

[19] Dock, et al., *History of American Red Cross Nursing*: 1065.

[20] "Army Nurses Ask Congress to Accord Them Official Rank," *New York Tribune*, February 16, 1919.

[21] "Army Nurses to Ask Congress for Military Rank," *New York Tribune*, September 17, 1918.

[22] Helen Hoy Greeley, "Rank for Nurses," *American Journal of Nursing* 14, no. 11 (August 1919): 840.

[23] *Proceedings of the Twenty-fifth Annual Convention of the National League of Nursing Education in Chicago on June 24 to 28, 1918* (Baltimore: Williams and Wilkins Company, 1919), 196.

[24] "Editorials," *Johns Hopkins Nurses Alumnae Magazine* 18, no. 2 (May 1919): 48-49.

[25] Gertrude Bowling, "Side-Lights on Life With a Shock Team," *Johns Hopkins Nurses Alumnae Magazine* 18, no. 2 (May 1919): 69.

[26] "Army Nurses to Ask Congress for Military Rank," *New York Tribune*, September 17, 1918.

[27] "Bill Would Grant Pay to U.S. Nurses Captured by Foe," *New York Tribune*, September 3, 1918.

[28] Sarnecky, *A History of the U.S. Army Nurse Corps*, 147.

[29] "Army Nurses to Ask Congress for Military Rank," *New York Tribune*, September 17, 1918.

[30] Flanagan, *One Strong Voice: The Story of the American Nurses' Association*, 427.

CHAPTER THIRTEEN

[1] *Johns Hopkins Nurses Alumnae Magazine* 35, no. 3 (July 1936): 158-159.

[2] Ibid.

[3] Ibid.

[4] Alice Fitzgerald, "Clara D. Noyes – An Appreciation," *The Trained Nurse and Hospital Review* 97, no. 1 (July 1936): 21.

[5] *Johns Hopkins Nurses Alumnae Magazine* 35, no. 3 (July 1936): 158-159.

[6] Ruth Agnes Abeling, "Forget Yourself," *Portsmouth Daily Times* (Portsmouth, OH), October 31, 1921.

[7] Ibid.

[8] "Queen of All the Nurses," Uncited Press Clipping in Red Cross Files. Records of the American National Red Cross, 1881-2008, Series: Historical Nurse Files, 1916-1959. Folder: Clara D. Noyes, Red Cross Badge No. 6215.

[9] "Noyes, Clara Dutton (1869-1936)," McHenry, Robert, ed., *Famous American Women: A Biographical Dictionary from Colonial Times to the Present* (Mineola, NY: Dover Publications, Inc., 1983), 305-306.

[10] Kernodle, *The Red Cross Nurse in Action*, 244.

[11] Ibid, 242-243.

[12] Clara D. Noyes, "Subnurses? Why Not Subdoctors?" *Pictorial Review*, no. 28 (December 1921), 78-80.

[13] "Sub-Nurses and Sub-Doctors," *The Medical Standard* 45, no. 2 (February 1922): 9.

[14] Kernodle, *The Red Cross Nurse in Action*, 243.

[15] Pryor, *Clara Barton: Professional Angel*, 341.

[16] Johns et al., *The Johns Hopkins School of Nursing: 1889-1949*, 76.

[17] Betty Frandsen, "Nursing Leadership: Management and Leadership Styles," a publication of the American Association of Nurse Assessment Coordination, 2014, accessed October 13, 2015, http://www.aanac.org/docs/white-papers/2013-nursing-leadership---management-leadership-styles.pdf?sfvrsn=6.

[18] The NOPHN allowed non-nurses in its membership, which complicated some of the governance rules with its ANA affiliation. The ANA only allowed nurses on its board, and only nurses were permitted as voting members of the ANA, requiring NOPHN corporate members to choose nurse delegates from within their organizations to serve as voting members on ANA matters. See M. Louise Fitzpatrick, *The National Organization for Public Health Nursing, 1912-1952: Development of A Practice Field* (New York: National League for Nursing, 1975).

[19] Fitzpatrick, *The National Organization for Public Health Nursing, 1912-1952*, 58-59.

[20] Ibid, 59.

[21] Clara D. Noyes, "Department of Red Cross Nursing," *American Journal of Nursing* 21, no. 3 (December 1920): 169.

[22] Kernodle, *The Red Cross Nurse in Action*, 357-359.

CHAPTER FOURTEEN

[1] Clara D. Noyes, "The Red Cross," *American Journal of Nursing* 19, no. 5 (February 1919): 367.

[2] "Tells of Red Cross Work: Prominent Executive Talks to Luncheon Guests," *Los Angeles Times*, July 9, 1922.

[3] Dock et al., *History of American Red Cross Nursing*, 1135.

[4] American Red Cross, *The American National Red Cross Annual Report for the Fiscal Year Ended June 30, 1921* (Washington, DC: American Red Cross, 1921), 56.

[5] "Miss Noyes to Inspect Work Abroad," *The Red Cross Bulletin* 4, no. 39 (September 20, 1920): 8.

[6] Clara D. Noyes, "The School of Nursing at Sofia Bulgaria," July 1925 (according to a penciled note on the document). Records of the American National Red Cross 1917–1934, Record Group 200, folder 963.52, "Bulgaria, Sofia, School for Nurses Special Reports, 1925-33," 8.

[7] Clara D. Noyes, "Department of Red Cross Nursing: American Red Cross Nurses in Foreign Lands," *American Journal of Nursing* 28, no. 5 (May 1928): 509.

[8] Ibid.

[9] American Red Cross, *The American National Red Cross Annual Report for the Fiscal Year Ended June 30, 1921* (Washington, DC: American Red Cross, 1921), 59.

[10] "Tells of Red Cross Work: Prominent Executive Talks to Luncheon Guests," *Los Angeles Times*, July 9, 1922.

[11] "Foreign Nursing Impressions: Miss Noyes Writes of Experiences on Her Tour of Inspection in European Countries," *The Red Cross Bulletin* 4, No. 48 (November 22, 1920): 6.

[12] Clara D. Noyes, "Department of Red Cross Nursing: The Schools of Nursing in the Old World (Prague)," *American Journal of Nursing* 22, no. 6 (March 1922): 445.

[13] "Foreign Nursing Impressions: Miss Noyes Writes of Experiences on Her Tour of Inspection in European Countries," *The Red Cross Bulletin* 4, no. 48 (November 22, 1920): 6.

[14] Clara D. Noyes, "Department of Red Cross Nursing: The Schools of Nursing in the Old World (Prague)": 445.

[15] Dock, et al., *History of American Red Cross Nursing*, 1151.

[16] Clara D. Noyes, "Department of Red Cross Nursing: The Schools of Nursing in the Old World (Prague)": 448.

[17] Clara D. Noyes, "Department of Red Cross Nursing," *American Journal of Nursing* 21, no. 8 (May 1921): 552.

[18] Ibid, 554.

[19] Ibid, 557.

[20] "Notables of Nursing and Medical Professions Assemble to Honor War Service Women," *San Francisco Chronicle*, July 8, 1922.

[21] Dock, et al., *History of American Red Cross Nursing*, 1158.

[22] Ibid, 1160.

[23] Red Cross files identify the anonymous nurse as Miss Hughes of Milton, Massachusetts, who was Frederick A. Delano's niece, according to a memo filed December 30, 1920 from Ernest Bicknell. Records of the American National Red Cross 1917–1934, Record Group 200, folder 947.52, "Poland, Warsaw, Training Schools for Nurses."

[24] Clara D. Noyes, "The Schools of Nursing in the Old World: Warsaw," *American Journal of Nursing* 22, no. 7 (April 1922): 539.

[25] Clara D. Noyes, "The Schools of Nursing in the Old World: Warsaw, Part II," *American Journal of Nursing* 8, no. 22 (May 1922): 633.

[26] "Bulgaria (Leaves from the Note Book of Miss Noyes)." Records of the American National Red Cross 1917–1934, Record Group 200, folder 963.52, "Bulgaria, Sofia, School for Nurses, 1920-25," 5.

[27] Dock et al., *History of American Red Cross Nursing*, 1168.

[28] Ibid.

[29] Ibid, 1175.

[30] "Recent Tour of Miss Noyes and Miss Hay to Various Commissions in Europe," Paris, December 30, 1920. Records of the American National Red Cross 1917–1934, Record Group 200, folder 940.11/06, "Department of Nursing Visits and Inspection Trips."

[31] Ibid.

[32] Dock et al., *History of American Red Cross Nursing*, 1184-1186.

[33] American Red Cross, *The American National Red Cross Annual Report for the Fiscal Year Ended June 30, 1921* (Washington, DC: American Red Cross, 1921), 57.

[34] Clara D. Noyes, "The Red Cross: Establishment of Foreign Training Schools," *American Journal of Nursing* 19, no. 12 (September 1919): 948.

[35] "Revolution in Japan Pending, Red Cross Nurse Says," *Ogden Standard-Examiner* (Ogden, UT), September 4, 1920.

[36] Ida F. Butler to Anna Tittman, 14 September 1920. Records of the American National Red Cross, 1881-2008, Series: Historical Nurse Files, 1916-1959. Folder "Tittman, Anna Louise," Red Cross Badge No. 6072.

[37] Ibid.

[38] Anna Tittman to Ida F. Butler, 27 September 1920. Records of the American National Red Cross, 1881-2008, Series: Historical Nurse Files, 1916-1959. Folder "Tittman, Anna Louise," Red Cross Badge No. 6072.

[39] Ida F. Butler to Anna Tittman, 29 September 1920. Records of the American National Red Cross, 1881-2008, Series: Historical Nurse Files, 1916-1959. Folder "Tittman, Anna Louise," Red Cross Badge No. 6072.

[40] Dock et al., *History of American Red Cross Nursing*, 933.

[41] Clara D. Noyes, "The Siberian Commission," *American Journal of Nursing* 20, no. 2 (November 1919): 134.

[42] Ibid, 135.

[43] Leonard A. Humphreys, *The Way of the Heavenly Sword: The Japanese Army in the 1920s* (Stanford, CA: Stanford University Press, 1995), 26.

[44] Ibid, 28.

[45] "Bristol Chapter Represented at Red Cross Meeting," *The Bristol Daily Courier* (Bristol, PA), May 13, 1921.

[46] Ibid.

[47] "Notables of Nursing and Medical Professions Assemble to Honor War Service Women," *San Francisco Chronicle*, July 8, 1922.

[48] Ibid.

[49] Ibid.

[50] Clara D. Noyes, "Department of Red Cross Nursing," *American Journal of Nursing* 21, no. 6 (March 1921): 392.

[51] R. Indie Albaugh, Chairman Special Committee of the Joint National Committee of the ANA, NLNE and NOPH, to Susan C. Francis, Director of Nursing for the Pennsylvania-Delaware Division of the American Red Cross, 18 February 1920. The American Nurses Association Collection, Howard Gotlieb Archival Research Center at Boston University, N 87, box 180, folder 7.

[52] "Dedication of the American Nurses' Memorial, Florence Nightingale School, Bordeaux, France," *American Journal of Nursing* 22, no. 10 (July 1922): 799.

[53] Clara D. Noyes, "To the Bordeaux School: A Message to the Florence Nightingale School, Bordeaux, France, Upon the Occassion of the Dedication of the Completed Memorial June 25, 1931," *American Journal of Nursing* 31, no. 9 (September 1931): 1059.

[54] Dock, et al., *History of American Red Cross Nursing*, 527.

[55] "Their Standards Improved Maintains French Nurse," *Washington Post*, April 27, 1934.

56 Clara D. Noyes, "Department of Red Cross Nursing: Visiting Bulgaria," *American Journal of Nursing* 26, no. 3 (March 1926): 219-222.

57 Ibid.

58 Clara D. Noyes, "The School of Nursing at Sofia Bulgaria," July 1925 (according to a penciled note on the document). Records of the American National Red Cross 1917–1934, Record Group 200, folder 963.52, "Bulgaria, Sofia, School for Nurses Special Reports, 1925-33," 15.

59 Clara D. Noyes, "Department of Red Cross Nursing: Visiting Bulgaria," *American Journal of Nursing* 26, no. 3 (March 1926): 219-222.

60 Clara D. Noyes to Hazel Goff, 6 October 1925. Records of the American National Red Cross 1917–1934, Record Group 200, folder 963.52, "Bulgaria, Sofia, School for Nurses Special Reports, 1925-33."

61 Clara D. Noyes, "Department of Red Cross Nursing: Visiting Bulgaria": 222.

62 Helen L. Bridge to Clara D. Noyes, 4 June 1923. Records of the American National Red Cross 1917–1934, Record Group 200, folder 947.52, "Poland, Warsaw, Training Schools for Nurses."

63 Ernest Bicknell to Clara Noyes, undated cover note attached to a series of letters from Helen L. Bridge in the fall of 1922. Records of the American National Red Cross 1917–1934, Record Group 200, folder 947.52, "Poland, Warsaw, Training Schools for Nurses."

64 Albert Ross Hill, Vice Chair in Charge of Foreign Operations, to Ida Butler, 15 September 1922. Records of the

American National Red Cross 1917–1934, Record Group 200, folder 947.52, "Poland, Warsaw, Training Schools for Nurses."

[65] Clara D. Noyes, "Report to the Vice-Chairman of the American Red Cross on Visit to Schools of Nursing and other Red Cross Nursing Activities in Poland." The report is undated but follows an August 3, 1923 visit to Warsaw. Records of the American National Red Cross 1917–1934, Record Group 200, folder 947.52, "Poland, Warsaw, Training Schools for Nurses."

[66] Ibid.

[67] Ibid.

[68] Clara D. Noyes to Helen L. Bridge, 7 September 1923. Records of the American National Red Cross 1917–1934, Record Group 200, folder 947.52, "Poland, Warsaw, Training Schools for Nurses."

[69] Helena Witkiewicz, Chairman of the WNS Graduates' Circle, "History of the Warsaw Nursing School in Warsaw, 78 Koszykowa Street," accessed February 2, 2016, http://www.wmpp.org.pl/en/nursing-schools/the-warsaw-nursing-school.html.

[70] "Extracted from Letter from Miss Hay to Miss Noyes Mar. 23, 1922" and "Ans. by Miss Noyes April 20, 1922." Records of the American National Red Cross 1917–1934, Record Group 200, folder 958.52, "Commission to Czecho-Slovakia, W.W. I, Prague School of Nursing, July 1922-Dec. 1926."

[71] Clara D. Noyes to Marion Parsons, 11 October 1922. Records of the American National Red Cross 1917–1934, Record Group 200, folder 958.52, "Commission to

Czecho-Slovakia, W.W. I, Prague School of Nursing, July 1922-Dec. 1926."

72 See Clara D. Noyes to Ernest P. Bicknell, 17 March 1923 and Ernest P. Bicknell to Clara D. Noyes, 16 March 1923. Records of the American National Red Cross 1917–1934, Record Group 200, folder 958.52, "Commission to Czecho-Slovakia, W.W. I, Prague School of Nursing, July 1922-Dec. 1926."

73 Clara D. Noyes to Ernest P. Bicknell, 13 March 1923. Records of the American National Red Cross 1917–1934, Record Group 200, folder 958.52 "Commission to Czecho-Slovakia, W.W. I, Prague School of Nursing, July 1922-Dec. 1926."

74 "Student News: Czechoslovakian Students," *American Journal of Nursing* 48, no. 5 (May 1948): 343.

75 Kristina Popova, in discussion with the author, February 20 and 27, 2016.

CHAPTER FIFTEEN

1 Clara D. Noyes, "Department of Red Cross Nursing: Widespread Disasters," *American Journal of Nursing* 26, no. 12 (December 1926): 967.

2 Clara D. Noyes, "Department of Red Cross Nursing: Tributes to Red Cross Nurses in the Near East," *American Journal of Nursing* 24, no. 7 (April 1924): 567.

[3] "Woman Heads Red Cross Aid: World-Wide Activities Center at Desk of Miss Clara D. Noyes," *Milwaukee Journal*, September 7, 1927.

[4] Ibid.

[5] "This Button and That," *The Evening News* (Harrisburg, Pennsylvania), August 25, 1927.

[6] Clara D. Noyes, "Department of Red Cross Nursing: Red Cross Nurses Finish Work in Mississippi Valley," *American Journal of Nursing* 27, no. 10 (October 1927): 857.

[7] American Red Cross, *The Mississippi Valley Flood Disaster of 1927: Official Report of the Relief Operations* (Washington, DC: American National Red Cross, 1929), 7.

[8] Ibid, 6.

[9] Ibid, "Appendix VII: Persons Cared For In Camp," 127-130.

[10] Ibid, 4.

[11] Ibid, 104.

[12] "Out of Flood Depths Rises People's Hope," *Warren Tribune* (Warren, OH), October 24, 1927.

[13] American Red Cross, *The Mississippi Valley Flood Disaster of 1927: Official Report of the Relief Operations* (Washington, DC: American National Red Cross, 1929), 111.

[14] "Miss I. Malinde Havey, Red Cross Public Health Nursing Director and World War Nurse Heroine Dies in Boston," The American Red Cross News Service (press release), September 8, 1938. Records of the American National Red Cross, 1881-2008, Series: Historical Nurse Files, 1916-1959. Folder "I Malinde Havey," Red Cross Badge No. 6004.

[15] American Red Cross, *The Mississippi Valley Flood Disaster of 1927: Official Report of the Relief Operations*, 6.

[16] Clara D. Noyes, "Department of Red Cross Nursing: Red Cross Nurses Finish Work in Mississippi Valley": 858.

[17] I. Malinde Havey's Narrative Report of Nursing Activities Week Ending July 9, 1927. Records of the American National Red Cross 1917–1934, Record Group 200, folder DR 224.08, "Mississippi River Valley Flood Week ending July 2."

[18] Ibid.

[19] Records of the American National Red Cross 1917–1934, Record Group 200, folder DR 224.08, "Mississippi Valley Flood 3/30/27 Reports and Statistics."

[20] "Report of the Sub-Committee of the Colored Advisory Commission On the Mississippi Flood Disaster." Records of the American National Red Cross 1917–1934, Record Group 200, folder DR-224.91/08, "Mississippi River Valley Flood, Negro Commission June 1927 Survey," 49.

[21] James Frieser to All Chapter Chairmen, 3 August 1927. Records of the American National Red Cross 1917–1934, Record Group 200, folder DR-224. 08, "Mississippi River Valley Flood 3/30/27 Reports and Statistics."

[22] John M. Barry, *Rising Tide: The Great Mississippi Flood of 1927 and How It Changed America* (New York: Simon and Schuster, 1997).

[23] Ibid, 414.

[24] Ibid, 311.

[25] Ibid, 315.

[26] Herbert Hoover to Walter White, 21 June 1927. Records of the American National Red Cross 1917–1934, Record Group 200, folder DR 224.91, "Negro Relations."

[27] J. Winston Harrington, "Refugees Herded Like Cattle To Stop Escape From Peonage," *Chicago Defender*, May 7, 1927.

[28] Undated confidential memorandum. Records of the American National Red Cross 1917–1934, Record Group 200, folder DR 224.91, "Negro Relations."

[29] W.E.B. Dubois, "The Flood, The Red Cross and the National Guard," *The Crisis*, February 1928.

[30] "Report of the Sub-Committee of the Colored Advisory Commission On the Mississippi Flood Disaster." Records of the American National Red Cross 1917–1934, Record Group 200, Folder DR-224.91/08, "Mississippi River Valley Flood, Negro Commission June 1927 Survey," 26.

[31] Ibid.

[32] Ibid, 34.

[33] Ibid, 36.

[34] Ibid, 35.

[35] Ibid, 37.

[36] Ibid, 39.

[37] N.R. Bancroft, Major, A.R.C. to Henry Baker, subject "Refugees in camps," 14 May 1927. Records of the American National Red Cross 1917–1934, Record Group 200, folder DR 224.91, "Negro Relations."

[38] DeWitt Smith to George E. Scott, 20 October 1928. Records of the American National Red Cross 1917–1934, Record Group 200, folder DR 224.91 "Negro Relations."

[39] A.L. Schafer to Dewitt Smith, 2 June 1927. Records of the American National Red Cross 1917–1934, Record Group 200, folder DR-224.91, "Mississippi River Valley Flood 3/30/27, Criticisms and Controversial Subjects."

[40] "Hoover Meets Colored Advisory Flood Commission; Abuses to Be Corrected, Red Cross Does Good Job," Special Release, 14 June 1927. Records of the American National Red Cross 1917–1934, Record Group 200, folder DR 224.91, "Negro Relations."

[41] "Report of the Sub-Committee of the Colored Advisory Commission On the Mississippi Flood Disaster." Records of the American National Red Cross 1917–1934, Record Group 200, folder DR-224.91/08, "Mississippi River Valley Flood, Negro Commission June 1927 Survey," 40.

[42] Ibid, 43.

[43] "Mississippi Valley Flood 1927" (report). Records of the American National Red Cross 1917–1934, Record Group 200, folder DR 224.08 "Mississippi River Valley Flood 3/30/27 Reports and Statistics."

CHAPTER SIXTEEN

[1] Joachim Fest, *Hitler* (1973; English transl., New York: Harcourt Brace & Company, 1974), 483.

[2] Greenberg, David, "Help! Call the White House!: How the 1927 Mississippi Flood Created Big Government," Salon.com, September 5, 2006, accessed January 5, 2016, http://www.slate.com/articles/news_and_politics/history _lesson/2006/09/help_call_the_white_house.html.

[3] Phoebe Pollitt and Camille N. Reese, "Nursing and the New Deal: We Met the Challenge," *Public Health Nursing* 14, no. 6 (December 1997): 373–382.

[4] Clara D. Noyes, "Department of Red Cross Nursing: Nature at Her Worst," *American Journal of Nursing* 36, no. 6 (June 1936): 624.

[5] Barbara Tomblin, *G.I. Nightingales: The Army Nurse Corps in World War II* (Lexington, KY: The University Press of Kentucky, 1996), 188.

[6] Ira Rutkow, *Seeking the Cure: A History of Medicine in America* (New York: Scribner, a Division of Simon & Schuster, 2010), 216.

[7] Fest, *Hitler*, 487-490.

[8] Ibid, 506.

[9] Richard Bessel, *Nazism and War* (New York: Modern Library Paperback Edition, 2006), 54.

[10] Kristina Popova, *The Joy of Service: Biopolitics and Biographies Between New York, Sofia and Grna Dzhumaja in the First Half of the 20th Century.* CAS Working Paper Series No. 5/2013: Sofia 2013. Advanced Academia programme, a project of the Center for Advanced Study Sofia, 37.

[11] Ibid, 39.

[12] Ibid, 55.

[13] "Graduating Nurses Hear Miss Noyes," *Hartford Courant*, June 1, 1932.

[14] Ibid.

[15] Ibid.

[16] James Noyes (Clara Noyes's nephew), in discussion with the author, November 13, 2015.

[17] Ibid.

[18] "Miss Clara Noyes, Red Cross Head, Dies Today," *The Day* (New London, CT), June 3, 1936.

[19] "The Passing of a Great Leader," *Red Cross Courier* 16, no. 1 (July 1936): 11-12.

[20] The address of the former hospital is listed among "Benevolent Institutions" in various Congressional Documents.

[21] "Miss Clara Noyes of Red Cross Dead," *New York Times*, June 4, 1936.

[22] "The Passing of a Great Leader," *Red Cross Courier*: 11-12.

[23] *Johns Hopkins Nurses Alumnae Magazine* 35, no. 3 (July 1936): 166.

[24] "She Sleeps a Holy Sleep," *British Journal of Nursing* vol. 84 (August 1936), 212.

[25] "Miss Noyes' Body Will Be Brought Here For Burial," *The Day* (New London, CT), June 4, 1936.

[26] Ida F. Butler to Mary M. Roberts, 9 June 1936. Records of the American National Red Cross, 1881-2008, Series:

Historical Nurse Files, 1916-1959. Folder "Clara D. Noyes," Red Cross Badge No. 6215.

[27] "She Sleeps a Holy Sleep," *British Journal of Nursing* vol. 84 (August 1936), 212.

[28] Clara D. Noyes, "Department of Red Cross Nursing," *American Journal of Nursing* 36, no. 7 (July 1936): 730.

[29] Ibid.

[30] "Editorials: Clara Dutton Noyes," *American Journal of Nursing* 36, no. 7 (July 1936): 701.

[31] Alice Fitzgerald, "Clara D. Noyes – An Appreciation," *The Trained Nurse and Hospital Review* 97, no. 1 (July 1936): 21.

[32] "Reserve Nurses – Army Nurse Corps: Assignments," *Trained Nurse and Hospital Review* 60, no. 1 (January 1918): 46.

[33] See "In the Nursing World: Army Nurse Corps," *Trained Nurse and Hospital Review* 61, no. 2 (August 1918): 112-115; and *Maryland in the World War 1917-1919 Military and Naval Service Records In Two Volumes and Case of Maps Volume II* (Baltimore: Maryland War Records Commission, 1933), 2331.

[34] "Nurse Delegation Here For Tribute to Red Cross Head," *The Day* (New London, CT), June 6, 1936.

[35] "Press Notices Upon The Death of Miss Noyes," *Johns Hopkins Nurses Alumnae Magazine* 35, no. 3 (July 1936): 161.

[36] "A Resolution." Records of the American National Red Cross, 1881-2008, Series: Historical Nurse Files, 1916-1959. Folder: Clara D. Noyes, Red Cross Badge No. 6215.

[37] Anabel Parker M'Cann, "American Nurse Wins Memorial Scholarship," *New York Sun*, August 11, 1938.

BIBLIOGRAPHY

Clara Noyes was a prolific writer. The research for this book was helped by the wealth of resources written in her own words: her regular contributions to the *American Journal of Nursing*; innumerable letters she wrote to and from nurses in the field; and, especially, the seminal *History of American Red Cross Nursing*, for which she was chairman of the editorial committee and coauthor along with Lavinia L. Dock, Sarah Elizabeth Pickett, Fannie F. Clement, Elizabeth G. Fox and Anna R. Van Meter. These primary sources were enhanced by several contextual examinations of the American Red Cross, nursing, and general history books on this period that formed a core of research about her life, along with the thousands of newspaper articles where Clara Noyes and her Red Cross work were examined.

Newspapers

"157 Pass 1st Bi-Racial Examination." *Washington Post,* July 14, 1954.

Abeling, Ruth Agnes, "Forget Yourself." *Portsmouth Daily Times* (Portsmouth, OH), October 31, 1921.

"A Big Walnut Tree." *New York Times,* January 28, 1894.

"Army Nurses Ask Congress to Accord Them Official Rank." *New York Tribune,* February 16, 1919.

"Army Nurses Honor Memory of Chief." *New York Tribune*, May 9, 1919.

"Army Nurses to Ask Congress for Military Rank." *New York Tribune*, September 17, 1918.

"Attends Seattle Meeting: Miss Clara Noyes Leaves for Conclave of Registered Nurses." *Washington Post*, June 17, 1922.

"Bill Would Grant Pay to U.S. Nurses Captured by Foe." *New York Tribune*, September 3, 1918.

"Bristol Chapter Represented at Red Cross Meeting." *The Bristol Daily Courier* (Bristol, PA), May 13, 1921.

Bryant, H.E.C. "Secretary Daniels Will Review Red Cross Parade in New York." *News and Observer* (Raleigh, NC), October 3, 1917.

"Clara D. Noyes." editorial, *Wilkes-Barre Record* (Wilkes-Barre, PA), June 9, 1936.

"College Grads in Negro WAC Band, Chorus." *Chicago Defender*, December 4, 1943.

"Davidson Remarried: Former Mayor of Baltimore Weds Nurse with Whom He Eloped." *Washington Post*, November 16, 1905.

"Discredited by Mother: Mrs. Noyes Does Not Believe Daughter Eloped with Davidson." *Washington Post*, May 25, 1905.

Du Bois, W.E.B. "The Flood, The Red Cross and the National Guard." *The Crisis*, February 1928.

"Ex-Mayor Davidson Weds: Baltimorean Marries the Nurse with Whom He Eloped in This City." *New York Times*, November 16, 1905.

"Former Mayor and a Trained Nurse Elope." *San Francisco Call*, May 24, 1905.

"Graduating Nurses Hear Miss Noyes." *Hartford Courant*, June 1, 1932.

"Happenings of Interest in Washington Society Circles." *Washington Post*, May 18, 1933.

Harrington, J. Winston. "Refugees Herded Like Cattle To Stop Escape From Peonage." *Chicago Defender*, May 7, 1927.

"Maryland Brevities." *The Evening Times* (Washington, DC). November 7, 1898.

M'Cann, Anabel Parker. "American Nurse Wins Memorial Scholarship." *New York Sun*, August 11, 1938.

McFadden, Robert D. "Ex-Rep. Jeanette Rankin Dies; First Woman in Congress, 92." *New York Times*, May 20, 1973.

Moriarty, Edith. "With the Women of Today." *The Charlotte News*, June 4, 1922.

"Miss Clara Noyes of Red Cross Dead." *New York Times*, June 4, 1936.

"Miss Clara Noyes, Red Cross Head, Dies Today." *The Day* (New London, CT), June 3, 1936.

"Miss Noyes' Body Will Be Brought Here For Burial." *The Day* (New London, CT), June 4, 1936.

"Miss Olive Boggess Marries." *Chicago Defender*, October 4, 1919.

"Mrs. Davidson Free: Court Grants Her Divorce and $50,000 Alimony." *Washington Post*, November 11, 1905.

"Mrs. M'Adoo Lauds Women in the War: President's Daughter, Speaking for Loan, Praises Heroism of Red Cross Nurses." *New York Times*, April 24, 1919.

"National Investigation of Slander Against Red Cross." *Los Angeles Times*, January 6, 1918.

"News of the State: Events of Interest Here and There Yesterday and Today." *The News* (Frederick, MD), May 29, 1902.

"No Conservation of Life of Child: Midwife not recognized." *Huntington Herald* (Huntington, IN), September 30, 1912.

"Notables of Nursing and Medical Professions Assemble to Honor War Service Women." *San Francisco Chronicle*, July 8, 1922.

"Nurse Delegation Here For Tribute to Red Cross Head." *The Day* (New London, CT), June 6, 1936.

"Nurses in Convention Condemn Kitchen Duty." *Chicago Daily Tribune*, June 5, 1912.

"Old Lyme: Red Cross Work Described." *The Day* (New London, CT), September 5, 1917.

"Only Third of Nurses Ready Used in Camps." *Chicago Daily Tribune*, January 26, 1918.

"Out of Flood Depths Rises People's Hope." *Warren Tribune* (Warren, OH), October 24, 1927.

"Pacifists in Suffrage Ranks Object to Preparedness Plan." *Brooklyn Daily Eagle*, February 21, 1917.

"Protest Loss of Pay: Army Nurses in Captivity Off Rolls, Comptroller Says." *Washington Post*, September 2, 1918.

"Queen of All the Nurses." Uncited Press Clipping in Red Cross Files. Records of the American National Red Cross, 1881-2008, Series: Historical Nurse Files, 1916-1959. Folder: Clara D. Noyes, Red Cross Badge No. 6215.

"Red Cross Plans Base Hospitals: Miss Clara Noyes Reveals Fact in Address to Women's Section of Navy League." *The Washington Times*, March 7, 1917.

"Revolution in Japan Pending, Red Cross Nurse Says." *Ogden Standard-Examiner* (Ogden, UT), September 4, 1920.

"Scarcity of Nurses: Hospitals Have Trouble in Recruiting Training Classes." *New York Tribune*, May 18, 1912.

"Suffrage Wins in the House Without One Vote to Spare; Democrats Divided on Issue." *New York Tribune*, January 11, 1918.

"Tells of Red Cross Work: Prominent Executive Talks to Luncheon Guests." *Los Angeles Times*, July 9, 1922.

"Their Standards Improved Maintains French Nurse." *Washington Post*, April 27, 1934.

"This Button and That." *The Evening News* (Harrisburg, Pennsylvania), August 25, 1927.

"To Guide Red Cross Nurses: Head of the Bellevue School is Made Superintendent." *New York Times,* August 1, 1916.

"Use Red Cross Nurses As Lure: Girls Promised Positions as Nurses Fall Victims to Bad Men." *Washington Post,* June 23, 1918.

"WAC Band Gets Final Okeh By War Department." *Chicago Defender,* September 2, 1944.

Willer, Robb and Matthew Feinberg. "The Key to Political Persuasion." *New York Times,* November 15, 2015.

"Win Their Diplomas." *Washington Post,* June 9, 1913.

"Woman Heads Red Cross Aid: World-Wide Activities Center at Desk of Miss Clara D. Noyes." *Milwaukee Journal,* September 7, 1927.

"World War Red Cross Nursing Director Visitor During Illinois Convention Here." *Peoria Journal Transcript* (Peoria, IL), October 14, 1934.

Bible Verses

Acts 16: 6-10 (Revised Standard Version).

Genesis 5:21-24 (Revised Standard Version).

Genesis 8:4 (Revised Standard Version)

Magazines

"Bellevue Gives Another Official." *American Red Cross Magazine* 11, no. 1 (1916): 355.

Catt, Carrie Chapman. "Poison Propaganda." *The Woman Citizen*, no. 14 (May 31, 1924): 32-33.

"Foreign Nursing Impressions: Miss Noyes Writes of Experiences on Her Tour of Inspection in European Countries." *The Red Cross Bulletin* 4, no. 48 (November 22, 1920): 6.

"Miss Noyes to Inspect Red Cross Work Abroad." *The Red Cross Bulletin* 4, no. 39 (September 20, 1920), 8.

Noyes, Clara D. "Subnurses? Why Not Subdoctors?" republished in the *Indianapolis Medical Journal* 24, no. 21 (December 1921): 315-16. Originally published in *Pictorial Review*, no. 28 (December 1921).

Noyes, Roger L. "Home Care Emergency Response: Hurricane Sandy Lessons Learned and Actions Taken." *Caring Magazine* (June 2013): 10-14.

"Official Program, National Convention of the Women's Party, Washington, DC, February 15-18, 1921." *Suffragist* 9, no. 1 (January to February 1921): 342.

"Speeches Through Radiotelephone Inspire New York Crowds." *Electrical Review* (May 31, 1919): 895-897.

"The Passing of a Great Leader." *Red Cross Courier* 7, no. 1 (July 1936): 11-12.

1930 United States Census, s.v. "Nelon [*sic*], Senetta B.," Precinct 2, District of Columbia, Washington, April 13 to 15, 1930.

American Red Cross. *The American National Red Cross Annual Report for the Fiscal Year Ended June 30, 1918* (Washington, DC: American Red Cross, 1918).

American Red Cross. *The American National Red Cross Annual Report for the Fiscal Year Ended June 30, 1921* (Washington, DC: American Red Cross, 1921).

American Red Cross. *The Mississippi Valley Flood Disaster of 1927: Official Report of the Relief Operations* (Washington, DC: American National Red Cross, 1929).

"Bulgaria (Leaves from the Note Book of Miss Noyes)." Records of the American National Red Cross 1917–1934, Record Group 200, folder 963.52, "Bulgaria, Sofia, School for Nurses, 1920-25."

"Bureau of Investigation: Detection of Violations of Federal Laws." *Annual Report of the Attorney General of the United States for the Year 1917* (Washington, DC: Government Printing Office, 1917).

Department of Justice Report, "Re: Eleanor Von Boehmer, German Neutrality Matter," completed by Agent

Arthur T. Bagley, 24 June 1916. Records of the American National Red Cross 1917–1934, Record Group 200, folder 109.1, "Sabotage – World War #1."

District of Columbia, Select Marriages, 1830-1921. Salt Lake City, Utah: FamilySearch, 2013. FHL Film Number: 2051925, Reference ID: 93377.

Electronic Army Serial Number Merged File, ca. 1938-1946 (Enlistment Records). National Archives and Records Administration, box 0021, film reel no. 1.21#.

Havey, I. Malinde, Narrative Report of Nursing Activities Week Ending July 9, 1927. Records of the American National Red Cross 1917–1934, Record Group 200, folder DR 224.08, "Mississippi River Valley Flood Week ending July 2."

"Itinerary of Miss Noyes' Tour, 1917-18." Records of the American National Red Cross, 1881-2008, Series: Historical Nurse Files, 1916-1959. Folder: Clara D. Noyes, Red Cross Badge No. 6215.

Laboratory Hospital Center, Savenay France (May 12, 1919). Death Certification, signed by Lt. Col. J.S. Coulter. Series: Historical Nurse Files, 1916-1959. Jane A. Delano files: 301, folder labeled "Delano, Jane, April 1-23, 1919."

Maryland. Cecil County. Deed of Sale. Folio 242, no. 7, April 23, 1864. Cecil County Circuit Court Land Records.

Maryland. Cecil County. Deed of Sale. Folio 519, no. 2, May 23, 1898. Cecil County Circuit Court Land Records.

Memo with extracts of quotes attributed to Red Cross Vice Chairman Willoughby G. Walling and Frederick C. Monroe, General Manager at Red Cross, 28 January 1919. Records of the American National Red Cross 1917–1934, Record Group 200, folder 803.3, "Epidemics, Influenza, Personnel."

Memo with extracts of quotes attributed to Red Cross War Council Member George B. Case and Charles Scott, Jr., Vice Chairman of the American Red Cross in Charge of Finance, 13 January 1919. Records of the American National Red Cross 1917–1934, Record Group 200, folder 803.3 "Epidemics, Influenza, Personnel."

"Mississippi Valley Flood 1927" (report). Records of the American National Red Cross 1917–1934, Record Group 200, folder DR 224.08, "Mississippi River Valley Flood 3/30/27 Reports and Statistics."

National Association of Colored Graduate Nurses records, 1908-1958. Schomburg Center for Research in Black Culture of the New York Public Library, SC Micro R-6565.

New York State Census, s.v., "Noes, Carrie D. [sic.], Head of Nurses Residence." Election District No. 4, Ward No. 21, New York City.

Noyes, Clara D. "American Nurses' Association: Federal Legislative Measures and the American Nurses' Association." The American Nurses Association

Collection, Howard Gotlieb Archival Research Center at Boston University, N 87, box 328, folder 13.

Noyes, Clara D. "Report to the Vice-Chairman of the American Red Cross on Visit to Schools of Nursing and other Red Cross Nursing Activities in Poland." The report is undated but follows an August 3, 1923 visit to Warsaw. Records of the American National Red Cross 1917–1934, Record Group 200, folder 947.52, "Poland, Warsaw, Training Schools for Nurses."

Noyes, Clara D. "The School of Nursing at Sofia Bulgaria," July 1925 (according to a penciled note on the document). Records of the American National Red Cross 1917–1934, Record Group 200, folder 963.52, "Bulgaria, Sofia, School for Nurses Special Reports, 1925-33."

Undated confidential memorandum. Records of the American National Red Cross 1917–1934, Record Group 200, folder DR 224.91, "Negro Relations."

"Nurses Defended Against Sen. Watson; Col. James R Church, Medical Corps, Quotes Records on Immorality Charges: Article by Gen. Winter, who investigated slanderous report, re-issued here." Records of the American National Red Cross 1917–1934, Record Group 200, folder 109.1, "Nurses – Charged with Immorality 1917-1918."

"Proposed Department of Education: Hearing Before the Committee on Education, House of Representatives, Seventieth Congress, First Session on H.R. 7.

April 25, 26, 27, 28 and May 2, 1928" (Washington, DC: Government Printing Office, 1928).

"Recent Tour of Miss Noyes and Miss Hay to Various Commissions in Europe," Paris, December 30, 1920. Records of the American National Red Cross 1917–1934, Record Group 200, folder 940.11/06, "Department of Nursing Visits and Inspection Trips."

Records of the American National Red Cross 1917–1934, Record Group 200, folder 803.08, "Epidemics, Influenza, Reports and Statistics."

Records of the American National Red Cross 1917–1934, Record Group 200, folder DR 224.08, "Mississippi Valley Flood 3/30/27 Reports and Statistics."

Records of the American National Red Cross 1917–1934, Record Group 200, folder 109.1, "Nurses – Charged with Immorality 1917-1918."

Records of the American National Red Cross, 1881-2008. Series: Historical Nurse Files, 1916-1959. Folder: Clara D. Noyes, Red Cross Badge No. 6215.

Records of the American National Red Cross, 1881-2008. Series: Historical Nurse Files, 1916-1959, Jane A. Delano files: 301, folder labeled "Delano, Jane, April 1-23, 1919."

"Report of the Sub-Committee of the Colored Advisory Commission On the Mississippi Flood Disaster." Records of the American National Red Cross 1917–1934, Record Group 200, folder DR-

224.91/08, "Mississippi River Valley Flood, Negro Commission June 1927 Survey."

"The Influenza Epidemic." Records of the American National Red Cross 1917–1934, Record Group 200, folder 803, "Epidemics, Influenza."

Undated and untitled report. Records of the American National Red Cross 1917–1934, Record Group 200, folder 803.11, "Epidemics, Influenza, Alaska."

Interviews

Noyes, James (Clara Noyes's nephew), in discussion with the author, November 13, 2015.

Popova, Kristina, in discussion with the author, February 20 and 27, 2016.

Books

Barry, John M. *Rising Tide: The Great Mississippi Flood of 1927 and How It Changed America*. New York: Simon and Schuster, 1997.

Bellevue and Allied Hospitals Ninth Annual Report 1910. New York: Lecouver Press Company, 1910.

Bessel, Richard. *Nazism and War*. New York: Modern Library Paperback Edition, 2006.

Birnbach, Nettie and Sandra Beth Lewenson, eds. *Legacy of Leadership: Presidential Addresses from the Super-*

intendents' Society and the National League of Nursing Education, 1894-1952. New York: National League of Nursing Press, 1993.

Cook, William Grant. *William Grant Cook, his ancestors and descendants.* Chicago: Privately Published, 1942.

Coss, Clara, ed. *Lillian D. Wald, Progressive Activist.* New York: Feminist Press of the City University of New York, 1989.

Cunningham, Edward. *The Port Hudson Campaign: 1862-1863.* Baton Rouge, LA: Louisiana State University Press, 1963.

Delano, Daniel, Jr. *Franklin Delano and the Delano Influence.* Pittsburgh, PA: James S. Nudi Publications, 1946.

Dock, Lavinia L., Sarah Pickett, and Clara D. Noyes. *History of American Red Cross Nursing.* New York: Macmillan Company, 1922.

Doolittle, Jan Wilson. *Women's Joint Congressional Committee and the Politics of Materialism, 1920-30.* Champaign, IL: University of Illinois Press, 2007.

Du Bois, W.E.B. *The Souls of Black Folk.* 1903, repr., New York: Bantam Books, 1989.

Dubois, Ellen Carol. *Feminism and Suffrage: The Emergence of an Independent Women's Movement in America, 1848-1869.* Ithaca, NY: Cornell University Press, 1978.

Ellison, Ralph. *Invisible Man.* 1952, repr., New York: Vintage Books, 1990.

Ettinger, Laura E. *Nurse-Midwifery: The Birth of a New American Profession*. Columbus, OH: Ohio State University Press, 2006.

Fest, Joachim. *Hitler*. 1973; English transl., New York: Harcourt Brace & Company, 1974.

Fitzpatrick, M. Louise. *The National Organization for Public Health Nursing, 1912-1952: Development of A Practice Field*. New York: National League for Nursing, 1975.

Garvey, Amy Jacques, ed. *The Philosophy and Opinions of Marcus Garvey, Or, Africa for Africans*. Dover, MA: The Majority Press, 1986.

Flanagan, Lyndia. *One Strong Voice: The Story of the American Nurses' Association*. Kansas City: American Nurses' Association, 1973.

Hemingway, Ernest. *A Farewell To Arms: The Hemingway Library Edition*. 1929; repr., New York: Scribner, 2012.

Humphreys, Leonard A. *The Way of the Heavenly Sword: The Japanese Army in the 1920s*. Stanford, CA: Stanford University Press, 1995.

Irwin, Julia. *Making The World Safe: The American Red Cross and a Nation's Humanitarian Awakening*. Oxford: Oxford University Press, 2013.

Jensen, Kimberly. *Mobilizing Minerva: American Women in the First World War*. Urbana, IL: University of Illinois Press, 2008.

Johns, Ethel and Blanche Pfefferkorn. *The Johns Hopkins School of Nursing: 1889-1949*. Baltimore: Johns Hopkins Press, 1954.

Jones, Heather. *Violence Against Prisoners of War in the First World War: Britain, France and Germany, 1914-1920*. Cambridge: Cambridge University Press, 2011.

Jones, Marian Moser. *American Red Cross from Clara Barton to the New Deal*. Baltimore: Johns Hopkins University Press, 2013.

Kernodle, Portia. *The Red Cross Nurse In Action*. New York: Harper and Brothers, 1949.

Kert, Bernice. *The Hemingway Women*. New York: Norton, 1983.

Lewenson, Sandra Beth. *Taking Charge: Nursing, Suffrage and Feminism in America: 1873-1970*. New York: National League for Nursing Press, 1996.

LeMay, Michael C. *Doctors at the Borders: Immigration and the Rise of Public Health*. Santa Barbara, CA: Prager, 2015.

Maryland in the World War 1917-1919 Military and Naval Service Records In Two Volumes and Case of Maps Volume II. Baltimore: Maryland War Records Commission, 1933.

Malka, Susan Gelfand. *Daring To Care: American Nursing and Second-Wave Feminism*. Chicago: University of Illinois Press, 2007.

McDonald, William, ed. *The Obits: Annual 2012*. New York: Workman Publishing Company, 2011.

McHenry, Robert, ed. *Famous American Women: A Biographical Dictionary from Colonial Times to the Present*. Mineola, NY: Dover Publications, Inc., 1983.

Mundinger, Mary O'Neil. *A Path to Nursing Excellence: The Columbia Experience*. New York: Springer Publishing Company, 2014.

Norman, Elizabeth M. *We Band of Angels: The Untold Story of American Nurses Trapped on Bataan by the Japanese*. New York: Random House, 1999.

Noyes, Clara D. "Service of Women in Time of War." *Twenty-Third Annual Convention of the American Nurses Association, Held at Philadelphia, PA, April 26 to May 2, 1917*. Baltimore: Williams & Wilkins Company, 1917.

Noyes, Henry E. and Harriette E. Noyes. *Genealogical Record of Some Noyes Descendants, Volume II*. 1904; repr. Salem MA: Higgins Book Company, 2015.

Opdycke, Sandra. *The Flu Epidemic of 1918: America's Experience in the Global Health Crisis*. New York: Routledge, 2014.

Pennock, Meta Rutter, ed. *Makers of Nursing History*. New York: Lakeside Publishing Company, 1940.

Proceedings of the Twenty-fifth Annual Convention of the National League of Nursing Education in Chicago on June 24 to 28, 1918. Baltimore: Williams and Wilkins Company, 1919.

Pryor, Elizabeth Brown. *Clara Barton: Professional Angel.* University of Pennsylvania Press, 1987.

Reverby, Susan M. *Ordered to Care: The Dilemma of American Nursing, 1850-1945.* Cambridge: Cambridge University Press, 1987.

Rimby, Susan. *Mira Lloyd Dock and the Progressive Era Conservation Movement.* University Park, PA: Pennsylvania State University Press, 2012.

Rooks, Judith Pence. *Midwifery and Childbirth in America.* Philadelphia: Temple University Press, 1997.

Rutkow, Ira. *Seeking the Cure: A History of Medicine in America.* New York: Scribner, a Division of Simon & Schuster, 2010.

Sandler, Stanley, ed. *Ground Warfare, An International Encyclopedia, Volume I A-G.* Santa Barbara, CA: ABC-CLIO, 2002.

Sarnecky, Mary T. *A History of the U.S. Army Nurse Corps.* Philadelphia: University of Pennsylvania Press, 1999.

Sicherman, Barbara and Carol Hurd Green, eds. *Notable American Women: The Modern Period: a Biographical Dictionary.* Cambridge, MA: The Belknap Press of Harvard University Press, 1980.

Silber, Nina. *Daughters of the Union: Northern Women Fight for the Civil War.* Cambridge, MA: Harvard University Press, 2005.

Slavin, Sarah, ed. *U.S. Women's Interest Groups: Institutional Profiles*. Westport, CT: Greenwood Publishing Group, 1995.

Smith, Norma. *Jeanette Rankin: America's Conscience*. Helena, MT: Montana Historical Society Press, 2002.

Staupers, Mabel Keaton. *No Time For Prejudice: A Story of the Integration of Negroes in Nursing in the United States*. New York: Macmillan Company, 1961.

Tjomsland, Anne, M.D. *Bellevue in France: Anecdotal History of Base Hospital No. 1*. New York: Froben Press, 1941.

Tomblin, Barbara. *G.I. Nightingales: The Army Nurse Corps in World War II*. Lexington, KY: The University Press of Kentucky, 1996.

Tucker, Sherrie. *Swing Shift: "All-Girl" Bands of the 1940s*. Durham, NC: Duke University Press, 2000.

Twenty-fourth Annual Report of the National League of Nursing Education: 1918. Baltimore: Williams & Wilkins Company, 1919.

Tyndall, Rose and Mary Murphy. *A History of the Bellevue School for Midwives: 1911-1936*. Series 1, box 2. Bellevue Hospital School of Nursing Alumnae Association Records, 1873-2009 (MC19). Bellevue Alumnae Center for Nursing History, Foundation of New York State Nurses. Guilderland, NY.

Zeiger, Susan. *In Uncle Sam's Service: Women Workers with the American Expeditionary Force, 1917-1919*. Ithaca, NY: Cornell University Press, 1999.

Zwerdling, Michael. *Postcards of Nursing: A Worldwide Tribute*. Philadelphia: Lippincott Williams & Wilkins, 2003.

Journals and Journal Articles

Baker, Bessie. "An Outline of The Work of Our Nursing Unit." *Johns Hopkins Nurses Alumnae Magazine* 18, no. 2 (May 1919): 58-61.

Bowling, Gertrude. "Side-Lights on Life With a Shock Team." *Johns Hopkins Nurses Alumnae Magazine* 18, no. 2 (May 1919): 61-69.

"Care of Nurses Taken By the Enemy." *American Journal of Nursing* 19, no. 5 (February 1919): 372-373.

Castle, Cora Sutton. "A Statistical Study of Eminent Women." repr. from the *Archives of Psychology* 4, no. 27 (New York: August 1913): 1-90.

Coile, H.P., M.D. "The Hydrotherapy of Typhoid Fever, and Improved Bath Apparatus for its Successful Implementation." *Transactions of the Seventieth Annual Session of the Tennessee State Medical Association, Nashville, 1903* (Nashville: Southern Publishing Association, 1903): 172-178.

Dawley, Katy. "Origins of Nurse-Midwifery in the United States and its Expansion in the 1940s." *Journal of Midwifery & Women's Health* 48, no. 2 (March/April 2003): 86-95.

"Dedication of the American Nurses' Memorial, Florence Nightingale School, Bordeaux, France." *American Journal of Nursing* 22, no. 10 (July 1922): 799-800.

Edgar, Clifton J. "Why the Midwife?" *The American Journal of Obstetrics and Diseases of Women and Children* 78, no. 1 (July 1918): 242-255.

"Editorial Comment." *Pacific Coast Journal of Nursing* 27, no. 8 (August 1922): 474-477.

"Editorials." *Johns Hopkins Nurses Alumnae Magazine* 18, no. 2 (May 1919): 48-49.

"Editorials: Clara Dutton Noyes." *American Journal of Nursing* 36, no. 7 (July 1936): 701-702.

Fitzgerald, Alice. "Clara D. Noyes – An Appreciation." *The Trained Nurse and Hospital Review* 97, no. 1 (July 1936): 19-21.

Greeley, Helen Hoy. "Rank for Nurses." *American Journal of Nursing* 14, no. 11 (August 1919): 840-852.

Hacker, David J., Libra Hilde, and James Holland Jones. "The Effect of the Civil War on Southern Marriage Patterns." *Journal of Southern History* 76, no. 1 (February 2010): 39-70.

"History In Brief of Base Hospital No. 18." *Johns Hopkins Nurses Alumnae Magazine* 18, no. 2 (May 1919): 55-57.

"In the Nursing World: Army Nurse Corps." *Trained Nurse and Hospital Review* 61, no. 2 (August 1918): 112-115.

Jammé, Anna C. "Recollections." *Johns Hopkins Nurses Alumnae Magazine* 36, no. 1 (January 1937): 13-16.

Johns Hopkins Nurses Alumnae Magazine 1, no. 1 (December 1901): 22.

Johns Hopkins Nurses Alumnae Magazine 35, no. 3 (July 1936): 156-166.

Keeling, Arlene W. "'A Most Alarming Situation': Responding to the 1918 Influenza Epidemic in Alaska." *Windows in Time*, University of Virginia School of Nursing 21, no. 2 (October 2013): 6-11.

Keeling, Arlene W. "'Alert to the Necessities of the Emergency': U.S. Nursing During the 1918 Influenza Pandemic." *Public Health Report*, 2010; 125 (Suppl 3): 105-112.

Noyes, Clara D. "A Modern Laundry." *American Journal of Nursing* 8, no. 7 (April 1908): 513-519.

Noyes, Clara D. "Address to the Graduating Class of 1917." *Johns Hopkins Nurses Alumnae Magazine* 16, no. 3 (August 1917): 100-106.

Noyes, Clara D. "Department of Red Cross Nursing: Widespread Disasters." *American Journal of Nursing* 26, no. 12 (December 1926): 967-971.

Noyes, Clara D. "Department of Red Cross Nursing." *American Journal of Nursing* 18, no. 4 (January 1918): 318-321.

Noyes, Clara D. "Department of Red Cross Nursing." *American Journal of Nursing* 21, no. 3 (December 1920): 169-172.

Noyes, Clara D. "Department of Red Cross Nursing." *American Journal of Nursing* 21, no. 6 (March 1921): 389-392.

Noyes, Clara D. "Department of Red Cross Nursing." *American Journal of Nursing* 21, no. 8 (May 1921): 552-557.

Noyes, Clara D. "Department of Red Cross Nursing." *American Journal of Nursing* 25, no. 5 (May 1925): 405-409.

Noyes, Clara D. "Department of Red Cross Nursing." *American Journal of Nursing* 36, no. 7 (July 1936): 730-734.

Noyes, Clara D. "Department of Red Cross Nursing: American Red Cross Nurses in Foreign Lands." *American Journal of Nursing* 28, no. 5 (May 1928): 509-513.

Noyes, Clara D. "Department of Red Cross Nursing: Nature at Her Worst." *American Journal of Nursing* 36, no. 6 (June 1936): 623-624.

Noyes, Clara D. "Department of Red Cross Nursing: Nursing Ex-Service Men." *American Journal of Nursing* 21, no. 11 (August 1921): 800-801.

Noyes, Clara D. "Department of Red Cross Nursing: Red Cross Nurses Finish Work in Mississippi Valley." *American Journal of Nursing* 27, no. 10 (October 1927): 857-860.

Noyes, Clara D. "Department of Red Cross Nursing: The Fifth Annual Roll Call." *American Journal of Nursing* 22, no. 1 (October 1921): 32-36.

Noyes, Clara D. "Department of Red Cross Nursing: The Schools of Nursing in the Old World (Prague)." *American Journal of Nursing* 22, no. 6 (March 1922): 445-448.

Noyes, Clara D. "Department of Red Cross Nursing: Tributes to Red Cross Nurses in the Near East." *American Journal of Nursing* 24, no. 7 (April 1924): 567-570.

Noyes, Clara D. "Department of Red Cross Nursing: Visiting Bulgaria." *American Journal of Nursing* 26, no. 3 (March 1926): 219-222.

Noyes, Clara D. "Department of Red Cross Nursing: Widespread Disasters." *American Journal of Nursing* 26, no. 12 (December 1926): 967-971.

Noyes, Clara D. "For Extraordinary Heroism." *American Journal of Nursing* 19, no. 7 (April 1919): 531-532.

Noyes, Clara D. "Sailing of the Units." *American Journal of Nursing* 17, no. 11 (August 1917): 1094-1097.

Noyes, Clara D. "The Midwifery Problem." *American Journal of Nursing* 12, no. 6 (March 1912): 466-471.

Noyes, Clara D. "The Red Cross." *American Journal of Nursing* 17, no. 7 (April 1917): 621-627.

Noyes, Clara D. "The Red Cross." *American Journal of Nursing* 19, no. 5 (February 1919): 367-376.

Noyes, Clara D. "The Red Cross." *American Journal of Nursing* 20, no. 5 (February 1920): 395-399.

Noyes, Clara D. "The Red Cross: Establishment of Foreign Training Schools." *American Journal of Nursing* 19, no. 12 (September 1919): 947-951.

Noyes, Clara D. "The Schools of Nursing in the Old World: Warsaw." *American Journal of Nursing* 22, no. 7 (April 1922): 539-543.

Noyes, Clara D. "The Schools of Nursing in the Old World: Warsaw, Part II." *American Journal of Nursing* 8, no. 22 (May 1922): 633-636.

Noyes, Clara D. "The Siberian Commission." *American Journal of Nursing* 20, no. 2 (November 1919): 134-138.

Noyes, Clara D. "Training of Midwives in Relation to the Prevention of Infant Mortality." *American Journal of Obstetrics and Diseases of Women and Children* (New York: William Wood and Company, 1912): 1051-1059.

Noyes, Clara D. "Training School for Midwives at Bellevue and Allied Hospitals." *American Journal of Nursing* 12, no. 5 (February 1912): 417-422.

Patterson, Andrea. "'Black Nurses in the Great War' Fighting for and with the American Military in the Struggle for Civil Rights." *Canadian Journal of History* 47.3 (2012): 545-566.

Pollitt, Phoebe and Camille N. Reese. "Nursing and the New Deal: We Met the Challenge." *Public Health Nursing* 14, no. 6 (December 1997): 373-382.

Popova, Kristina. *The Joy of Service: Biopolitics and Biographies Between New York, Sofia and Grna Dzhumaja* in the *First Half of the 20th Century*. CAS Working Paper Series No. 5/2013: Sofia 2013. Advanced Academia programme, a project of the Center for Advanced Study Sofia: 3-58.

Poslusny, Susan M. "Feminist Friendship: Isabel Hampton Robb, Lavinia Lloyd Dock and Mary Adelaide Nutting," *The Journal of Nursing Scholarship* 21, no. 2 (June 1989): 64-68.

"Press Notices Upon The Death of Miss Noyes." *Johns Hopkins Nurses Alumnae Magazine* 35, no. 3 (July 1936): 160-162.

"Report of the Section of Nursing and Social Work of the American Association for the Study and Prevention of Infant Mortality." *American Journal of Nursing* 12, no. 4 (January 1912): 328-335.

"Reports from Camps on Influenza Show a Total of 144,095 Cases." *The Official U.S. Bulletin*, October 7, 1918: 3.

"She Sleeps a Holy Sleep." *British Journal of Nursing* vol. 84 (August 1936): 212.

Shulman, Jean. "They Were Giants In Those Days." *Nursing Matters Past and Present*, a publication of the American Red Cross National Nursing Committee, 18th edition (Spring 2015): 5-7.

Stock, Pauline. "Experiences With A 'Shock Team'." *Johns Hopkins Nurses Alumnae Magazine* 18, no. 2 (May 1919): 70-73.

"Student News: Czechoslovakian Students." *American Journal of Nursing* 48, no. 5 (May 1948): 343.

"Sub-Nurses and Sub-Doctors." *The Medical Standard* 45, no. 2 (February 1922): 9.

Taubenberger, Jeffrey. "The Origin and Virulence of the 1918 'Spanish' Influenza Virus." *Proceedings of the American Philosophical Society* 150, no. 1 (March 2006): 86-112.

"The American Medical And Surgical History of the War." *Army and Navy Register* 64, no. 1999 (November 9, 1918): 528.

"Reserve Nurses – Army Nurse Corps: Assignments." *Trained Nurse and Hospital Review* 60, no. 1 (January 1918): 45-48.

Webb, L.H. "Vaccine in Typhoid Therapy." *The Charlotte Medical Journal: A Southern Journal of Medicine and Surgery* 76, no. 1 (July 1917): 12-14.

Williams, J. Whitridge. "Medical Education and the Midwife Problem in the United States." *Journal of the American Medical Association* 58, no. 1 (January 6, 1912): 1-12.

Yale, Louise P. "Clara D. Noyes," poem as printed in the *Johns Hopkins Nurses Alumnae Magazine* 35, no. 3 (July 1936): 157-158.

Ziegler, Charles Edward. "The Elimination of the Midwife." *Journal of the American Medical Association* 60, no. 1 (January 4, 1913): 32-38.

Pamphlets

Catt, Carrie Chapman. *The Ballot and the Bullet.* New York: Published for the National American Woman Suffrage Association, 1897.

Irises 1932, by Cooley's Gardens; Henry G. Gilbert Nursery and Seed Trade Catalog Collection.

The Story of the American Journal of Nursing, 4th revision, March 1950.

Yale University. *Leaders in Nursing* (1924). Clara Noyes Biofile. The Alan Mason Chesney Medical Archives of the Johns Hopkins Medical Institutions, Baltimore.

Letters

Albaugh, R. Indie, Chairman Special Committee of the Joint National Committee of the ANA, NLNE and NOPH, to Susan C. Francis, Director of Nursing for the Pennsylvania-Delaware Division of the American Red Cross, 18 February 1920. The American Nurses Association Collection, Howard Gotlieb Archival Research Center at Boston University, N 87, box 180, folder 7.

Bancroft, N.R., Major, A.R.C. to Henry Baker, subject "Refugees in camps," 14 May 1927. Records of the

American National Red Cross 1917–1934, Record Group 200, folder DR 224.91, "Negro Relations."

Bartlett, Miss to Jane Delano, 18 February 1918, subject "Execution of nurse, at Camp Sevier, Greenville, S.C." Records of the American National Red Cross 1917–1934, Record Group 200, folder 109.1, "Sabotage – World War #1."

Bicknell, Ernest P. to Clara Noyes, undated cover note attached to a series of letters from Helen L. Bridge in the fall of 1922. Records of the American National Red Cross 1917–1934, Record Group 200, folder 947.52, "Poland, Warsaw, Training Schools for Nurses."

Bielaski, Alexander B., Chief of the United States Department of Justice, to Charles Magee, Secretary of American National Red Cross, 5 July 1916. Records of the American National Red Cross 1917–1934, Record Group 200, folder 109.1, "Sabotage – World War #1."

Bielaski, Alexander B., Chief of the United States Department of Justice, to Charles Magee, Secretary of American National Red Cross, 13 April 1917. Records of the American National Red Cross 1917–1934, Record Group 200, folder 109.1, "Sabotage – World War #1."

Bridge, Helen L. to Clara D. Noyes, 4 June 1923. Records of the American National Red Cross 1917–1934, Record Group 200, folder 947.52, "Poland, Warsaw, Training Schools for Nurses."

Butler, Ida F. to Anna Tittman, 14 September 1920. Records of the American National Red Cross, 1881-

2008, Series: Historical Nurse Files, 1916-1959. Folder "Tittman, Anna Louise," Red Cross Badge No. 6072.

Butler, Ida F. to Anna Tittman, 29 September 1920. Records of the American National Red Cross, 1881-2008, Series: Historical Nurse Files, 1916-1959. Folder "Tittman, Anna Louise," Red Cross Badge No. 6072.

Butler, Ida F. to Mary M. Roberts, 9 June 1936. Records of the American National Red Cross, 1881-2008, Series: Historical Nurse Files, 1916-1959. Folder "Clara D. Noyes," Red Cross Badge No. 6215.

Coulson, George to Johns Hopkins School of Nursing, 11 January 1894. "Clara Noyes, JHH SON Student Records," box 2, folder 14, 1894, Alan Mason Chesney Medical Archives of the Johns Hopkins Medical Institutions, Baltimore.

Delano, Jane to Clara D. Noyes, 7 June 1916. Records of the American National Red Cross, 1881-2008, Series: Historical Nurse Files, 1916-1959. Folder: Clara D. Noyes, Red Cross Badge No. 6215.

Delano, Jane to Miss Alice Meggison of Haverhill, MA, 15 May 1918. Records of the American National Red Cross 1917–1934, Record Group 200, folder 109.1, "Nurses – Charged with Immorality 1917-1918."

Delano, Jane to Surgeon General William Gorgas, 15 February 1918. Records of the American National Red Cross 1917–1934, Record Group 200, folder 109.1, "Nurses – Charged with Immorality 1917-1918."

Dorr, Frederick to Clara D. Noyes, 15 July 1918. Records of the American National Red Cross 1917–1934, Record Group 200, folder 109.1, "Nurses – Brutal Treatment By Germans."

"Extracted from letters from Miss Hay to Miss Noyes, May 4, 1922" and "Ans. By Miss Noyes, May 20, 1922." Records of the American National Red Cross 1917–1934, Record Group 200, folder 958.52, "Commission to Czecho-Slovakia, W.W. I, Prague School of Nursing, July 1922-Dec. 1926."

Francis, Susan to Clara D. Noyes, 2 January 1919. The American Nurses Association Collection, Howard Gotlieb Archival Research Center at Boston University, N 87, box 180, folder 7.

Frieser, James to All Chapter Chairmen, 3 August 1927. Records of the American National Red Cross 1917–1934, Record Group 200, folder DR-224.08, "Mississippi River Valley Flood 3/30/27 Reports and Statistics."

Garner, Agnes to Clara D. Noyes, 21 November 1929. Records of the American National Red Cross, 1881-2008. Series: Historical Nurse Files, ca. 1916-ca. 1959. File Unit: Stanfield, Mrs. Agnes H. (Wm. C).

General Letter No. 1, Subject: "Request from Surgeon General Blue, U.S.P.H.S," Frank Persons to all Division Managers, 3 October 1918. Records of the American National Red Cross 1917–1934, Record Group 200, folder 803, "Epidemics – Influenza, 1918, Divisions."

Hill, Albert Ross, Vice Chair in Charge of Foreign Operations, to Ida Butler, 15 September 1922. Records of the American National Red Cross 1917–1934, Record Group 200, folder 947.52, "Poland, Warsaw, Training Schools for Nurses."

Hoover, Herbert to Walter White, 21 June 1927. Records of the American National Red Cross 1917–1934, Record Group 200, folder DR 224.91, "Negro Relations."

Jammé, Anna C. to Clara Noyes, 19 April 1919. Records of the American National Red Cross, 1881-2008, Series: Historical Nurse Files, 1916-1959. Jane A. Delano files: 301, folder labeled "Delano, Jane, April 1-23, 1919."

Melhorn, K.C. to Clara D. Noyes, 28 November 1928. Records of the American National Red Cross, 1881-2008 Series: Historical Nurse Files, ca. 1916-ca. 1959 File, Unit: Stanfield, Mrs. Agnes H. (Wm. C).

National Director of the Nursing Service to Agnes Stanfield, 5 December 1928. Records of the American National Red Cross, 1881-2008. Series: Historical Nurse Files, ca. 1916-ca. 1959. File Unit: Stanfield, Mrs. Agnes H. (Wm. C).

National Director of the Nursing Service to Dr. K. C. Melhorn, 19 December 1928. Records of the American National Red Cross, 1881-2008. Series: Historical Nurse Files, ca. 1916-ca. 1959. File Unit: Stanfield, Mrs. Agnes H. (Wm. C).

Noyes, Clara D. to Agnes Von Kurowsky, 5 January 1918. Records of the American National Red Cross, 1881-2008 Series: Historical Nurse Files, ca. 1916-ca. 1959 File, Unit: Stanfield, Mrs. Agnes H. (Wm. C).

Noyes, Clara D. to Ernest P. Bicknell, 13 March 1923. Records of the American National Red Cross 1917–1934, Record Group 200, folder 958.52, "Commission to Czecho-Slovakia, W.W. I, Prague School of Nursing, July 1922-Dec. 1926."

Noyes, Clara D. to Ernest P. Bicknell, 17 March 1923 and Ernest P. Bicknell to Clara D. Noyes, 16 March 1923. Records of the American National Red Cross 1917–1934, Record Group 200, folder 958.52, "Commission to Czecho-Slovakia, W.W. I, Prague School of Nursing, July 1922-Dec. 1926."

Noyes, Clara D. to Frederick Daw [sic.], 12 July 1918. Records of the American National Red Cross 1917–1934, Record Group 200, folder 109.1, "Nurses – Brutal Treatment By Germans."

Noyes, Clara D. to Georgiana Ross, 7 July 1907. Class of 1896, Alan Mason Chesney Medical Archives of the Johns Hopkins Medical Institutions, Baltimore.

Noyes, Clara D. to Hazel Goff, 6 October 1925. Records of the American National Red Cross 1917–1934, Record Group 200, folder 963.52, "Bulgaria, Sofia, School for Nurses Special Reports, 1925-33."

Noyes, Clara D. to Helen L. Bridge, 7 September 1923. Records of the American National Red Cross

1917–1934, Record Group 200, folder 947.52, "Poland, Warsaw, Training Schools for Nurses."

Noyes, Clara D. to Lillian Wald, 14 August 1914. Lillian Wald Papers, Rare Book and Manuscript Library, Columbia University in the City of New York.

Noyes, Clara D., to Lillian White, 3 June 1919. Records of the American National Red Cross 1917–1934, Record Group 200, folder 803.11, "Epidemics, Influenza, Alaska."

Noyes, Clara D. to Lillian White, 12 June 1919. Records of the American National Red Cross 1917–1934, Record Group 200, folder 803.11, "Epidemics, Influenza, Alaska."

Noyes, Clara D. to M. Adelaide Nutting, 8 April 1917. New York Nursing Archives, Teacher's College.

Noyes, Clara D. to Marion Parsons, 11 October 1922. Records of the American National Red Cross 1917–1934, Record Group 200, folder 958.52, "Commission to Czecho-Slovakia, W.W. I, Prague School of Nursing, July 1922-Dec. 1926."

Noyes, Clara D. to Miss Dick, undated letter (probably from 1908, according to a note in the file). "Correspondence, Class of 1896." Alan Mason Chesney Medical Archives of the Johns Hopkins Medical Institutions, Baltimore.

Noyes, Clara D. to Superintendent of Nurses at Johns Hopkins Hospital, 27 January 1894. "Clara Noyes, JHH SON Student Records," box 2, folder 14, 1894, Alan Mason Chesney Medical Archives of the Johns Hopkins Medical Institutions, Baltimore.

Noyes, Clara D. to Susan Francis, 28 December 1918. The American Nurses Association Collection, Howard Gotlieb Archival Research Center at Boston University, N 87, box 180, folder 7.

Noyes, Clara D. to The American National Red Cross, undated correspondence. Records of the American National Red Cross, 1881-2008, Series: Historical Nurse Files, 1916-1959. Jane A. Delano files: 301, folder labeled "Delano, Jane, April 1-23, 1919."

Red Cross Acting Vice Chairman to Secretary of the Navy Josephus Daniels, 30 September 1918. Records of the American National Red Cross 1917–1934, Record Group 200, folder 803.08, "Epidemics, Influenza, Reports and Statistics."

Schafer, A.L. to Dewitt Smith, 2 June 1927. Records of the American National Red Cross 1917–1934, Record Group 200, folder DR-224.91, "Mississippi River Valley Flood 3/30/27, Criticisms and Controversial Subjects."

Smith, DeWitt to George E. Scott, 20 October 1928. Records of the American National Red Cross 1917–1934, Record Group 200, folder DR 224.91, "Negro Relations."

Taft, William Howard to Maj. Gen. Murray, 30 June 1916. Records of the American National Red Cross, 1881-2008, Series: Historical Nurse Files, 1916-1959. Folder: Clara D. Noyes, Red Cross Badge No. 6215.

Tittman, Anna to Ida F. Butler, 27 September 1920. Records of the American National Red Cross, 1881-2008, Series: Historical Nurse Files, 1916-1959. Folder "Tittman, Anna Louise," Red Cross Badge No. 6072.

Von Kurowsky, Agnes to Clara D. Noyes, 2 January 1918. Records of the American National Red Cross, 1881-2008, Series: Historical Nurse Files, 1916-1959, File Unit: Stanfield, Mrs. Agnes H. (Wm. C).

Wald, Lillian to Chapin Brinsmead, 18 August 1914. Lillian Wald Papers, Rare Book and Manuscript Library, Columbia University in the City of New York.

Wald, Lillian to Clara D. Noyes, 13 August 1914. Lillian Wald Papers, Rare Book and Manuscript Library, Columbia University in the City of New York.

White, Lillian to Clara D. Noyes, 26 July 1919. Records of the American National Red Cross 1917–1934, Record Group 200, folder 803.11, "Epidemics, Influenza, Alaska."

Press Releases

"HCA Seeks Passage of Bills Supporting Home Care's Role in Medicaid Redesign." June 11, 2013 press release from the Home Care Association of New York State (HCA), accessed October 13, 2015, http://hca-nys.org/wp-con-

tent/uploads/2015/03/PRHCA2013SessionPrioritie
s.pdf.

"Hoover Meets Colored Advisory Flood Commission;
Abuses to Be Corrected, Red Cross Does Good
Job." Special Release, 14 June 1927. Records of the
American National Red Cross 1917–1934, Record
Group 200, folder DR 224.91 "Negro Relations."

"Miss Clara D. Noyes, National Red Cross Nursing Head
Dies." Press release from the American Red Cross
News Service (June 3, 1936), private collection of
James Noyes, Old Lyme, CT.

"Miss I. Malinde Havey, Red Cross Public Health Nursing Director and World War Nurse Heroine Dies
in Boston." The American Red Cross News Service (press release), September 8, 1938, Records of
the American National Red Cross, 1881-2008, Series: Historical Nurse Files, 1916-1959. Folder "I
Malinde Havey," Red Cross Badge No. 6004.

Radio Address by Miss Clara Noyes, National Director of
Nursing Service, American Red Cross: "Anniver-
sary of Florence Nightingale's Birth Adopted as
National Hospital Day." Press release from the
American Red Cross News Service (May 12,
1921), private collection of James Noyes, Old
Lyme, CT.

Online Sources

Barton, Rick. "Cecil County Farmer: Mt. Ararat." *Cecil
Soil Magazine*, March/April 2009, accessed November 13, 2015,

http://www.bluetoad.com/article/Cecil+County+F
armer%3A+Mt+Ararat/117972/0/article.html.

Frandsen, Betty. "Nursing Leadership: Management and Leadership Styles," a publication of the American Association of Nurse Assessment Coordination, 2014, accessed October 13, 2015, http://www.aanac.org/docs/white-papers/2013-nursing-leadership---management-leadership-styles.pdf?sfvrsn=6.

Greenberg, David. "Help! Call the White House!: How the 1927 Mississippi Flood Created Big Government." Salon.com, September 5, 2006, accessed January 5, 2016, http://www.slate.com/articles/news_and_politics/history_lesson/2006/09/help_call_the_white_house.html.

Keylor, William. "The Long-forgotten Racial Attitudes and Policies of Woodrow Wilson." *Professor Voices*, Boston University, March 4, 2013, accessed October 13, 2015, http://www.bu.edu/professorvoices/2013/03/04/the-long-forgotten-racial-attitudes-and-policies-of-woodrow-wilson/.

Knox, Richard. "Home Health Care Proves Resilient In Face Of Sandy Destruction." *National Public Radio*, November 2, 2012, accessed October 13, 2015, http://www.npr.org/sections/health-shots/2012/11/02/164207669/home-health-care-proves-resilient-in-face-of-sandy-destruction.

"Lest We Forget." Lymeline.com. May 27, 2013. Accessed October 1, 2015, http://lymeline.net/2013/05/lest-we-forget/.

U.S. National Library of Medicine. "Certified Nurse-midwife: History of the Profession," *MedlinePlus,* accessed October 13, 2015, https://www.nlm.nih.gov/medlineplus/ency/articl e/002000.htm.

Witkiewicz, Helena. Chairman of the WNS Graduates' Circle. "History of the Warsaw Nursing School in Warsaw, 78 Koszykowa Street," accessed February 2, 2016, http://www.wmpp.org.pl/en/nursing-schools/the-warsaw-nursing-school.html.

Dissertations

Piemonte, Robert V., *A History of the National League of Nursing Education 1912-1932: Great Awakening in Nursing Education.* Dissertation Submitted for the Degree of Doctor of Education in Teachers College, Columbia University (1976).

INDEX

Barton, Clara: absence
from Red Cross
iconography, 69,
224-225; influence
on Red Cross
volunteers, 11-12;
ouster from Red
Cross and feuds
with Mabel
Boardman, 91, 166

Base Hospitals: No. 1,
71-72; No. 5, 111;
No. 11, 111; No.
21, 81; No. 27, 133;
No. 36, 204; No. 69,
133

Bellevue Hospital
Nurse Training
School: Clara
Noyes role at, 37,
47, 70, 73, 78, 160,
226; early status as
elite nursing
school, 16, 21, 33,
70; formation of
Base Hospital No.
1, 71-72; midwife
school at, 38-39, 44-
47; segregation at,
56-59

Bernatzikova, Marie,
196

Bible verses: Acts, 85;
Genesis, xi, 4, 9

Bicknell, Ernest, 196

Boardman, Mabel:
conflicts with Clara
Noyes over nurses'
aides, 168-169;
controversies with
Clara Barton, 90-91,
165-166;
restructuring of
American Red
Cross, 73, 165

Bordeaux School of
Nursing: Clara
Noyes speech for
opening, 189-190;
Clara Noyes visit
to, 188;
development of
school, 173-174;
fundraising efforts,
188-189

Bowling, Gertrude,
110, 155

Bridge, Helen L., 193

Brinsmead, Chapin,
58-59

Bulgaria: school of
nursing in Sofia,

Noyes statements on, 52-53; nurses' role in the movement, 3, 50-53, 148-149; passage of suffrage amendment, 154, 157; suffrage movement and pacifism, 63-67. *See also* Nineteenth Amendment

Szlenkier, Zofia, 195

Taft, William Howard: appointment of Clara Noyes to Red Cross, 76, 78; as Chairman of the Committee on Nurses Rank, 78, 152; role in the American Red Cross, 78, 90

Thompson, Elnora, 189

Thoms, Adah, 97, 106

Tittman, Anna, 183-186

Torrance, Rachel, 191

Treaty of Versailles, 213, 217

Typhoid: Clara Noyes training in treatment of, 24-25; during Mississippi Flood of 1927, 201, 203, 209; outbreak in Siberia, 185; treatment of, 35

Universal Negro Improvement Association, 60

USS Red Cross, 64. *See also* Mercy Ship

Von Kurowsky, Agnes: application and assignment to Red Cross, 115-117; Haiti service of, 119-120; inspiration for *A Farewell to Arms*, 117; marriage of, 120; questions about father's German heritage, 115; relationship with Ernest Hemingway, 117;

CPSIA information can be obtained
at www.ICGtesting.com
Printed in the USA
FFOW04n0815270317
33747FF